worship

city,
church and
renewal

John F. **baldovin**, SJ

The Pastoral Press

Washington, DC

Acknowledgments

Acknowledgment is gratefully made to the following publishers and editors for permission to use the following material: *Liturgy* (Journal of the Liturgical Conference, Washington, D.C. for "The City as Church, the Church as City," *Liturgy: Holy Places* 3:4 (1983); "Sunday Liturgy in Jerusalem," *Liturgy: With All the Saints* 5:2 (1985); Scholars Press for "Worship in Urban Life: The Example of Medieval Constantinople," from Peter S. Hawkins, ed., *Civitas: Religious Interpretations of the City* (Atlanta, GA: Scholars Press, 1986); the United States Catholic Conference for "Sacraments and the Paschal Presence of the Bishop," from a forthcoming book, edited by Kenneth Jenkins and to be published by the United States Catholic Conference, on the Ceremonial of Bishops; *The Way* for "The Nature and Function of the Liturgical Homily," from *Spirituality and Liturgy: Supplement to the Way* 67 (1990); Liturgy Training Publications (Chicago, IL) for "The Bible and the Liturgy," from *Catechumenate* 11:5 and 11:6 (1989); The Liturgical Press (Collegeville, MN) for "On Feasting the Saints," *Worship* 54 (1980), "Concelebration: A Problem of Symbolic Roles in the Church," *Worship* 59 (1985), "Kyrie Eleison and the Entrance Rite of the Roman Eucharist," *Worship* 61 (1987); "The Liturgical Year: Calendar for a Just Community," from Eleanor Bernstein, ed., *Liturgy and Spirituality in Context* (Collegeville: The Liturgical Press, 1990); "Liturgical Renewal 1963-1988," from Lawrence Madden, ed., *The Gift Half-Understood: The State of Liturgy Twenty-Five Years after the Council* (Collegeville: The Liturgical Press, 1991); the Notre Dame Center for "Liturgical Presidency: The Sacramental Question," which will be published in a forthcoming collection.

ISBN: 0-912405-78-3

The Pastoral Press
225 Sheridan Street, N.W.
Washington, D.C. 20011
(202) 723-1254

The Pastoral Press is the publications division of the National Association of Pastoral Musicians, a membership organization of musicians and clergy dedicated to fostering the art of musical liturgy.

Printed in the United States of America

Contents

For Barbara, John, and Tim

Introduction

THE FIFTEEN PAPERS COLLECTED IN THIS VOLUME REPRESENT MY DI-
vergent scholarly and pastoral interests over the past ten
years. I was extremely grateful to Virgil Funk for suggesting
that I assemble them for, if nothing else, putting this collection
together helped me to take stock of my own preoccupations as
a liturgical historian and theologian. I have been very fortunate to be able to teach both in a university setting (Fordham)
and in a seminary/graduate school (Jesuit School of Theology
and the Graduate Theological Union). Encounters with colleagues and students in both places as well as invitations to
speak at a number of national and regional conferences on liturgy have forced me to think long and hard about problems
facing the church and its worship today. These studies represent the results of that thought.

This book is divided into three parts, which represent both
my different interests and in many ways the diverse roles I
play in the church and academy. The first part concentrates on
a popular presentation of my research on the historical setting
of Christian worship in the first millennium. Through research
into the stational liturgies, I became convinced that it was not
only the texts of the various Christian liturgies that influenced
the formation of worshiping communities, but also the context
of those liturgies. Hence an attempt to flesh out in a more
phenomenological way the impact of various urban centers
and the culture of the Late Antique Mediterranean world on

the development of the ethos of the classic Christian liturgies. This yields a modest contribution to social history, for the most interesting question about liturgy (to me, at any rate) is—what is (was) it that people actually experience when they worship? No doubt the findings of the essays on the city and liturgy have relevance today in showing us how deeply our own culture influences the way we worship, not to mention the need to interact creatively with our own culture or cultures in the formation of contemporary Christian worship.

The second part of the books consists of studies on the eucharist and on Christian ministry. These studies reflect most clearly my own primary occupation as a seminary professor of liturgy and sacramental theology, especially in view of the specific needs and problems facing the contemporary Roman Catholic Church. In the essays on the entrance rites, concelebration, and frequency, one should be able to discern an interest not so much in texts and the theology that can be derived from them as with the whole presentation and setting of worship. Much of the current discussion of the relation between the rule of prayer and the rule of belief (*lex orandi / lex credendi*) would, in my opinion, benefit from a fuller appreciation of the fact that the "rule of prayer" consists not only in the texts that are prayed but also the manner in which they are prayed and the social and ecclesial setting in which they take place. Thus the issues dealt with are as much ecclesiological as they are liturgical. In fact, it has been my conviction that an adequate treatment of liturgy must always reflect a well thought-out ecclesiology—a gain that has been most evident in contemporary sacramental theology. My concern with the liturgy has gone hand-in-hand with considerations on those who have special responsibility in liturgical life, the ordained ministers of the church. Thus, the essays in the latter half of this second section deal with the nature of liturgical presidency and the service of the ordained to the church as a whole. It should be evident, especially in the essay on the relation between the office of bishop and the sacraments that I do not hold a merely functionalist view of ministry. My attempt to de-mythologize or de-construct traditional views has been an effort to gain some clarity on contemporary questions facing the ordained ministry of the church.

With some minor alteration I have decided to let stand what

I have to say in the essays that have been reprinted in this second part. If I were to make a "retraction," it would be in the essay on the frequency of the eucharist. It is the article on which I have received the most critical comment, and correctly so, since this is a most sensitive issue. I am not sure I would write it precisely the same way today, since in the first place I have often been understood to be arguing against daily worship, which is far from the case, And in the second place, it has been my experience that when the "Catholic instinct" for daily Mass is ignored, the celebration of the eucharist has not been replaced by other forms of liturgical worship but rather with a vacuum. In any case, I would still want to insist on the qualitative difference between weekday eucharistic celebration and Sunday worship, where, it seems to me, so much more is at stake. Perhaps the best direction to pursue would be a much simpler form for the weekday eucharist—one that would differentiate it clearly from the Sunday celebration as the weekly assembly of the people of God.

The studies in the third part of this book represent my reflections on the future of Roman Catholic worship in the context of the contemporary liturgical reform. In some way these most reflect my position not only as an academician but also as a practitioner both in my experience of contemporary Roman Catholic liturgies and as a leader. For this aspect of my life I am most grateful for those communities which have welcomed me as a presider and preacher, as well as those in which I have participated as an "ordinary" member of the faithful. It seems to me that contemporary writers on liturgy ignore the latter kind of experience to their peril.

If anything like a method is represented by these essays, it most clearly shows in the pieces on concelebration and on frequency, where I try to combine insights from history, doctrine, and pastoral experience to form an assessment of a particular question. It seems to me that none of these factors can be ignored in the responsible treatment of questions that face the church today. In particular, I would point to the necessity of historical understanding, for (especially when viewed with a mild hermeneutic of suspicion) history constantly instructs us as to both continuities in the Christian experience and the profound ways in which social and intellectual contexts have shaped the worship of any particular era.

A collection such as this merits recognition of an enormous debt of gratitude. First of all, I am thankful to Lawrence Johnson of The Pastoral Press, who has done wonders in putting this material in order. That my thinking and writing have been by no means wholly original is indicated by many of the names found in the notes to the various pieces. It is a tribute both to the size of the field of liturgical studies and to the dedication with which scholars participate in it that I can count many of these people not only as mentors and partners in intellectual exchange but also as friends. I am also grateful to my colleagues and students, especially at the Jesuit School of Theology at Berkeley, as well as to numerous people who invited or inspired me to write a number of these pieces. Among them (although I am sure to leave some out) are: Aidan Kavanagh, John Cook, Leo Klein, Kenneth Untener, Donald Buggert, Margaret O'Brien Steinfels, Ron Krisman, David Lonsdale, John Gallen, Lawrence Madden, Mary Alice Piil, and Eleanor Bernstein. This book is dedicated to my sister, brother-in-law, and nephew who have been a constant source of love and support.

CHRISTIAN WORSHIP IN SPACE AND TIME

1

The City as Church, the Church as City

THE CITY HAS LONG HELD A POWERFUL ATTRACTION OVER THE HU-
man imagination. A city involves a certain concentration of
population brought together for various social, economic, and
political reasons. But a city is more than this, just as it is more
than its number of buildings, streets, and public places. The
city is a powerful idea, a symbol of human society. The Roman
concept of *civitas*, for example, stood for the city as well as for
civilization. A city is a public symbol expressing and forming
a society's concept of itself.

In the past Christian worship has had an intimate connection with the idea of the city, This is not surprising, since liturgy, as the cult of Christians, is deeply embedded in the society
whose faith it expresses. How has the city been conceived as a
religious symbol? How did Christians appropriate the city as a
space for worship after the fourth century? How did the
church incorporate both the idea and the image of the city into
its liturgy? What relation can the city and the church have today? These are the questions that set the framework for everything that follows.

The City as Sacred

The writer of Revelation uses the image of a city to describe heaven (21:2, 10-21). The city has associations that are not only symbolic of society itself, but also of society's intimate connection with sacred reality. This is true both for early Christianity and for a wide diversity of traditional societies. The Deuteronomic reform in the religion of Israel emphasizes the cult's unification by the temple and by Sion, the city of David. Here in this city, above all, God meets this people. Beyond the traditions of the Near East, a number of ancient cities were either sacred centers in origin or became primarily ritual cities; for example: cities in China, Teotihuacan in Mexico, and Macchu Picchu in Peru. Lewis Mumford argues that the origins of the meaning of the city are found in its sacredness.[1] A city is bounded off from the chaotic outside world of nature just as villages are, but it also has a permanence that villages cannot have.

Moreover, in the ancient world no strict differentiation occurred between political society and religion. Pluralism and religious tolerance are modern ideas, requiring the city to be a secular and not a sacred space. But for the social world into which Christianity was introduced, the civil religious cult determined and expressed how a particular society thought itself related to the sacred. This idea is perhaps the major reason for the persecution of Christians. Those who refused to worship the state's gods had to be atheists; it was both crazy and evil not to participate in the civil cult, the center of social and political life. That such a civil cult existed is beyond doubt; it can be seen in the great religious procession of the *Panathenaia* at Athens and in numerous other religious processions and triumphs in Republican and Imperial Rome.

Early Christianity was very much an urban phenomenon.[2] The missions of early Christianity were carried mainly to urban centers. But in the period before Constantine, Christian worship seems to have been practiced mainly in private houses. Even when persecution grew less violent, Christians did not constitute anything like a public cult in and for the city. With the toleration and subsequently the imperial legitimation of Christianity in the fourth century, this situation changed, and radically so.

The Church as City

The Constantinian era presented Christianity with an opportunity to express the symbolic meaning of an entire society. Preaching and theology alone were not sufficient to galvanize a whole social world, but worship, which is essentially symbolic, can perform this task—and it did. One of the significant means by which the church made Christianity a social as well as religious phenomenon was to make various aspects of its liturgy public. To be sure, there were still mysterious aspects of Christian liturgy. Baptism took place not in public, but rather in the closed world of the baptistery, where nakedness and religious symbols acted in concert to produce an awesome religious experience. The celebration of the eucharist was reserved to the baptized faithful, as the rites of dismissal in Eastern Christian liturgies show.

But a whole range of liturgical services could be made public. Thus, different churches and shrines were employed on different fast days and feasts for the celebration of either the eucharist or a special service of prayer. In many cases these services also involved public processions from a meeting place to the church or shrine where the liturgy was celebrated with the bishop or his representative presiding. This phenomenon has been called stational liturgy. Although the urban stational liturgies had a common goal, they differed in their origins and character in each major urban center.

Let us concentrate first on the common goal presented by the stational liturgy. For the early church, liturgy was ideally a centralized, unifying event. Each community assembled around its spiritual and liturgical leader, the bishop. At least during the fourth and fifth centuries the eucharist was celebrated in one place in the city on a given fast or feast day. On Sundays a number of smaller churches also housed the eucharistic celebration, but the primary liturgy of the city was that presided over by the bishop, the stational liturgy. The modern practice of a Mass (or more than one Mass) in every church on every day was foreign to a mentality that conceived of the eucharist as a symbol of the profound corporate unity that Christians shared. This unity was "publicized" by the stational liturgy.

Jerusalem, Rome, and Constantinople are good examples of this urban stational liturgy, for they exercised great influence on Christian worship in other cities, as well as on the development of the eucharist and calendar throughout wide areas

of Christianity. Jerusalem served as a natural setting for the
development of the stational liturgy. The city and its environs
contained a number of holy places associated with the life of
Christ and the paschal mystery: Sion (the meeting place of the
apostles), the Mount of Olives, Bethlehem, and above all the
Holy Sepulcher-Golgotha complex. These sites and a number
of others were used at times appropriate to the feast on important days or significant seasons. This stational round of
services was first described by the pilgrim Egeria late in the
fourth century.

Rome had the largest Christian community in the mediterranean world. No one church building could possibly have ac-
commodated all Christians in the city. In addition, an increasing number of pilgrims came to venerate the shrines of
Christianity's many martyrs, especially of Peter and Paul.

The origins of the Roman stational liturgy are hazy. Arche-
ologists have discovered a number of pre-Constantinian sites
at which house churches probably stood. The original stational
liturgy of this city may have been a means of uniting these
churches; not only their numbers required this but also the
ethnic and linguistic diversity that they represented. (A liturgy demonstrating unity among Polish, Italian, Hispanic, African-American, and French Roman Catholic parishes in a modern American city would be analogous.) Thus the Roman
stational liturgy might have been an early attempt to unite
what had been disparate communities.[3]

Another way of manifesting this unity was the common
veneration of martyrs at their burial places in cemeteries outside the city limits. Whatever the origins of Roman stational
practice, there was a large number of well-endowed churches
and shrines to be found in the city by the late fifth century.
These were used especially during Lent for a liturgical system
that covered the entire city. During Lent the pope (or his representative) and the people gathered with him celebrated the
eucharist on the afternoon of each fast day (except Thursdays
until the eighth century). As might be expected, larger basilicas were used on Sundays and more important days; smaller
basilicas, called titular churches, were used on the ordinary
weekdays of Lent.

The Roman stational model also spread to other Northern

European cities likes Metz, Ravenna, and Milan. These latter cities modeled their urban liturgies on the Roman pattern, substituting their own churches and shrines for the Roman ones.

Constantinople represents a third example of the city employed as a church. Since processions were so central to this liturgy, we shall now shift our attention to them. Constantinople was founded partly at least as a ceremonial city. It was Constantine's imperial showcase. Thus it not only had a splendid palace, a great church (Hagia Sophia), other churches and shrines, hippodrome, and baths; it also had broad thoroughfares and plazas. Of the latter, the most important was the Forum of Constantine, located about five hundred meters from Hagia Sophia.

Our first complete evidence of a liturgical calendar for this city (in the ninth or tenth century) shows that Constantinople had a highly processional liturgy. Processions often began at Hagia Sophia, proceeded to the forum for a brief prayer service, and then went on to the church or shrine of the day. At times this meant a procession of seven miles length. A number of shrines (many of them dedicated to the Virgin Mary and made sacred by various other relics) formed a ring around the city and served as sites for the celebration of the eucharist. Other churches and shrines were located within the city itself.

The tenth-century liturgical calendar for Constantinople indicates that on almost every day a special celebration was held at one or another of these churches. Each of these celebrations could not have been stational in the sense that the patriarch presided over it, but we do know of sixty-eight occasions in the course of the year when liturgical processions were held. This considerable number does not even include the state processions of the emperor from his palace across a courtyard to Hagia Sophia. These medieval public expressions made the city of Constantinople a church, a space for God's people to assemble.

We have earlier evidence as well. At the beginning of the fourth century John Chrysostom gives an example of a special procession, the transfer of the relics of the martyr Phocas from Asia Minor to a church outside the city:

Yesterday our city was aglow, radiant and famous, not because it had colonnades, but because a martyr arrived in procession from Pontus . . . Did you see the procession in the forum? . . . Let no one stay away from this holy assembly; let no virgin stay shut up in her house, no woman keep to her own home. Let us empty the city and go to the grave of the martyr, for even the emperor and his wife go with us . . . Let us make the sea a church once again, going forth to it with lamps.[4]

This is only one example of a liturgical procession in fourth-century Constantinople. Many more were held besides as supplications in times of great civic need. Chrysostom seems to have been especially fond of speaking about the city as a church. While still a presbyter at Antioch, he preached on processions in time of great civic turmoil, saying: "the whole city has become a church for us."[5]

Thus in medieval Jerusalem, Rome, Constantinople, and many other cities besides, a world in which Christianity formed the symbolic basis for social life, worship was not confined to the neighborhood church. It was public; it acclaimed the society's connectedness with the sacred; it made the streets and plazas sacred places in addition to the churches and shrines. To put it simply, the city became a church.

The Church as City

But what of the other statement in our title? How is it that the church could be conceived as a city? The answer to this question requires some discussion of spaces employed for Christian worship in the period after Constantine. As I see it, we are faced here with a complex development. Christian churches consisted basically of two types: the assembly hall and the shrine.

The assembly hall was essentially a public meeting place. Most early Christian basilicas were not new or specialized forms of architecture, but were adapted from secular halls used to conduct public business. A certain transformation of the secular basilica did take place, however. The assembly was focused on a sanctuary area containing the altar and seats for the ordained ministers. The Christian buildings were also lavishly decorated with gold, silver, mosaics, marble, and numerous lamps.

Shrines, on the other hand, connote a very different kind of space. A shrine is localized and focuses on a special site, usually the tomb of the martyr. Some early Christian basilicas combined the two types of building. One example is St. Peter's on the Vatican Hill, a large basilica acting as a covered cemetery and focusing on a shrine, the tomb of Peter. Liturgical arrangements, like the altar, were probably originally portable.[6]

We shall concentrate here not on the shrines but on the more usual type of early Christian church—the assembly hall (or basilica) for conducting the public business of the Christian *ecclesia*, namely, the liturgy. This kind of building did not separate Christians from the city, like a kind of sacred oasis but rather brought the city and its concerns into the church. Augustine makes this clear when he states: "The house of God is itself a city. For the house of God is the people of God."[7] For Augustine, of course, the city was the symbol of civilization and its possibilities.

In an important sense, the early churches were not only part of the city, they represented it. They were a miniature representation of public life. Thus churches were essentially public buildings that lay at the heart of the social symbol system.

Church and City Today

At this point it must be obvious that the picture we have drawn of early Christian worship in its relation to the city is not strictly applicable to contemporary society in the United States. In the first place, a single common symbol system no longer dominates our culture except perhaps as civil religion and that in the most tenuous sense. Second, we live in a society that affirms a healthy pluralism in which, in principle, no single religious group or church can demand adherence of all citizens. Several consequences follow from this.

The first consequence is that in a democratic and pluralistic society the state replaces the church as a universal symbol system. Thus, symbolically speaking, the city must be secular and not directly related to the sacred. Presidential inaugurations and celebrations of Thanksgiving and the Fourth of July tend to replace strictly religious feasts as truly social events. Ritualization of such events is best noted in Leni Rienfenstahl's documentary film, *Triumph of the Will*, which recounts the Nazi party's Nuremberg rally in 1936. This massive display of public civil ritual had no relation at all to the sacred. In fact, it reinforced the symbolic status and power of a purely secular state that had taken on the aura of the sacred.

Second, in a pluralistic society the whole of life, and *a fortiori* religious belief, become a highly privatized affair.[8] This phenomenon can be seen especially in cities where (except perhaps in ethnic neighborhoods) church attendance is a voluntary activity. The voluntary nature of church attendance can be both a good and a disturbing sign. It is good because regular churchgoers are people who want to be there. It can be disturbing in that a wider social base for the church is lost. The problem is this: how can one worship voluntarily and be a real participant in the wider civil society at the same time?

A third consequence of pluralism follows from the first two. The church is understood as a refuge from the city, a sanctuary from civil life. "Politics doesn't belong in the pulpit" is the familiar refrain, for religion has come to represent something that is strictly separate from public life.

Each of these factors seriously hampers an authentic understanding of Christian worship. Liturgy is essentially a corporate act involving whole persons and expressing their ultimate belief about the nature of human life. Christian liturgy, especially the eucharist, expresses and forms our relation to God through and with one another. Therefore, it is imperative that we work to bring the church and the city, *ecclesia* and *civitas*, closer together.

This is not a call for a return to a traditional, non-pluralistic concept of society. That would be both impossible and undesirable in our contemporary social situation. The church, however, need not act like a shrinking violet at the fringes of society. Recently the Roman Catholic Church in America has begun to speak and to act as a whole on social and political issues. This is a healthy sign of natural ecclesial concern for the whole of life. How can it be expressed liturgically?

My response is at the same time simple and difficult—the church must be itself. By this I mean that it must take its liturgy seriously as a corporate act. Concerns for justice and civil welfare must be evident not only in preaching but also in the manner in which liturgy itself is celebrated. Real attention must be given to the dignity of the whole gathered assembly. As Augustine said, the church is a city because the house of God is the people of God.

By the same token, the church should be bolder in asserting its right to be in public. Celebrations of the eucharist in civic stadiums and squares as well as liturgical processions through the streets and public places are means of proclaiming the public nature of the church and its concerns. These are not mere curiosities or gimmicks to gain the attention of all, but rather expressions that the public life of the city is also a sphere of salvation.

To return to our beginning, the city is a symbol. But symbols are by their very nature ambivalent. To some the city may be a symbol of evil, corruption, and decay. To others, and especially the church, it can be a symbol of life, human cooperation, and corporate salvation. Even the city can be gathered into the great hymn of God's praise.

Notes

1. Lewis Mumford, *The City in History* (New York: Harcourt, Brace and Jovanovich, 1961) 68-69.

2. See Wayne Meeks, *The First Urban Christians* (New Haven: Yale University Press, 1983) 13; also John G. Gager, *Kingdom and Community: The Social World of Early Christianity* (Englewood Cliffs, NJ: Prentice Hall, 1975) 107. For a more complete description of stational liturgy, see John F. Baldovin, *The Urban Character of Christian Worship: The Origins, Development, and Meaning of Stational Liturgy*, Orientalia Christiana Analecta, vol. 228 (Rome: Pontificium Institutum Studiorum Orientalium, 1987) esp. 35-38.

3. See Giorgio LaPiana, "The Roman Church at the End of the Second Century," *Harvard Theological Review* 18 (1925) 201-277.

4. John Chrysostom, "On the Holy Martyr Phocas" (PG 50:699).

5. John Chrysostom, "Homily 15 on the Statues" (PG 49:155).

6. See Richard Krautheimer, *Early Christian and Byzantine Architecture*, 2d ed. (Harmondsworth: Penguin Books, 1975) 39ff.

7. Augustine, *Ennarationes in Psalmos* 126:3.

8. Richard Sennett, *The Fall of Public Man* (New York: Alfred A. Knopf, Inc., 1977).

2

Worship in Urban Life: The Example of Medieval Constantinople

THE CITY OF THE MOTHER OF GOD CONSECRATES ITSELF TO HER AS AN offering, for she resides in it. Through her the city is both protected and powerful. And so the city cries to her: "Hail, O hope of all the ends of the earth."[1]

The city in question is, of course, Constantinople. This poetic prayer accompanied psalmody at morning prayer (or *orthos*) at Constantinople on the fifth Sunday of Lent, and acted as a refrain to a processional psalm on the anniversary of the city's dedication, 11 May. Such allusions to the protection of Constantinople, the God-guarded city, by the Mother of God are not at all rare in the city's medieval liturgy. In fact, anyone who attempts to reconstruct the tenth- and eleventh-century system of worship at Byzantium cannot help but notice how frequently the city is referred to in liturgical texts, and how much the city itself figures in worship.

I would like to lay out the relationship between the Christian worship and the urban milieu of Constantinople in the Middle Byzantine period, that period for which our sources are particuarly rich. I will do this in three parts, showing first, how the history of Constantinople was celebrated throughout its yearly cycle of worship; second, how the city itself, and not merely its churches and shrines, acted as a *locus* for Christian worship; and finally, how the city was considered to be sanctified by worship.

The City in the Liturgical Year

The *Typicon* of the Great Church, a book of directions for the patriarch's liturgical services at Constantinople in the tenth century, provides us with a rather complete picture of the city's major liturgical services. It shows a number of days that were given over, not to the celebration of a particular facet of Christian faith, such as the Epiphany, the Exaltation of the Holy Cross, or the Ascension, nor to the memory of particular Christian saints, but rather to anniversaries of specific events in the history of Constantinople. By my count, there are twenty such commemorations listed in the tenth-century *Typikon*. And all but two of these commemorations involved liturgical processions.

By far the most important of these celebrations was the anniversary of the city's dedication, an event that took place on 11 May 330, some four years after Constantine had decided to make the old Byzantium into his capital. To what extent the city's dedication in 330 was specifically Christian is a point of some discussion. It seems most reasonable to follow Gilbert Dagron, who in his masterful history of the city's first hundred years, *Naissance d'une capitale*,[2] claims that Constantinople was not so much dedicated to the Christian God or to pagan deities as it was to the glory of the emperor after whom it was named. Nevertheless, it was not long before the city was thought to have been dedicated to Christ or to the God of the Martyrs.[3] By the seventh century Mary, the Mother of God, was considered the object of dedication, especially after she was credited with defending the city in the siege of 626. And so in the tenth-century *Typicon* it is Mary the Mother of God who has pride of place in the anniversary of Constantinople's dedication. The title for the day reads: "11 May. The commemoration of the birthday of this God-protected and royal city" (*Typikon* 1.286).

The liturgical celebration began, as do all major feasts in the Byzantine church year, with evening prayer or *paramonie* on the previous evening. This was a solemn affair held in the

Great Church (Hagia Sophia) and followed by a monastic vigil service called *pannychis*. The next morning the Great Church was again the locale for the celebration of *orthos*. At both evening prayer and morning prayer the special chant of the day was the one which introduces this essay: "The City of the Mother of God consecrates itself to her . . ." Since Mary was responsible for the city's welfare and dominion, Constantinople owed her its allegiance.

After *orthos* a liturgical procession (involving participation of the whole people and not merely officials) moved from the Great Church down the major boulevard of the city, the Mese, to the most important plaza, the Forum of Constantine. It was here, precisely at the porphyry column topped by a statue of Constantine portrayed as a Christianized sun-god, that the original dedicatory service had been held. The small oratory at the base of the prophyry column, the chapel of Constantine and Helen, was the focus for the anniversary celebration. The place was made even more significant by its legendary associations, for it was said to contain not only nails from the cross of Christ but also the Palladium of old Rome. More than any other place in the city, therefore, this plaza with its column represented the noble ancestry of Constantinople: Constantinian, Christian, and Roman.

The outdoor liturgical celebration of the city's birthday was one of five such yearly services that included special readings before the procession moved elsewhere for the celebration of the eucharist. The choice of readings at this service illustrates the way the citizens of Constantinople made a connection between their city and their religious faith. The first reading, Acts 18:1-11, contains two verses that the Constantinopolitans would especially apply to themselves (although they had to stretch for references, since Byzantium is not mentioned in the New Testament). The first is Paul's announcement: "From now on I will go to the Gentiles." The second is the word of the Lord in reference to Corinth: "For I have many people in this city." The gospel for the service was also specially chosen for its applicability to Constantinople. One phrase in John's Last Supper discourse, John 15:9-16, reads: "You did not choose me, but I chose you, that you should go out and bear fruit, and that your fruit should abide . . ." No doubt the Byzantines thought the statement applicable to themselves.

Those accustomed to the concept of civil religion will perhaps smile; for here church, crown, and city are virtually identified with each other. The inhabitants of Constantinople, at
least in their prayers, considered themselves to have a very
special place in the world and attributed that prominent position to God's continuing providence. Medieval Byzantines believed in general that their *civitas* or civilization was to play a
special eschatological role as the remnant of the redeemed.
This role is even more evident in the chant used on 11 May for
the procession's return to the Great Church.

> O Lord, deliver your city, the eye of the world, from all your
> just threats; conserve it always as the ornament of the imperial
> sceptre. Grant us, by the help of the Mother of God, protection
> from the barbarians and safety from all dangers. (*Typicon* 1,
> 286)

Of course, the city's birthday was an obvious day on which
to relate its history to its established religious faith. But there
were nineteen days besides, in which a civic anniversary was
celebrated liturgically. Each of these commemorations referred
to a time when the city was saved from disaster by God and
the Mother of God. These near-catastrophes included fires,
barbarian attacks, and earthquakes. Earthquakes, especially,
evoked not only immediate liturgical response but lasting memorial observances. They must have been terrifying events, all
the more so because they were understood as particular signs
of divine displeasure. There are nine such earthquake memorials in the tenth-century *Typikon* of the Great Church. Most of
the services related to these commemorations took place outside the city walls or at the edge of the city, where there was
much open space. (The city never grew to the extent of the
fifth-century Theodosian Walls.) This choice of liturgical site
probably reflects the tendency of the population to flee to
open areas in case of earthquake, as we would do today.

Other commemorations referred to the city's salvation from
human threats, namely attacks and sieges. Here the Mother of
God played an especially active role in the city's defense. One
of the most vivid examples is that of the attack of the Avars
and Persians in 626, when Heraclius was fighting Persians

elsewhere and the army was for the most part absent from the city. On this occasion, according to Byzantine tradition, it was a relic, the robe of the Virgin, kept in a chapel at the shrine of Blachernae near the northernmost point of the city walls, which saved the day. The patriarch Sergius paraded this new palladium around the city walls, and the enemies fell back in disarray. Thus the chant for the Feast of the Deposition of the Virgin's Robe, on 2 July (a feast still celebrated in Byzantine churches today), reads in the *Typikon*:

> Mother of God, ever Virgin, protector of all peoples, you have given to your city your Robe and Cincture as sure protection. By your virginal conception, you remained incorruptible, for in you time and nature have entered a new way. And so we beg you: Give peace to our empire, and to our souls great mercy. (*Typikon* 1.328))

Earthquakes, barbarian invasions, sieges, fires, and other disasters all provided likely occasions for services of prayer if not panicked supplication. What is so remarkable about the worship system of medieval Constantinople is not that these events were times for immediate liturgical expression, but that their anniversaries were commemorated year after year for centuries. In the west, Rome and Gaul knew supplicatory processions that occurred every year on fixed days, or according to the date of the Feast of the Ascension; but none were so closely tied to specific local memories. The notion of Constantinople as a sacred, God-guarded city was strong enough to shape the Byzantine liturgical year around events in the city's own history. For this reason alone, Constantinople is an extraordinary example of the conjunction of urban life and Christian worship.

THE CITY AS A PLACE OF WORSHIP

One of the difficulties we moderns have in reconstructing the worship of late ancient and medieval societies is that we take an anachronistic view of their liturgical life. We tend to think of worship services as isolated events, distinct from the ongoing life of the culture. This was not the case in medieval Constantinople.

Not that Constantinople was unique in its employment of the whole city for worship. Every major urban center of late antiquity had an elaborate liturgical system, in which the major liturgical celebration of each feast of fast occurred in a particular church. This pattern may be called episcopal liturgy, because it was presided over by the bishop of the city or his representative. It has also been called stational liturgy, from the Roman idea that each major liturgical assembly was a *statio*, a "standing on guard duty of God's people."[4] Rome, Jerusalem, Antioch, Alexandria, Ravenna, Milan, Mainz, Metz—all of these cities had stational systems of worship in which different churches or shrines in and around the city were employed on different days. For the most part, this would be the city's only liturgical celebration on that day; but the station could also stand for the most important liturgical celebration, while less grand events were held in other churches for the convenience of the faithful. In either case, stational liturgies were major public celebrations that linked Christian worship with the ongoing everyday life of the city, especially by means of processions.

Constantinople also followed this pattern. To be sure, it had a more centralized focus for the celebration of the eucharist on major feasts. The Great Church, Hagia Sophia, was located at the heart of the city's monumental center, close by the Imperial Palace, the Hippodrome, and the Forum of Constantine. The great feasts of the liturgical year, such as Christmas, Epiphany, the Paschal Vigil, Easter Sunday, the Transfiguration (6 August), and the Exaltation of the Holy Cross (14 September), were all celebrated in the Great Church. Aside from these, however, a great number of feasts were celebrated at different churches in or around the city. These were not minor celebrations, for the tenth-century *Typikon* of the Great Church indicates that they, too, included liturgical processions.

All in all, some sixty-eight processions were held during the year. Moreover, this evidence is corroborated by the *De Ceremoniis Aulae Byzantinae* ("On the Ceremonies of the Byzantine Court") compiled by the tenth-century emperor-scholar, Constantine VII Porphyrogenitus. This source describes among other things the invovement of the imperial court in liturgical processions.[5] The emperor and his retinue participated in twenty-six liturgical processions in the course of the year. Of these, nine were processions from the imperial palace to the Great Church. These short but highly stylized progresses were not really popular processions but rather what I like to call "personage-centered" processions. On seventeen other occasions the emperor and his court joined with popular liturgical processions that had as their *terminus* a church other than Hagia Sophia.

In any case, an imperial processions was a splendid affair. One of these is described by Harum-ibn-Yahya, an Arab captive at the court of Basil I, the Maccedonian, in the last quarter of the ninth century. I shall quote here from A.A. Vasiliev's translation:

> The Emperor commands that on his way from the Gate of the Palace to the Church for the common people (the Great Church), which is in the middle of the city, be spread mats and upon them be strewn aromatic plants and green foliage, and that on the right and left of his passage the walls be adorned with brocade. Then he is preceded by 10,000 elders wearing clothes of red brocade; their hair reaches their shoulders, and they wear no upper cloak. Then behind them come 10,000 young men wearing clothes of white brocade. Then come 10,000 servants wearing clothes of brocade of the color of the blue sky; in their hands they hold axes covered with gold. Behind them follow 5,000 chosen eunuchs wearing white Khorasanian clothes of half-silk; in their hands they hold golden crosses. Then after them come 10,000 Turkish and Khorasanian pages wearing clothes of colored brocade, in their hands they have golden censers perfumed with aloes. Then come twelve chief patricians wearing clothes woven with gold; each of them holds a golden rod. Then come a hundred pages wearing clothes trimmed with borders and adorned with pearls; they carry a golden case in which is the Imperial Robe for the Emperor's prayer. Then before the Emperor comes a man called al-Ruhum, who makes the people be silent and says "Be silent." Then comes an old man holding in his hand a golden washbasin and a golden jug adorned with pearls and rubies. Then comes the Emperor wearing his festival clothes, that is, silk clothes woven with jewels; on his head there is a crown; he wears two shoes, one of them black, the other red. The prime minister follows him. In the hand of the Emperor there is a

small golden box in which is a bit of earth. He goes on foot. Whenever he makes two paces, the minister says in their own language *"Memnēsthe tou thanatou,"* which means in translation "Remember the death." When the minister says this to him, the Emperor pauses, opens the box, looks at the earth, kisses it, and weeps. He proceeds in this way until he reaches the gate of the Church.[6]

Doubtless, Harun-ibn-Yahya's estimate of over fifty-five thousand participants in the imperial procession from palace to church is grossly exaggerated. But one certainly gets the impression that these processions were extragavent affairs, for the *De Ceremoniis* informs us that there were also stopping points along the way in which the leaders of the various traditional urban factions (Blues, Greens, Whites, and Reds) greeted the emperor with acclamations, many of a religious character. There are clear indications that the public worship of Constantinople linked court, church, and society very closely together.

Let us return to the *Typikon's* description of the liturgical processions. I have already mentioned that there were sixty-eight popular processions in the course of a year. These processions always had an appropriate church or shrine for their destination. For example, they went to a church dedicated to the Virgin Mary on her feast days; or on 18 October, the feast of St. Luke, they went to the Church of the Holy Apostles where his relics were deposited. Many of these processions involved travelling considerable distances, since the starting point was usually the Great Church. The *Typikon* indicates that eleven processions went to the Holy Apostles (five kilometers from the Great Church), ten to the shrine of the Mother of God at Blachernae (seven kilometers), and three to the Hebdomon, the former army camp outside the city walls on the Via Egnatia to Rome (ten kilometers). These were by no means the only long processions in the course of the liturgical year.

In order to give an idea of what these processions were like, I will follow the *Typikon's* description of what happened on 25 September. The reason given for the procession is "the terrors which announced the resurrection," namely, an earthquake in 437, when Theodosius II was emperor and Proclus was patri-

arch (*Typikon* 1.45-49ff). According to a legend chronicled by
Theophanes, it was during the procession of the terrified sup-
plicants on 25 September 437 that the *Trisagion* was miracu-
lously revealed. Each year on the anniversary the patriarch,
clergy, and people would assemble in the Great Church after
morning prayer (which ended around dawn) and go in procession to the Forum of Constantine, where they would stop for a
brief service of prayer and litanies. They would then proceed
down the Mese to the Golden Gate, where they would again
stop briefly. Then they processed, singing all the while, to the
open-air Tribunal of the Hebdomon, where a number of emperors were crowned or acclaimed by the army. The chant for
the procession was, of course, the *Trisagion*, which had been
revealed on this day. After the procession came to a halt, there
was a service of psalms, scripture readings, and litanies. Finally, the procession moved to the Church of St. John the Theologian (the Apostle) where the eucharist was celebrated. The
procession and the revelation of the *Trisagion* are pictured together in the Menologion of Basil II, a product of the eleventh
century.[7]

Notice the elements of the liturgical procession: participation of both clergy and people, litanies, the use of open-air
spaces for services, and the constant employment of an easily
repeatable chant. Especially the use of the city's boulevard's
and open-air plazas alert us to the public nature of medieval
Constantinopolitan worship. Such processions through the
streets may have been even more frequent in the pre-
Iconoclast period than the *Typikon* indicates. This at least is my
suspicion, because Greek church historians of the mid-fifth
century, namely, Socrates and Sozomen, both refer to religious
processional practice in Constantinople. The account of Sozomen speaks for itself:

> The Arians, deprived of their churches in Constantinople dur-
> ing the reign of Theodosius [the Great], held their liturgical
> meetings outside of the city walls. They previously assembled
> by night in the public porticoes, and were divided into bands,
> so that they sang antiphonally, for they had composed certain
> refrains which reflected their own doctrine. At the break of day
> they marched in procession, singing these hymns, to their litur-

gical assemblies. They proceeded in this manner on all solemn festivals and on Sundays and Saturdays . . . John [Chrysostom] was fearful that any of his own people be led astray by witnessing these processions, and therefore commanded them to sing hymns in the same manner. The orthodox became more distinguished, in a brief time surpassing the heretics in number and processions.[8]

Here we may well have a witness to the origins of liturgical processions in Constantinople. Their frequency in this account (all Sundays, Saturdays, and festivals) has led me to suspect that popular processions were much more frequent in Constantinople in the pre-Iconoclast period than in the ninth and tenth centuries. Moreover, this witness confirms the contention of Juan Mateos and Robert Taft that the introductory rites of the Byzantine eucharist were influenced directly by Constantinople's stational processions.[9] In addition to the frequency of occurrence and effect on the structure of the eucharistic celebration, these processions also show that Christian worship was not confined to the churches, shrines, and monasteries of Constantinople, but that it was an open, public affair. Liturgy took place on the streets and not only in the churches. In describing the relation between religion and culture in late antique Byzantium, historian Peter Brown has put this same idea very well:

Styles of liturgy and preaching show how easily the street flowed into the basilica; and the receding tide brought out much of the holy into the street.[10]

Our sources have shown that the city itself was employed as the scene for Christian worship. In one sense this liturgy of the streets was a means of religious propaganda, advocating the superiority of one or another ecclesiastical party. But eventually this type of public worship also showed that urban society and the religious faith that it was underpinning were inextricably intertwined. For the medieval Byzantine, worship was not a matter of personal idiosyncrasy or private taste, confined to the walls of a building; rather, it was a manifestation of the culture itself.

In the same vein one must note the importance of public plazas for liturgical celebrations. In forty-six of the sixty-eight liturgical processions that we have identified in the *Typikon* of the Great Church, there was a special service in the city's main plaza, the Forum of Constantine. In terms of urban religious life, then, this Forum was nearly as important as the Great Church itself.

A CITY SANCTIFIED BY WORSHIP

Over the so-called Beautiful Doors of the southwest vestibule of Hagia Sophia, an entrance regularly used by the emperor and his retinue, a tenth-century mosaic shows the Mother of God seated on a throne with the child Jesus on her lap. She is receiving two gifts. On her left stands the Emperor Justinian holding his rebuilt Great Church. On the right stands the Emperor Constantine with his gift to the Virgin, the city of Constantinople itself. Few representations could so well manifest the idea of Constantinople. It was (at least from the seventh century on) considered to be dedicated to Mary, the *Theotokos*, the Mother of God. Moreover, it was dedicated entirely—not just its shrines and churches, but the whole city.

In return, of course, the Mother of God was the major protector of the city. Her most sacred relics (there were no bodily relics according to the tradition that her body had been assumed into heaven at her death) were her robe and her cincture. These Constantinople possessed and kept at the shrines of Blachernae and Chalkoprateia respectively. Symbolically, it was she who assumed the posture of the city's main military defender, as the following *troparion*, employed twice in the Lenten liturgy, shows:

> You have provided our city with an unvanquishable rampart,
> the Virgin who bore you, O Savior, through her save our souls,
> we pray you, from the dangers that assail us all about. (*Typikon*
> 2.52,58)

It was the Virgin who saved the city several times in the seventh century and again in the ninth century, as the Patriarch Photius made clear in two of his homilies on the siege of the

Rus in 860. In the first he excoriated the populace for being lax in their attendance at liturgical services, except of course when their lives were in danger. In the second homily he described what happened when the Virgin's robe was taken out of its special chapel at Blachernae to repulse the Russian invaders:

> When the whole city was carrying with me her rainment for the repulse of the besiegers and protection of the besieged we offered freely our prayers and performed the litany [i.e., in procession], thereupon with ineffable compassion she spoke out in motherly intercession . . . Truly is the most holy garment the raiment of God's Mother. It embraced the walls, and the foes inexplicably showed their backs; the city put around itself, and the camp of the enemy was broken up as at a signal; the city bedecked itself with it . . .[11]

Not only did relics of the Mother of God act as special protection devices for the city, but the very positioning of shrines dedicated to her manifest the idea of the Virgin Mary as the city's protective patroness. Among the one hundred-twenty-three shrines, churches, and monasteries that Raymond Janin lists for Constantinople, several stand out as protective shrines.[12] Just as the martyrial shrines of Peter, Paul, and Lawrence encircled Rome, so did the shrines of the Mother of God at Blachernae, located at the very northern tip of the city, at the Palaia Petra, just north of the Adrianople Gate, and the Pege (the Virgin of the Miraculous Source), located to the northwest of the Golden Gate. Each of these (and most often Blachernae) acted as a *terminus* for liturgical processions (i.e., supplications for the city and its inhabitants) during the course of the church year. In addition to the Mother of God, Constantinople had two other protectors, John the Apostle and John the Baptist, both of whom had shrines at the Hebdomon along the Via Egnatia to Rome.

We should not underestimate the drawing power of these shrines. They were not merely located in pleasant surroundings outside the city walls (Constantinople always had plenty of open green space within the Theodosian Walls); they also symbolized divine protection for the city itself. As early as the fourth century Jerome could say: *Movetur urbs sedibus suis,* "the city has changed its very location"[13]—so popular were the shrines of the saints containing their powerful relics or attesting astounding miracles. It is only with slight exaggeration that Peter Brown has recently written: "Late antique Christianity, as it impinged on the outside world, *was* shrines and relics."[14] This held true throughout the medieval period as well. Constantinople had a "manifest destiny," "because it was protected by supernatural defenders. The urban liturgy repeatedly reminded the population of this fact.

Constantinople was the very heart of the Byzantine Empire. Even when there was precious little empire to be capital over, it was *the* city, and without it there could be nothing like an empire, as the emperors in exile found out in Nicaea and Trebizond after the Latin conquest in 1204. The city itself was the symbol of an eschatological vocation, for it had been entrusted with keeping the true faith alive until the end of time.[15] Of course, all cities in the ancient and medieval worlds were held together by some sort of ideology of the sacred. All of them, right from the very beginnings of history, centered their urban social life on the sacred.[16] In a particular way, however, the urban liturgy of Constantinople was intimately tied to the sacredness of the city and to the idea of divine protection. It was due to this close tie, as well as to the city's political centrality, that the liturgy of Constantinople was so influential on all the Greek churches and their descendants.

Through the liturgical use and the dynamic interplay of churches, streets, plazas, and extra-urban spaces, the entire city became something like a church. By its very structure the liturgy of Constantinople identified the participants as inhabitants of a sacred city. Urban worship, therefore, was part of the seamless whole of life in medieval Constantinople. It was an indispensable factor for a society that considered itself special and sacred, protected by God and by the Mother of God. Not unlike modern urban dwellers, the people of Constantinople called their city "The City." And they called themselves *Romaioi*, the inheritors of the first Rome. For their predecessors, *civitas* meant not only walls, buildings, streets, and social relationships; it connoted civilization itself. For the medieval Byzantine, this *civitas* was inconceivable without worship at its most public.

Notes

1. Juan Mateos, *Le Typicon de la grande église (Ms. HS 40)*, Oriental-ia Christiana Analecta, vol. 165 (Rome: Pontificium Institutum Orientalium Studiorum, 1963) 1:286. Abbreviated in text as *Typikon*.

2. Gilbert Dagron, *Naissance d'une capitale: Constantinople et ses institutions de 330 à 451* (Paris: Presses Universitaires de France, 1974) 41.

3. Eusebius, *Vita Constantini* 3.48. See also D. Lathoud, "La consé-cration et dédicace de Constantinople d'après la tradition byzan-tine," *Echos d'Orient* 23 (1924) 289-314 and 24 (1925) 180-201, and Richard Krautheimer, *Three Christian Capitals: Topography and Politics* (Berkeley and Los Angeles: University of California, 1983) 41-68.

4. See my two essays, "La liturgie stationale à Constantinople," *La Maison-Dieu* 147 (1981) 85-94; and "The City as Church, the Church as City," *Liturgy* 3:4 (1983) 69-73. Reprinted as Chapter 1 of this vol-ume. See also Geoffrey G. Willis, "Roman Stational Liturgy," *Further Essays on Early Roman Liturgy*, Alcuin Club Collections, vol. 50 (Lon-don: SPCK, 1968) 3-20.

5. Johann Jacob Reiske, ed., *De Ceremoniis Aulae Byzantinae*, Cor-pus Scriptorum Historiae Byzantinae, vols. 8 and 9 (Bonn: Weber, 1829-1840).

6. A.A. Vasiliev, "Harum Ibn-Yahya and His Description of Con-stantinople," *Seminarium Kondokovianum* 5 (1932) 158-160.

7. *Il Menologio de Basilio II (Cod. Vat. gr. 1613)* (Turin, 1907) 2:65, 142, 350, 353, 355.

8. Sozomen, *Ecclesiastical History* VIII:8. A readily available Eng-lish translation of Sozomen by Charles D. Hartraupt is available in *A Select Library of Nicene and Post-Nicene Fathers of the Christian Church*, second series, eds., Philip Schaff and Henry Wace (New York: Chris-tian Literature Company, 1890).

9. Juan Mateos, *La Célébration de la parole dans la liturgie byzantine*, Orientalia Christiana Analecta, vol. 191 (Rome: Pontificium Institu-tum Orientalium Studiorum, 1971) 34-38; Robert Taft, "How Litur-gies Grow: The Evolution of the Byzantine 'Divine Liturgy'," *Orien-talia Christiana Periodica* 43 (1977) 364-365.

10. Peter Brown, "Eastern and Western Christaintiy in Late Antiq-uity: A Parting of the Ways." In Derek Baker, ed., *Church History* 12 (1976) 20-21.

11. Cyril Mango, trans., *The Homilies of Photius, Patriarch of Con-stantinople*, Dunbarton Oaks Studies, vol. 9 (Washington, D.C.: Dun-barton Oaks Research Library and Collection, 1958) 102.

12. Raymond Janin, *La Géographie écclésiastique de l'empire byzan-*

tine, 2d ed. (Paris: Institut Français d'Etudes Byzantines, 1969), vol. 3 (*Les Eglises et les monastères*); entry "*Theotokos.*"

13. Jerome, *Epistle* 107.1.

14. Peter Brown, *The Cult of the Saints: Its Rise and Function in Latin Christianity* (Chicago: University of Chicago Press, 1981) 12.

15. Cyril Mango, *Byzantium: The Empire of New Rome* (London: Weldenfeld and Nicolson, 1980) 201-217; Robert Browning, *The Byzantine Empire* (New York: Scribner, 1980) 96; Peter Brown, *The Cult of the Saints* 92-93.

16. Lewis Mumford, *The City in History* (New York: Harcourt, Brace & World, 1961) 68.

3

Sunday Liturgy in Jerusalem: A Pilgrim's View

AS YOU RISE FROM YOUR HARD PILGRIM'S BED WITH SLEEP STILL IN your eyes, you say to yourself: "I've never been to a service this early in the morning." But the monks who tend your hostel have told you that this service is not to be missed, unlike any you have experienced in your home country across the Mediterranean. This is your first Sunday in Jerusalem, and it is Lent. Considering the length and difficulty of your journey, you are determined not to miss a single part of the worship in this holy city. The pilgrims with you share your feelings. You have all been astonished by this place ever since you arrived in midweek; anticipation overtakes you because you will be allowed to pray in the holiest places, those sanctified by the Lord's presence.

Your hosts gather your group of pilgrims. Luckily, they can translate everything into Latin for you since you don't understand Greek, the languages used here for liturgies. You've noticed that some people who come to the daily services need a translator since they speak only Syriac, which seems to be the native tongue around here. Your guides lead you into the courtyard of the *Anastasis*, the large rotunda that covers the holy tomb of the Lord. They tell you that everyone must wait here until cockcrow for only then will the doors to this building be opened. Everyone seems to arrive early—this beautiful courtyard is packed with people. You join in singing the psalms—or perhaps they are hymns?

At cockcrow you notice that some of the clergy are clearing a path for the bishop who is coming to the *Anastasis* from his chambers nearby. As he enters the courtyard, all doors are opened. You and your companions are fortunate because you can see the bishop entering the chancel gates which are in front of the tomb.

Your guides describe the service. First, there are three psalms led by a priest, a deacon, and another member of the clergy in turn. As in your vigils back home, prayers are said after each psalm. At the completion of the psalms there is a long prayer, which you learn is a prayer of intercession for the church and the world. You remember your own small church, which seems far away indeed as you absorb the breathtaking sight of the dome and the lamps that make the interior dance in their flickering light.

The smell of incense startles you, since you've only smelled it in the processions of the imperial officials. Several censers are carried into the church, filling the place with the sweet smell. The bishop has now come to the chancel's entrance in front of the cave. He picks up a book and begins to read the gospel of the Lord's passion and resurrection. What better place to read it from than his own holy tomb? As the gospel is translated for you, you recall Matthew's account from which it is taken, and your cry merges with that of the crowd as all remember the Lord's suffering.

The bishop has finished reading the gospel, but the vigil hasn't ended. You follow in procession as he is led back into the courtyard before the large cross that surmounts holy Golgotha. Once the bishop arrives at the cross, the cantor begins another psalm, which is also followed by a prayer. Then the bishop blesses everyone; since you are nearby, you can approach him and kiss his hand, just as you do when taking leave of your town patron.

After a while the bishop returns to his house, but you follow your guides back to the *Anastasis* where the chanting of psalms continues until dawn. You can sleep any day, but here in this place you don't want to miss a thing.

In the Martyrium

At dawn you follow your guides and the crowd into the great church, called the *martyrium*. The eucharist is about to begin. Everyone enters at the same time, with the bishop and his clergy entering last. You marvel at the number of doors the church has. A psalm is being sung with most of the people responding to it, but since the liturgy is in Greek you cannot join in. Perhaps you will learn some responses before the end of your pilgrimage.

Now the bishop and clergy are taking their seats on the platform in the middle of the nave, which you are told is called a *bema*. It faces the marvelous sanctuary whose apse is surrounded by twelve pillars, each bearing a silver bowl on top. You imagine that these pillars represent the twelve apostles.

A reader stands to begin the first reading. Your translators tell you it is from the Letter to the Hebrews, which you have heard is read during Lent in a number of the churches in the east. The reading speaks of our firm hope in the promise made through Christ Jesus, our high priest after the order of Melchizedek (Heb 6:13-20). When the reader has finished, another psalm is chanted, this time with alleluia as its refrain. Then the deacon rises to proclaim the gospel, which is also translated for you. It is Mark's story about Jesus' cure of the boy with a dumb spirit, and it ends with the Lord's prediction of his own passion and resurrection (Mk 9:17-31).

Now something happens that you have never seen before. Each of the presbyters with the bishop preaches on the readings of the day. The bishop (whose name is Cyril) preaches last and eloquently about the Lord as high priest according to Melchizedek. The service takes much longer than the eucharist at home, but no one seems to be bothered by its length.

When the bishop has finished preaching, the deacon takes up the litany for the catechumens, the penitents, and the mentally disturbed. As none of these people may remain for the offering itself, each group is dismissed at the end of the prayers in its regard. Finally the deacon chants the litany for the church and the whole world.

Another psalm chant is taken up as the bishop and the clergy leave the platform in the nave and process to the holy of holies, the apse where the offering will be made. The deacons bring the gifts that will be offered in memory of the Lord who died for you. After the gifts have been placed on the holy table, something else occurs that you have never seen before. A deacon approaches the bishop and the clergy with a pitcher and a bowl and washes their hands. Clearly this washing symbolizes the purity required for the offering that is to come, since the bishop and the clergy have not even touched the gifts. Then the bishop asks everyone to greet one another in peace. The men greet the men and the women the women, of course, since they are standing on opposite sides of the nave.

The bishop is standing at the holy table facing all, that is, facing toward the east, the symbol of light against the darkness. He begins the dialogue of the great anaphora, as the eucharistic prayer is called here. You do not understand the words, but you are familiar with this part of the liturgy. Every now and again you catch a recognizable word. Certainly you recognize the name Sion toward the end of the prayer. It is appropriate that the mother church of all Christians should be mentioned in this most holy prayer in this most holy place.

At the end of the great prayer, the Lord's Prayer is said by everyone. Saying this prayer amidst the offering is a new experience, but it seems appropriate since you are praying for the bread of life that you are about to receive. As the consecrated bread is broken, the bishop proclaims: "Holy things for holy people." Everyone responds: "One is holy, One Lord, Jesus Christ." You realize that you are about to receive the holy one who died for you and was raised in this very place. Awe and gratitude fill your heart.

After the bishop and the clergy have received the life-giving body and blood of the Lord, you enter the procession to do the same. Your guides tell you that the cantors are singing Psalm 34, and you pick up the refrain: "Taste and see that the Lord is good." Like the others who receive, you extend your palms to receive the Lord's body, the right hand on the left; after saying "Amen," you touch it to your eyes before consuming it. Now you approach the cup of the Lord's precious blood, say "Amen," and drink from it. This time you make sure to take the moisture on your lips and touch it to your forehead and your eyes, knowing that every part of you must be sanctified by the holy communion with the Lord.

Next you join in the procession which leads across the courtyard of the cross to the holy *Anastasis* where the Lord himself was raised. Everyone sings along the way. When all have entered the *Anastasis*, the bishop goes to the cave of the resurrection and prays several prayers. Then he blesses everyone, and as many as possible come up to kiss his hand at the dismissal. Now you can return to your lodgings and get some food. You are still excited, but also a bit weary and hungry. You welcome the rest because the heat is greater here than in your country, and it is only the fourth Sunday of Lent. Besides, you will be returning to the church in a few hours.

Prayer at Evening

Just before the tenth hour (about two hours before sunset), your guides summon you once more—this time for a service you have been attending since your arrival: the prayer you call vespers or the prayer at evening which is here called *licinicon* or *lucernare*, lamplighting in your language. Entering the *Anastasis* for the final time, you can easily see how the service derived its name. Every lamp has been lit, and the place is dazzling with the brilliance of light that was taken from a lamp burning within the Lord's tomb.

The bishop is not yet here, but the service begins as usual with psalms and hymns. You are told that one selection is Psalm 141, a most fitting text, since it speaks of the lifting up of one's hands as an evening offering. Another, you are informed, is a very old hymn in praise of Christ the light, called in Greek, *Phos hilaron* ("O Gladdening Light").

Toward the end of the singing the bishop enters. He takes his place at his chair, as do the presbyters at the chairs that surround him. When the hymns and psalms have been completed, the bishop goes to the chancel in front of the tomb while a deacon begins to pray for individuals. A large children's choir responds to every name by singing *Kyrie eleison* (in your language "Lord, have mercy"). Then the bishop prays twice and the dismissals begin, first for the catechumens and then for the faithful.

At this last service of the day, the liturgy does not end in the *Anastasis*. Rather, while singing hymns, all process to the courtyard of the cross, where a prayer and the blessing of the catechumens and faithful is repeated. Finally, all process to the Great Church, where the eucharist was celebrated in the morning, and the same rite is repeated. As before, many people approach the bishop to receive his blessing individually as the service ends.

It has indeed been a long day; tomorrow you will rise early to pray again. You feel like an athlete in training for the liturgies of great (or holy) week and Easter which your neighbors have described to you. But for the moment you are well-pleased that you have spent this Lord's Day, Sunday, in the holiest place on earth. You've heard preachers say that this place is no more sacred than any place in which the community assembles to celebrate, and you believe that, but you still feel privileged to be here, knowing that Sunday has taken on a new meaning for you.

Analysis

The preceding hypothetical reconstruction of what Sunday liturgy might have looked like during Lent in the late fourth century in Jerusalem is based on the following sources: The Travel Diary of the pilgrim woman, Egeria (381-384); the Catechetical Lectures of Cyril, Bishop of Jerusalem; the Mystagogical Lectures of the same bishop Cyril or perhaps of his successor, John (386-417); the Old Armenian Lectionary, witnessing the state of the Jerusalem liturgy at the beginning of the fifth century; the Georgian Lectionary, which also reflects the liturgy of Jerusalem, but from the late fifth century up to the eighth century; and finally the Anaphora (or eucharistic prayer) of St. James, whose main lines are described in Cyril's fifth mystagogical lecture.

Scholars may take exception to several areas of this hypothetical reconstruction. The first is my hypothesis that Jerusalem used basically the same lectionary in Lent that was subsequently employed by the church of Constantinople and is fundamentally that of the Byzantine Rite today. My suggestion, however, is based on several comments in Cyril's catechetical lectures. The subject is, moreover, fully developed in my book *Liturgy in Ancient Jerusalem*.[1]

Second, there has been a considerable amount of debate as to what the Sunday eucharist looked like in Jerusalem. Some think that the liturgy of the word took place in the Great Church and that the procession to the *Anastasis* preceded the celebration of the liturgy of the eucharist proper. For a number of reasons, especially a comparison with the contemporary document, the *Apostolic Constitutions*, stemming from Antioch or its environs, I believe that the service in the *Anastasis* was a postcommunion service of prayer, blessing, and dismissal.

Third, I have suggested that the liturgy of the word took place in the name of the Great Church (*Martyrium*) based on the evidence of the Georgian Lectionary that a special chant of some length accompanied the washing of the hands, thus probably indicating a procession of some sort. We know that in a number of the Syrian churches the liturgy was divided between a liturgy of the word in the nave (at a *bema*) and the liturgy of the eucharist which in turn took place in the apse area or sanctuary.

If it seems to the reader that our pilgrim has spent a lot of time in church for one day, the impression is correct. This fact is attributable not only to the special pilgrimage nature of the Jerusalem church, but also to the zeal of people who express their priorities by the amount of time and attention they give to the assembly on the Lord's Day.

Note

1. John Baldovin, *Liturgy in Ancient Jerusalem*, Alcuin-Grove Studies in Worship, vol. 9 (Bramcote, Notts: Grove Books, 1989), chapter 5.

4

On Feasting the Saints

THE REFORM OF THE GENERAL ROMAN CALENDAR OF 1969 PLACED A major emphasis, in the celebration of the liturgical year, on the temporal cycle, and rightly so.[1] The goal of the reform was to bring out in sharp relief the centrality of Easter, especially the celebration of Sunday, and to clear much of the debris that inevitably settles in a communal calendar. One of the most striking effects of the reform was to reduce greatly the number of saints in the general (universal) Roman calendar and to simplify the classification of days by dividing them into three categories (solemnities, feasts, and memorials—both obligatory and optional). Priorities were set on the paschal triduum, Eastertide, Lent, and Sunday. Very few saints were assigned solemnities.[2] The result has been a widespread confusion as to what to do with the sanctoral aspect of the calendar. My purpose here is to show that, although the sanctoral may not be the most important part of the calendar, it has an integral role to play in the Christian celebration of time.

THE CELEBRATION OF TIME

Before dealing directly with saints' days, it will be useful to consider what Christians mean by the celebration of time. Celebration is a term which has become all too loose in application. When this word is used to denote every eucharist, it loses its force. Celebration is literally "outstanding" time. Its closest equivalent is festivity, which Juan Mateos has well described as "an exuberant manifestation of life itself standing out in contrast to the background rhythm of daily life . . . the feast [is] the communitarian, ritual and joyful expression of common experiences and longings, centered around a historical fact, past or contemporary."[3]

To celebrate, then is to feast. It should be obvious that when the eucharist is held daily, every eucharist cannot be a true celebration in the strict sense of the word. Part of the difficulty with the eucharist in contemporary practice is the failure to modulate it according to scale. It is a difficulty which the current liturgical books of the Roman Rite do little to alleviate. A true celebration is one in which the whole community (or at least a significant part of it) participates. There should be a clear distinction between authentic celebration of the communal eucharist and the day-to-day meetings of small groups at which the eucharist is the focus.

With regard to the latter, it is a mistake to consider the scaled-down daily celebration of the eucharist, to which many Roman Catholics are accustomed, as a feast, regardless of the dignity that the calendar assigns to the day. There is a difference between celebration and commemoration. A commemoration may consist of a few sentences of hagiographical information, diverse orations and prefaces, and even readings outside of the daily cycle, but this does not make for a feast. Only "the exuberant manifestation of life itself" does that, and it is closely allied to how people perceive time.

In Christianity there is no such thing as sacred as distinct from profane time.[4] To be sure, there are certain rhythms of the day and of the seasons, but in principle all time has been redeemed in Christ, and the fact that the end-time is upon us means that all chronological time exists to be made holy. Time is literally what we make of it. It is constructed out of human perception, individual and communal. All people have had the experience of duration seeming longer or shorter depending on various factors such as expectation, mood, and the presence or absence of light. This is what permits us to construct a calendar, one which can capitalize on external factors, such as the seasons, but need not be a prisoner of these factors. In short, the authentic celebration of a calendar will depend far more on the needs and shape of a particular Christian community than it will on external factors.

This is where the cult of the saints becomes important. It is not in the first place an attempt to support individual piety, but rather (and this is certainly true of its origins) a manifestation of ecclesial spirit. Certain individuals by their death (and life)[5] help to form the identity of a community by being models of Christ himself. They approximate the Christian mystery in a specific way which relates to a local community and so are aids in inserting that community into the mystery of Christ.

All this is not new. In fact, it has quite a good pedigree in the history of the church. Historians have consistently focused on the local nature of the cult of the saints and its growth out of the cult of the dead in general.[6] This much is clear from the first extant account of a martyr's cult, namely, *The Martyrdom of Polycarp*:

> So we later took up his bones, more precious than costly stones and more valuable than gold, and laid them away in a suitable place. There the Lord will permit us, as far as possible, to gather together in joy and gladness to celebrate the day of his martyrdom as a birthday, in memory of those athletes who have gone before, and to train and to make ready those who are to come hereafter.[7]

The martyr was celebrated by the extended family that made up the Christian community each year on the day of his or her *dies natalis* in the place where the body was buried. The celebration was limited for a long time to that local family, the particular church. Even the fourth-century Philocalian Calendar (A.D. 354) of Rome includes only three non-Roman saints.[8] The subsequent unversalization of the cult of the martyrs and the addition of categories like confessor, virgin, and bishop is too involved to go into here. It is sufficient to note that the origins of the cult of the saints attest to the desire of the local community for a concrete entry-point into the mystery of Christ. Such an interpretation of these origins provides the legitimation not for individual piety but for the ecclesial feast, the celebration by the whole community of the mystery of Christ manifest in this faithful witness, to whom it can relate rather directly.

With this in mind, let me proceed to deal with three questions: (1) Should local Christian congregations construct their own festal calendars? (2) What are the advantages and disadvantages in so doing? (3) What are the factors, then, which make for genuine celebration?

LOCAL FESTAL CALENDARS

The General Roman Calendar includes fourteen solmenities (four of which are movable[9]), twenty-five feasts (two are movable[10]), sixty-three obligatory memorials, and ninety-five optional memorials. All 179 days cannot be truly celebrated, given what was said above. Hence the creation of the category—memorial—for 158 of these days. It is difficult to imagine that even the thirty-nine solmnities and feasts can be kept with genuinely festal character, especially since thirty-two of them do not as a rule fall on Sundays. The usual solution has been to keep a number of solemnities (six in the U.S.A.) as days of obligatory Mass attendance. Among these days of obligation in the U.S. only three of them have any relation to the saints: All Saints (1 Nov.), the Assumption (15 Aug.), and the Immaculate Conception (8 Dec.).

Here an objection may be raised. How can one argue for the festal celebration of the day of a particular saint, when the days of obligation (except of course for Christmas) seem to be suffering from benign neglect? The response is quite simple. The days chosen for universal solemnization (among them the days of obligation) are selected on the basis of their relation to the Christian mystery in general, not for their relation to a particular celebrating community. What needs to be re-thought is how a particular church, community, or congregation can authentically celebrate. The general calendar provides the raw material for the feast but not the feast itself unless the feast happens to have a germane connection with the concrete worshiping community.

It is not beside the point that Christmas was chosen to fall on a day, the *Natalis Solis Invicti* (Birth of the Unconquered Sun, the old date of the Roman winter solstice), that had festal connections. The same can be said for another day in the fourth-century Philocalian Calendar, the *Cathedra Petri* (Chair of St. Peter), 22 February, which coincided with the *cara cognatio*, a Roman civil feast for honoring all the dead.[11] Again, 25 April was chosen for the Greater Litany not because of St. Mark's day, but because it coincided with an ancient Roman agricultural procession, *Robigalia*; and in Jerusalem the Feast of the Dedication of the Cathedral (the shrines of the Passion and Resurrection of Christ) was chosen to coincide with the date of the dedication of the Temple of Jupiter Capitolinus and perhaps also with the Jewish feast of Booths, 13 September. Such a process of selection is not foreign to modern times either. Witness the selection of May Day for the Feast (now memorial) of St. Joseph the Worker and the last Sunday of October (prior to the 1969 calendar) for the Feast of Christ the King in direct opposition to Reformation Sunday.[12] The point is that a feast day must be tied to some concrete, socially recognizable or historical event if it is to take hold in a community.

The General Roman Calendar and the Instruction on Particular Calendars both offer the opportunity for local churches to construct their festal time in such a concrete fashion. The *Normae Generales*, for example, read: "Individual churches or religious communities should honor in a special way those saints who are particularly associated with them."[13] From this follow a number of conditions which are spelled out in the instruction of 24 June 1970.[14]

Particular calendars must harmonize with the general calendar. The temporal cycle has priority. Therefore, solemnities or feasts of particular churches may not conflict with Sundays, Lenten weekdays, the octave of Easter, weekdays between 17 and 31 December, or with universal solemnities.[15] But in a local parish, for example, the following days might be solemnized: the national patron, the principal patron of the diocese, the principal patron of the city or town, the patron of the parish church, and the anniversary of the church's dedication.[16] The instruction urges that the selection of saints' days be made on the basis of the day that the person died (the *dies natalis*), but recognizes the possibility of using the anniversary of the translation of a saint's body or the day of (his) ordination. As with most Roman ecclesiastical documents, there is ample room for imagination:

Permitted celebrations will be fixed on days which are best suited to pastoral needs . . . Nothing prohibits the possibility of certain feasts being celebrated with greater solemnity in particular places within a diocese or religious order. If one observes this distinction carefully, the calendars will respond better to particular cases and needs.[17]

Thus the answer to our first question is that local churches not only can but should construct their own festal calendars. And the pastoral imagination is encouraged to find times that provide the possibility of authentic celebration, genuine feasts.

ADVANTAGES AND DISADVANTAGES

What then might be the advantages and disadvantages of constructing such a calendar? Dealing first with the disadvantages may shed more light on the advantages. In the first place, anyone concerned with liturgical celebration today is no stranger to the fact that celebration is impossible without a vibrant worshiping community, one rooted in a common experience of faith. Since authentic celebration calls for a vigorous community and not merely the adaptation of a daily eucharist which few attend, it seems that the possibility of genuine feasts of the saints is slender.[18]

Another disadvantage is that local calendars run the risk of an undesirable particularism—the possibility that local celebrations might eclipse not only saints of universal significance but also the priority of the temporal cycle, especially of Easter.

A third disadvantage has to do with the present situation of daily eucharist in the Roman Catholic Church. As was mentioned above, time needs to be modulated. If the eucharist is to remain the focus of every Catholic meeting for prayer, from solemnities to optional memorials, then such modulation will be difficult to come by. In other words, if every day is a celebration, it is likely that no day will be a true celebration.

The fourth and perhaps most significant disadvantage is that modern society does not lend itself well to feasts. The time off, necessary for the feast, does not seem easy to come by, and increasingly other activities compete for the time of Christians. Unless Christian feasts are made to coincide with civic holidays (a venerable solution), most feasts will be celebrated in the evening, after work.

Each of the disadvantages in the local celebration of feasts of the saints is matched by more significant advantages. First, with regard to the need to have a community in order to celebrate, one recognizes the community building aspect of the saints. This or that personage who has a strong tie to the community enhances the identity of the group. In this connection several ethnically oriented saints' celebrations come to mind. One is the feast of St. Patrick among the Irish Americans of New York and other cities and towns; other examples are the various Italo-American *feste* of specified saints and the Virgin; yet another is the Puerto Rican celebration of the Nativity of John the Baptist. Needless to say, these feasts are not solely or even primarily liturgical occasions, but it remains for the pastoral imagination to ritualize, to bring them further into the Christian orbit. Such feasts are the raw material we have for the integration of popular and ethnic piety with the wider Christian faith.

Second, a particularist Christianity is preferable to a bland one. The priority of the temporal cycle cannot mean that truly popular feasts are not to be celebrated with great fervor in local communities. The history of the Christian celebration of time shows that it is precisely the sanctoral which provided local identification for the church. A legitimate desire for identifiable models led even to the "invention" of the bodies of saints, especially in areas where there had been few martyrs.[19] Moreover, saints' feasts need not necessarily interfere with the temporal cycle.[20]

Finally, the antifestal situation of modern society does not demand immediate and unconditional surrender on the part of Christian communities. Faced with an impoverishment of time as well as an impoverishment of cult (as P. Jounel has described the phenomenon[21]), congregations and their leaders should realize that time need not be shaped by factors which are beyond their control. How individuals and communities order their time is an indication of their priorities. In an increasingly "de-natured" world, those priorities will have to be fought for. Thus there is something inherently evangelistic about the celebration of Christian feasts.

FACTORS MAKING GENUINE CELEBRATIONS

It remains, then, to discuss the shape that sanctoral feasts might take. The most important factor is that feasts are extraordinary. They lift people out of ordinary chronological time. Therefore, they must be few in number and carefully selected. It is possible that one or more could be chosen to coincide with a day that is already a holiday. As long as the priority of the temporal cycle is adhered to,[22] suitable days can be chosen with local peculiarities in mind.

Second, as was true of the practice of early Christians, the eucharist should always be associated with the celebration. But since feasts are not merely collective visible events but also "total social facts,"[23] the eucharist alone is probably not sufficient for a celebration of a genuine feast. Pulling all the stops out for a celebration means having it in a larger social context, something that the entire community can celebrate meaningfully. For example, the best day to choose for an ordination (with all its attendant celebration) might be the local patronal feast, just as religious often pronounce vows on days of special solemnity for their congregations.

These reflections have been an attempt to set the sanctoral in a festal perspective. Many other problems remain with the sanctoral cycle of the General Roman Calendar, especially with regard to its universal and ecumenical aspects.[24] But the concern here has been primarily with the relation of saints and their feasts to the identity of the local church. The saints can be the manifestation of an ecclesial spirit, which is a prime motive of liturgy. Few saints can be feasted authentically in any one church, and they will vary from community to community. What is important is that the saints who are recognized by feasts in their honor build up the faith of the community. That such a practice is consistent with Christian belief is clear in what follows:

> In genuine Christian theology the great updater of Jesus is the Holy Spirit. For the Second Person of the Trinity became incarnate in a particular time and a particular place; the Third Person did not. As the Spirit of Jesus, he can make Jesus present to

all times and places. Nevertheless, the Spirit, invisible in himself, is visible only in and through the Christian believer; and so we need models of how Jesus can be visible in disciples at other times and other places. This need explains the Church's presentation of saints for emulation.[25]

Notes

1. See *General Norms for the Liturgical Year and Calendar*, Liturgy Documentary Series, vol. 6 (Washington, D.C. United States Catholic Conference, 1976).

2. All these are New Testament saints: Mary (1 Jan., 15 Aug., 8 Dec.), St. Joseph (19 March), John Baptist (24 June), and Peter and Paul (29 June).

3. Juan Mateos, *Beyond Conventional Christianity* (Manila: East Asian Pastoral Institute, 1974) 225, 279.

4. Ibid. 305. See also an article that argues the same notion at some length, L.M. Chauvet, "La ritualité chrétien dans le cercle infernal du symbole," *La Maison-Dieu* 133 (1978) 31-77.

5. No doubt there is a danger here. It is well expressed by J. Hild, "Le mystère des saints dans le mystère chrétien," *La Maison-Dieu* 52 (1957) 6: "A honorer seulement quelques saints de prédilection et à copier devotement leur examples, on court le danger d'ignorer le véritable mystère de la sainteté chrétienne; au lieu de se former une âme ecclésiale on risque de la déformer par une piété individualiste."

6. See especially, Hippolyte Delehaye, *Les Origines du culte des martyrs*, 2d ed. (Brussels: Société des Bollandistes, 1933); idem, *Sanctus: Essai sur le culte des saints dans l'antiquité* (Brussels: Société des Bollandistes, 1927) 122-161. Also B. de Gaiffier, "Refléxions sur l'origine du culte des martyrs," *La Maison-Dieu* 52 (1957) 19-43 and Theodor Klauser, *Christliche Martyrerkult, heidnischer Heroenkult, und spätjudische Heiligenverehrung*, Veröffentlichung der Arbeitsgemeinschaft für Forschung des Landes Nordrhein-Westfalen, Geisteswissenchaften, vol. 19 (Cologne: Westdeutscher Verlag, 1960).

7. "The Martyrdom of Polycarp," 18:2-3; Eng. tr. in Cyril C. Richardson, ed. *The Early Christian Fathers* (New York: Macmillan, 1970) 156.

8. Perpetua and Felicity in Africa, 7 March, and Cyprian, 14 Sept. with celebration at the catacomb of Callistus.

9. That is, Holy Trinity, Corpus Christi, Sacred Heart, and Christ the King.

10. That is, Holy Family, Baptism of the Lord.

11. *Cathedra* here does not refer to the bishop's throne but to the empty seat left for the honored dead at the feast.

12. Shifts in the 1970 calendar are instructive here. St. Joseph the Worker remains on 1 May but has been reduced to an optional memorial. Christ the King is now celebrated as the last Sunday before Advent.

13. General Roman Calendar, no. 50 (n. 1 above) 11.

14. This instruction was available to me only in a French translation: "Instruction sur les calendriers particuliers." *La Maison-Dieu* 103 (1970) 96-113. I will cite the paragraph numbers given in the original document.

15. "Instruction," nos. 1, 2 (p. 97).

16. Ibid., nos. 8-11 (pp.99-100).

17. Ibid., nos. 22, 25 (pp.104, 105). The translation is mine.

18. P. Jounel, "La célébration de l'année liturgique renovée," *La Maison-Dieu* 133 (1978) 98, remarks: "Où ces célébrations sont d'une grande importance pour nourir la foi des baptisés et les entretenir dans une relation intime et savoreuse avec le monde invisible, celui où nous attendent les Témoins. Seul un effort pastoral soutenu, capable d'assumer les échecs, pourra surmonter la difficulté. Avouons qu'il n'est pas reconfortant de célébrer, le 24 juin, une messe debordante de joie dans une église vide."

19. For example, of Protase and Gervase by Ambrose of Milan, A.D. 386, and of Stephen in Jerusalem, A.D. 415. See Bernard Kötting, *Der frühchristliche Reliquienkult und die Bestattung im Kirchengebäude*, Veröffentlichung der Arbeitsgemeinschaft für Forschung des Landes Nordrhein-Westfalen, Geisteswissenschafter, vol. 123 (Cologne: Westdeutscher Verlag, 1965) and André Grabar, *Martyrium*, 3 vols. (Paris: Collège de France, 1943-1946).

20. P. Jounel, "Les oraisons du propre des saints dans le nouvel missel," *La Maison-Dieu* 105 (1971) 180-198, points out that many of the new sanctoral collects correspond well with the season in which the saint is celebrated; confer the collect for the Feast of Sts. Philip and James, 3 May.

21. P. Jounel, "La célébration," 90-91.

22. An example we have already seen, St. Patrick's Day, always falls within Lent. Its vigorous survival is testimony that a real feast cannot be suppressed.

23. F. Isambert, "Notes sur la fête comme célébration," *La Maison-Dieu* 106 (1971) 101.

24. Confer R. Nardone, "The Roman Calendar in Ecumenical Perspective, " *Worship* 50 (1976) 238-245; also J. Dubois, "Les saints du nouveau calendrier," *La Maison-Dieu* 100 (1969) 157-178. Far too

many saints are Roman and/or Italian. Out of 150 non-New Testament saints in the General Calendar, 123 are European. Clearly we have to find saints from elsewhere.

25. Raymond E. Brown, "The Meaning of Modern New Testament Studies for an Ecumenical Understanding of Mary," *Biblical Reflections on Crises Facing the Church* (New York: Paulist Press, 1975) 106, n. 104.

5

All Saints
in the
Byzantine Tradition

EVEN CASUAL VISITORS TO A CHURCH OF THE BYZANTINE CHRISTIAN
tradition risk feeling overwhelmed by the presence of a great
cloud of witnesses—the saints of Christian faith. Before a word
is spoken or a chant intoned, the visitors will sense that saints
are an integral aspect of Byzantine piety and devotion. Immediately they see the Virgin enthroned with the child in the apse
of the church and the icons of Christ and the *Theotokos*, the
Mother of God, which flank the holy doors on the ikon screen
leading into the sanctuary. In some buildings, such as San
Apollinare Nuovo, a sixth-century church in Ravenna, they
will be impressed by mosaics depicting a long line of martyrs—
men to the right and women to the left—who march with the
faithful down the nave of the church to the sanctuary. The glorious interior of many Byzantine churches is packed with
ikons, frescoes, and mosaics of saints whose timeless stares
provide companionship in divine worship to all Christians—
the "saints" as Paul called us—who still worship in the flesh.

If these western visitors also delve into the service books of
the various churches of the Byzantine tradition, they may be
impressed by the sheer number of the saints venerated in the
eucharist and liturgy of the hours in the course of the calendar

year. These include apostles, martyrs, confessors and virgins, monks and lay people, great bishops and ascetics, and even the famous holy men and women of Israel's faith.

This bounty comes as no surprise to Roman Catholics, of course, whose pre-Vatican II calendar included almost as many saints. Both the Roman and Byzantine calendars have been trimmed any number of times in the course of the centuries, yet it seems to be a law of Christian piety that after each reform the number of saints grows back just as lushly as before. Of course, churches in the Byzantine tradition vary in the saints who are venerated, depending on the national origin of the church and whether or not it is in communion with Rome, but in any case an enormous number of saints are objects of devotion in every contemporary Byzantine calendar.

The text of the Divine Liturgy of St. John Chrysostom, the eucharistic rite most frequently employed among Byzantine Christians, includes numerous references to all the saints. Most litanies, for example, end with the formula: "Let us remember our all-holy, spotless, most highly blessed and glorious Lady the Mother of God and ever-virgin Mary with all the saints, and commend ourselves and one another and our whole life to Christ God." All the saints are also featured in the weekday preparatory antiphons of the divine liturgy, in the prayer before the chant of the *trisagion* ("Holy God, Holy Mighty, Holy Immortal One, have mercy on us") and in the eucharistic prayer itself, in which forebearers, patriarchs, prophets, apostles, preachers, evangelists, martyrs, confessors, ascetics, and every holy soul are remembered.

Little wonder, then, as Robert Taft puts it, that "the communion of saints is one of the most profound impressions of Byzantine worship."[1] The saints provide a strong link with a common tradition that enables Byzantine piety to avoid much of the individualism that plagues contemporary Western Christianity. It is in this context of the ongoing devotional and liturgical piety of Eastern Christians that we can begin to appreciate the significance of the Feast of All Saints in the Byzantine calendar.

THE FEAST OF ALL SAINTS

Unlike the western celebration of All Saints, which has had

its own day on the calendar since the seventh century (originally 13 May and then 1 November), the Byzantine feast occurs on a Sunday within the temporal cycle; that is, its observance is governed by the date of Easter. Since the fourth
century it has been kept on the Sunday after Pentecost, although in some places it may have been celebrated on another
date.[2] To this day Byzantine Christians celebrate All Saints,
rather than the Feast of the Holy Trinity, on the Sunday following Pentecost.

For students of the liturgical year the feast of All Saints in
the east is an early departure from the very idea of Pentecost,
the great fifty days of Easter, as a unitive celebration of the
victory of Christ over the powers of death and his consequent
enthronement and pouring forth of the Holy Spirit. In Jerusalem, for example, it was not until the early fifth century that a
distinct celebration of the Ascension was held. And so, in the
sense of keeping the fifty days of Easter as a unity, celebrating
a related feast on the Sunday after the fifty days are over is a
somewhat unfortunate development.

Feasting all the saints on the Sunday after Pentecost signi-
fies that Easter itself is extended by an octave to include another important celebration. In the west, the week following
Pentecost became an octave of the Holy Spirit, a celebration of
the seven gifts of the Spirit, even though such a festive celebration was mitigated by the return to penitential practices symbolized by the ember days that always fell during this week.
In the east, something of the same sort happens. Fasting is re-
sumed at the end of Pentecost Sunday, which is marked by an
"Office of Genuflection," since one does not kneel during the
great fifty days. In any case, the Byzantine liturgical books of
chants and other hymnic material for the Easter Seasons, the
Pentecostarion, does not end with Pentecost Sunday but with
All Saints Sunday, a week later.

This development implies that Eastern Christians were early, and strongly, attracted not only to extending the feast of
Easter but to extending it specifically in the direction of feasting all the martyrs, the first of the saints to be venerated in this
feast. The Syrians also marked a day during Eatertide as a
commemoration for all dead Christians, as the homilies of the
sixth-century Monophysite patriarch of Antioch, Severus,
demonstrate.[3] Eastern Christian piety obviously needed to in-

clude all Christians, the living, the martyrs, and all the dead, in its celebration of Christ's victorious trampling down of death by his death.

Feasting all of the saints was important for Christians of the fourth and subsequent centuries because the saints themselves held an extremely important place in piety and devotional practice.[4] Christians in eastern and western parts of the Roman Empire honored the martyrs in their relics, their bodily remains, which every Christian center of importance possessed. These martyrs provided a sense of identity for particular communities by being a focus for the activity of the sacred in their midst. They also gave the local churches continuities with the past.

In both east and west the exchange of relics eventually became a way for communities to show their respect for one another as well as to demonstrate their unity in the worldwide church. In fact, in Peter Brown's estimation this practice provides historians with a map of social relations in the early medieval world.[5] Thus the veneration of martyrs was the first object of this feast in the fourth century. Already in the fourth century, however, as such outstanding Christians as Anthony of Egypt, Martin of Tours, and Paulinus of Nola, began to be venerated though they were not martyrs, the technical meaning of sainthood began to expand. Soon the feast became a way of honoring all holy men and women of outstanding Christian virtue, especially those who were not recognized by name and yet had witnessed to the faith.

The greatest Byzantine liturgical center of all, the city of Constantinople, capital of the Eastern Roman Empire, had adopted the feast of All Saints on the Sunday following Pentecost at least by the beginning of the sixth century. We know this because we possess a *kontakion* (a kind of sung homily) composed by Romanos Melodos, one of the greatest of Byzantine hymnodists. The title of the *kontakion* is "On all martyrs." This remarkable piece likens God to a gardener of all creation who receives the martyrs as the first fruits of his handiwork.

In a sense, according to Romanos, the feast calls all these martyrs into a holy assembly. They come from everywhere to invite the whole world to feast with them and to praise God. Their courage and endurance is highly praised for they are perceived to be intercessors with God, workers of miracles, protectors of the true faith, and companions for God's holy people.[6] In wonderfully poetic fashion Romanos' piece succeeds; it praises the God of the martyrs and it provides educational and inspirational examples of how the martyrs function as model Christians.

No treatment of this traditional Byzantine feast is complete until we have looked at the major piece of evidence for the Byzantine liturgical year that comes from the tenth century, the *Typicon* (or book of ceremonial direction) of the Great Church, Hagia Sophia in Constantinople. The significance of the *typicon*'s description of the feast reaches far more widely than tenth-century Constantinople, for the liturgy of this great center of Eastern Christianity has shaped all subsequent Byzantine liturgical practice. We learn from the *typicon* that, as with all major feasts of the year, All Saints included not only the celebration of the eucharist and liturgy of the hours but also a long procession to a special stational church, at which the eucharist for the feast was presided over by the patriarch of Constantinople or his representative.[7]

All Saints Day is one of sixty-eight such processional days in the tenth-century liturgy of this city. The feast also marked one of the seventeen feasts on which the emperor took part in the processional to the stational church.[8] This practice of having one church in the city where the eucharistic liturgy was celebrated with particular splendor was not unique to Constantinople: it was followed in many cities of the early medieval period. For a feast of the Virgin Mary, for example, one of the many important shrines to the Mother of God in the city or its environs was employed.

On All Saints the *typicon* informs us that the stational church was that of All Saints, a small church constructed next to the the church of the Holy Apostles, where the relics of Saints Luke and Timothy as well as the tomb of the founder of the city, Constantine, were located.[9] Since this church was constructed only in the tenth century by the emperor Leo VI in honor of his first wife, Theophano, the celebration must previously have taken place in another church or shrine. The best possibility is Holy Apostles, which already had memorials to all the apostles and tombs of a number of Byzantine emperors.

In the *Typicon* of the Great Church the title for the feast runs as follows: "The Memorial of the holy and victorious Martyrs in the whole world, who died for the sake of the name of our great God and Savior Jesus Christ." Even in the tenth century, then, the emphasis of the feast was placed on the witness of the martyrs. The *troparion*, or antiphon accompanying vespers, morning prayer, the procession to the church, and the procession at the beginning of the eucharistic liturgy can be translated thus:

> O Christ our God, your Church adorned as with purple and fine linen with the blood of all the martyrs throughout the world cries to you. Pour out your mercies on your people, give peace to the empire, by the prayers of the Theotokos. You alone are the lover of the human race.

The other chants in the eucharistic liturgy predictably emphasize the saints and their sufferings. The chant that accompanies the readings is Psalm 16:3, 8: "As for the saints in the land, they are the noble, in whom is my delight . . . I keep the Lord always before me, because he is at my right hand, I shall not be moved." The alleluia verse before the gospel is Psalm 34:18: "The Lord is near to the brokenhearted, he saves the crushed in spirit." Finally, the verse at communion is Psalm 33:1: "Rejoice in the Lord, you righteous; praise befits the upright."

The scripture readings for the eucharistic liturgy, on which we shall comment further, are Hebrews 11:33-12:2a-12:2a and Matthew 10:32-33, 37-38; 19:27-30. One should note further that All Saints Sunday was the only Sunday of the year in which a liturgical procession ended at a church other than Hagia Sophia. This is yet another indication that All Saints was considered to be most important in medieval Eastern Christian piety and worship.

THEOLOGY OF THE FEAST

The historical evidence we have considered here can help us to discern a theology of this great feast. Since the best interpreter of any feast is the lectionary, we turn first to the scripture readings for the day and to the position of All Saints in the Byzantine liturgical year.

The Byzantine liturgical year, like its Roman counterpart, focuses on preparation for and celebration of the great fifty days of Easter as well as on weekly repetition of the day of the Lord, Sunday.[10] Technically speaking, Sunday never celebrates anything other than the mystery of the passion, death, and resurrection of Jesus so that it is more appropriate to call Easter the "Great Sunday" than to call Sunday "a little Easter," as is commonly done. Be this as it may, both the Roman and the Byzantine traditions have shown a tendency to celebrate some Sundays as special feasts. This is the case with the Roman extension of Eastertide beyond Pentecost Sunday to include the Feast of the Holy Trinity and Corpus Christi (the latter at least in the United States) on the two subsequent Sundays. As we saw above, this impulse must have been felt among the Christians of the fourth century at Antioch, since John Chrysostom explicitly mentions a feast on this day in his homily "On all the martyrs." But why celebrate a feast of All Saints following Pentecost Sunday?

The clearest explanation of the date for this feast in the liturgical year is apparent from the scriptural readings for the day, which are the same today as they were in the *Typicon* of the Great Church, Hagia Sophia. The passage from Hebrews proclaims the suffering that holy women and men of old endured for their faith. It elaborates many different forms of suffering from torture, mockery, and scourging to imprisonment, stoning, and being sawn in two; it ends with the wonderful exhortation: "Therefore, since we are surrounded by so great a cloud of witnesses, let us also lay aside every weight, and sin which clings so closely, and let us run with perseverance the race that is set before us, looking to Jesus the pioneer and perfecter of our faith, who for the joy that was set before him endured the cross" (Heb 12:1-2a).

The gospel is a combination of verses from two distinct discourses by Jesus in Matthew. It links the idea of witnessing to Christ before the whole world with Jesus' promise to Peter and the other disciples that "everyone who has left houses or brothers or sisters or father or mother or children or lands for my sake, will receive a hundredfold, and inherit eternal life" (Mt 19:29).

great fifty days of Easter when Christians have celebrated in a most explicit way the risen life of Jesus Christ and the outpouring of that life by the Holy Spirit, their attention is drawn immediately to the necessity of discipleship. Celebrating all of the saints, and especially those who have given their lives in a violent manner, develops the logic of the gospel message.

Eastern Christians are reminded that not only has Christ experienced the passage through death to a life that will never end, but so have countless holy men and women down through the ages. Therefore (and the "therefore" of Hebrews 12:1 is one of the most powerful uses of that connective in the whole New Testament), we are encouraged to follow the example of the great multitude of saints who have imitated Jesus. Eastern Christians are further reminded that Christian life is not only adoring Christ Jesus as the savior of the human race, but taking up the cross and following his lead as pioneer and perfecter of our faith. This message is reiterated in the gospel for the Sunday following All Saints (Mt 4:18-23) which recounts the call of the apostles.

The Byzantine feast of All Saints, celebrated on the Sunday after Pentecost, might also be called, to borrow a phrase from Dietrich Bonhoeffer, the Sunday of "the cost of discipleship." Western Christians express the same motif first by reading the beatitudes on 1 November, second by concentrating on discipleship in the gospel selections for the Sundays following Pentecost. Perhaps Eastern Christians achieve a better sense of the connection between the passion, death and resurrection of Jesus, the multitude of his faithful ones who have gone before us, and the challenge to our own discipleship by placing this feast immediately after the Easter Season. Nevertheless, remembering and celebrating, in eastern or western fashion, the innumerable men and women of every race and tongue, of every historical era and every way of life who have manifested the graciousness of God and the truth of the gospel message and who form such a great cloud of witnesses—this is the joyful task for every generation of the saints.

Notes

1. Robert F. Taft, "The Spirit of Eastern Christian Worship," *Beyond East and West: Problems in Liturgical Understanding* (Washington, D.C.: The Pastoral Press, 1984) 118-119.

2. John Chrysostom, "Sermon in the Holy Martyrs" (PG 50:705): "It has been seven days since the feast of Pentecost."

3. This feast was celebrated sometime after Easter week. See François Graffin, ed., *Patrologia Orientalis* (Turnhout, Belgium) *Les Homiliae cathédrales de Sévère d'Antioch*, Homily 44 in Vol. 36:1, pp.96-107; Homily 49 in Vol. 35:3, pp.340-357.

4. See my "On Feasting the Saints," *Worship* 54 (1980) 338. Reprinted as Chapter 4 in this volume.

5. See Peter Brown, "The Rise and Function of the Holy Man in Late Antiquity," *The Journal of Roman Studies* 61 (1971) 80-101 as well as his *The Cult of the Saints: Its Rise and Function in Latin Christianity* (Chicago: University of Chicago Press, 1981).

6. See *Kontakia of Romanos, Byzantine Melodist*, vol. 2, *On Christian Life*, translated and annotated by Marjorie Carpenter (Columbia: University of Missouri Press, 1970) 291-296.

7. See my "The City as Church, the Church as City," *Liturgy* 3:4 (1983) 69-73. Reprinted as Chapter 1 in this volume.

8. Constantine Porphyrogenitus, *De Ceremoniis Aula Byzantinae*, eds., J.J. Reiske and I. Bekker (Bonn, 1840), Book 2, chapter 7.

9. Juan Mateos, ed., *Le Typicon de la grande église*, vol. 2, *Le Cycle des fêtes mobiles*, Orientalia Christiana Analecta, vol. 166 (Rome: Pontificium Institutum Orientalium Studiorum, 1963) 144-147; see also Glanville Downey, "The Church of All the Saints (Church of Saint Theophano) near the Church of the Holy Apostles at Constantinople," *Dumbarton Oaks Papers* 9/10 (1956) 301-305.

10. For the importance of the celebration of Sunday among Christians of the east, see Robert F. Taft, "Sunday in the Byzantine Tradition," *Beyond East and West* 31-48.

6

The Liturgical Year: Calendar for a Just Community

Then at last will all creation be one,
And we shall join in singing your praise
Through Jesus Christ our Lord.

Eucharistic Prayer A

Then I saw a new heaven and a new earth; for the first heaven and the first earth had passed away, and the sea was no more. And I saw the holy city, a new Jerusalem, coming down out of heaven from God, prepared as a bride for her husband; and I heard a great voice from the throne saying: "Behold the dwelling of God is with human beings. God will dwell with them, and they shall be God's people, and God will be with them. God will wipe away every tear from their eyes, and death shall be no more, neither shall there be any mourning nor crying nor pain any more, for the former things have passed away. (Rv 21:1-4)

THESE TWO VISIONS, THE FIRST FROM THE INTERNATIONAL COMMISsion on English in the Liturgy's experimental Eucharistic Prayer A, and the second from the Book of Revelation, sum up in a marvelous way the extraordinary Christian vision of the world as a place of reconciliation, freedom, healing, justice, and Shalom, God's peace. It is the Christian vision of the kingdom, the reign of God.

In the face of the privatization of religion in our own culture, we are beginning to realize increasingly that the Christian vision of the fullness of the end times—the eschatological vision—is intrinsically social or communal. No Christian community, which means no worshiping community, can afford any longer to stick its corporate head in the sand of individualistic salvation at the expense of concerns about society and the culture at large. Therefore, it is imperative that all people who are responsible for the church's liturgy—and this means in the last analysis the whole worshiping community but especially those charged, whether ordained or not, with special responsibility for the church's worship—must seek out ways for Christian worship to reflect a response to the contemporary world.

Before dealing with this question in terms of the liturgical calendar, it is necessary to clarify the biblical meaning of divine justice which must be the source of all Christian efforts. The Christian vision of divine justice is of a justice that transcends every political and economic system. Two of the parables of Jesus illustrate this important point. The first is the parable of the Prodigal Son or, better, the Merciful Father (Lk 15:11-32). One misses a vital aspect of this story if one confines its interpretation merely to the forgiveness and reconciliation of the individual sinner with God, for in it there is a message about divine justice. God does not require retribution of the wayward son, but rather conversion. Moreover, unlike an ordinary oriental patriarch, God becomes a fool by letting go of all the trappings of prestige to greet the wayward one and provide him with the very best. There is even more to the story, for at the end, a sobering and at the same time liberating point is made with regard to the elder son who is angered at the Father's profligacy. The elder son is called upon the recognize the depths of his own unrighteousness or injustice, and the listener is put in the place of that son. The parable is incomplete and calls for the response of the listeners; we are called upon to complete the story by our own response to the foolishness of divine justice.

The second parable may be even more disturbing to the normal, everyday, common-sense approach to a just world. It is Matthew's parable of the workers in the vineyard (Mt 20:1-16).

Here, the usual pay scale is turned topsy-turvy when the own-
er of the vineyard in his lavish generosity pays the same
amount to those who have worked for an hour as to those who
have worked all day. To be sure, the main point of the parable
is not about social justice but rather God's election. However,
the story is offensive to our normal sense of what is just. What
seems unjust by human standards pales before the abundance
of divine goodness, a compassion that relativizes all human attempts to be just.

These brief reflections on only two of the parables need to
be complemented by other images in the message of Jesus—
for example, the last-judgment scene in Matthew 25:31-46,
where salvation hinges on one's response to those in need, or
Jesus' own ministry of liberation in Luke 4:16-30. The transcendence of divine justice cannot absolve us of the divine
challenge to cooperate in the building of a just society by every available means, but it can serve as a warning that no political or social scheme is ultimate. The final realization of justice and peace will outdo all of our best efforts, but the call to
Christian social justice demands both a fidelity to the biblical
notion of justice and to the Christian tradition of working out
that justice in diverse cultural situations and historical periods. The U.S. Catholic Bishops' Pastoral, *Economic Justice for
All*, puts it this way:

> Our reflection on U.S. economic life today must be rooted in
> this biblical vision of the kingdom and discipleship, but it must
> also be shaped by the rich and complex tradition of Catholic
> life and thought. Throughout its history the Christian commu-
> nity has listened to the words of Scripture and sought to enact
> them in the midst of daily life in very different historical and
> cultural contexts.[1]

The incarnation of that vision in terms of the liturgical calendar's feasts and seasons is our concern here, for the Christian vision is normally reflected by the worship of the church.
To quote *Economic Justice for All* once again:

> Challenging U.S. economic life with the Christian vision calls
> for a deeper awareness of the integral connection between wor-
> ship and the world of work. Worship and common prayers are
> the wellsprings that give life to any reflection on economic

problems and that continually call the participants to greater fidelity and discipleship.[2]

It must be added that in the ongoing Sunday assembly Christians are formed by a liturgical cycle that must have political and economic consequences if those same Christians are to offer credible and authentic witness in the contemporary world. To arrive at some answers to the question, "How can the liturgical calendar aid us in manifesting the Christian vision of peace and justice?"—the third part of this essay—one should ask two questions beforehand: What is there about contemporary culture and therefore contemporary liturgical life that conflicts with this vision and general? And how have liturgical calendars shaped communal Christian belief and action in the past?

INDIVIDUALISM, COMMUNITY, AND THE CALENDAR

The liturgical calendar of the Roman Catholic Church and other mainline Christian Churches is indeed problematic today, for it presupposes in many ways a social and cultural world that no longer exists. James Sanders has criticized the church lectionary and calendar: "Most of the festivals in the Christian calendar are but ancient agricultural and fertility-cult seasonal celebrations, barely Christianized."[3]

There is some truth to this charge, but what the author fails to understand is that the Christians of the ancient Mediterranean world had little choice but to adapt their celebrations to the culture in which they lived—at least to the extent that Christianity was congruent with those cultures. The alternative was to become a small sectarian group, lamenting the ways of the world. Moreover, as Thomas Talley has shown, the origins of the various Christian feasts and seasons were far more complex than the mere adaptation of agricultural or pagan festivals. There was inevitably some adaptation to cultural conditions: as an example, the cooptation of the Roman festival of the dead—*cara cognatio* on 22 February—as the feast of the Chair of St. Peter. One must note that we have a tendency to argue for inculturation in the contemporary world while scorning it in the past. Such myopia will not serve us well in discerning how the liturgical year can be a vehicle for bringing about social justice.

But back to the problem at hand: the liturgical year and our own socio-cultural calendars do not match. It is extremely difficult for the liturgical year to mold people's everyday experience. The problem is much deeper than the calendar. We live in a world—at least this is true of assimilated, English-speaking North Americans—where a basic, gut-level commitment to common values and a common world view has broken down. Such a world has a great deal of trouble focusing on common symbols; this in turn weakens the liturgy which is rooted in the celebration of such symbols in ritual action. In other words, liturgy requires a passionate, even if implicit, commitment to a common view of the world. This does not imply that every liturgical experience is exclusively communal; there are times when individuals experience something completely different from the rest of the community depending on their mood or circumstances. However, today's problem is that we tend to bring fundamentally individualized experiences and expectations to liturgical life.

This fact has been well borne out by contributors to recent sociological literature. I will mention two examples. In *The Fall of Public Man* Richard Sennett demonstrates the gradual individualization of western people from the eighteenth century to the present.[4] In *Habits of the Heart*, case studies of individuals from different walks of life, Robert Bellah and his colleagues, in even more striking fashion, show how fragmented our contemporary American culture really is.[5] In terms of religion, it seems that the individuals who were subjects of the study are representative of Americans seeking personal experiences in the midst of their life's journey. Put simply, they have engaged in common worship for therapeutic purposes. It is difficult to step outside this scenario because the therapeutic life is as common as the air we breathe, as real to us as angels and demons were to our forebears.

This theme has not been lost on contemporary liturgical commentators. Aidan Kavanagh says that Christian worship has been transformed by a flight to suburbia, his metaphor for the church trying to escape the world, which he images as *civitas*, the city. The liturgy should be the world's workshop, but the church scorns the world in favor of attention to individual needs and desires. The old *civitas* becomes a garbage dump for liturgical suburbanites:

> The workshop [of the church in the world] relocates to suburbia and becomes no longer a civic affair but a series of cottage industries producing novelties and fads for passing elites.[6]

Though Kavanagh's analysis is somber, even a little depressing, and sounds like a liturgical commentary on George Orwell's *1984* or Aldous Huxley's *Brave New World*, he makes a valid point. The individualization of contemporary life, especially its affluence in our own culture, makes not only for a church out of touch with justice but a church out of touch with the world redeemed in Christ, a church that inevitably seeks a religious never-never land.

In a very different manner but with similar purpose, David Power has called for a critical reappropriation of symbols, of liturgical life, by attending in a particular way to the memory of those who are suffering, a memory we would frequently like to avoid.[7] These perceptive American liturgical commentators have made it possible to begin evaluating the problem of incarnating a justice oriented understanding of the liturgical calendar from a new starting point. The starting point is all important, for if one begins by presupposing that all that needs to be done is to add to the calendar and lectionary our immediate personal and social concerns, then one has missed the point. The whole way in which we celebrate the liturgical year needs reflection. In order to understand the justice implications of the Christian calendar, one also has to understand what it means and what it *has* meant to celebrate the year by means of a liturgical calendar.

HOW HAS THE CALENDAR
REFLECTED AND SHAPED CHRISTIAN BELIEF?

Tension between the "Already—Not Yet"

Obviously how the calendar has reflected and shaped Christian belief is a question that would take volumes to answer. We can only briefly develop three points here. The first point is that the liturgical year always manifests a real tension in the human and Christian experience of time. The very fact of the incarnation of Christ and his redemption of the world implies an irreducible tension between the already and the not-yet in the Christian experience of the world. We have been redeemed. God has definitively and irrevocably entered into the human condition and history; in a real sense the end—*telos*, goal—of the world has come. Yet at the same time we must continue to work out our salvation. Creation, to employ Paul's metaphor in Romans 8:22, is still groaning in anticipation of its consummation. The world still struggles with pain, conflict, injustice, and other forms of sin. The experience of the death and resurrection of Christ, which is at the center of every liturgical celebration, means that Christians have faith in God's saving activity in the past and the present, and at the same time are hopeful of that ultimate reconciliation and consummation mirrored in our eucharistic praying and in the passage from Revelation quoted at the beginning of this essay. There is no better example of how this tension bears itself out in terms of the liturgical year than the annual celebration of Advent with its many-leveled appreciation of the coming of the Lord, an event that has been experienced and is yet to *be* experienced. The celebration of the liturgical year as an event of justice does not allow this tension to be resolved.

Cultural Adaptation of the Calendar

The second reflection is that liturgical communities have traditionally taken the skeletal structure of the existing local liturgical cycle, the main feasts and seasons, and used them as the framework for the celebration of Christianity within their own cultures. A good example of this is the connection between the Feast of the Unconquered Sun at Rome on 25 December in the late third and early fourth centuries and the Christian celebration of Christmas. Even if the origin of this dating of Christmas may lie elsewhere than the pagan solar feast, a theory that has recently been rehabilitated,[8] Christians did make use of the counter-symbolism of Christ the "Sun of Righteousness" for their own purposes. Such a cooptation of the pagan winter solstice and sun worship was not a betrayal of Christianity but rather the sensible adaptation of Christian faith to the existing culture. After all, if God has truly and irrevocably entered into the human condition and human history, then Christian faith can legitimately make use of the symbolism that the world provides. This insight is at the root of Christian sacramentality. To celebrate Christ, the light of the world, in the darkest days of the year—at least in the northern hemisphere—makes a great deal of sense; it is not the survival of paganism but the recognition of God in nature as well as in human history.

Moreover, historical liturgical communities made their own social environments the setting for their worship. The cycle of the year was spun out not only in terms of ideas and words, but in terms of places and events in the history of the people as well. This phenomenon is called stational liturgy, in which different churches and shrines served as the place of a city's main liturgical celebration depending on the feast or commemoration.[9] The best example of this liturgical-cultural phenomenon is the liturgical year in medieval Constantinople, the center—or better, the trend-setter—for much of late-Byzantine liturgy. Tenth-century sources show that the church there held sixty-eight outdoor liturgical processions in the course of each year. These public manifestations of piety related Christian faith not only to events in the universal liturgical cycle like Easter and Christmas, but also to the saints and, in particular, to events in the history of the city itself. Many of the feasts were actually related to crucial moments in the social experience: the birthday or dedication of the city, a plague, an earthquake, the defeat of invaders in a siege. Here, God's power was made manifest and commemorated year after year in a tangible way to which people could relate; it was liturgy at its most popular.

Importance of the Saints

Liturgy at its best is owned by the people who celebrate it, relating their faith and worship to their experience of the world. This leads to the third point, namely, the permanent attraction of saints' days in the Christian liturgical calendar. People relate best in the final analysis not to ideas but to flesh-and-blood human beings who exemplify for them in the contemporary cultural circumstances what it means to be *in Christ*, to be grasped by the power of God. Saints here are far more than models for moral imitation; they are tangible reminders that God's power has been at work in human beings. This is the reason behind the perennial fascination with shrines, relics, and images in Christian life—they are connectors with people who have manifested the truth and power of Christianity.[10] No doubt the popularity of various saints will wax and wane according to cultural and historical circumstances, but to abandon the saints for a rationalized Christomonistic approach to Christian faith is to impoverish not only the liturgical calendar but Christian faith itself. The caution here is that saints are never independent agents; they are always to be related to Christ, the paschal mystery, as is the source of their attractiveness. That devotion to the saints has at times in the history of Christianity been perverted does not negate its usefulness.

One need not look only to the medieval period to find examples of individuals who provide a powerful focus for the liturgical expression of Christian faith. In our own time the Virgin of Guadalupe has served as an effective rallying point for a whole people's hopes for liberation and justice as well as an anchor for their Christian identity. Robert Orsi's recent and fascinating study of devotion to the Virgin of Mount Carmel and her *festa* in Italian Harlem from the late nineteenth to the mid-twentieth century has shown how even in American culture such a devotion can be intimately involved in a people's self-realization and aspirations.[11]

These three factors (the tension between realized and expected redemption, the cultural adaptations of the liturgical calendar, and the importance of human examples) have everything to do with discerning how the liturgical year can be a vehicle in the promotion of peace and justice.

SOCIAL JUSTICE AND THE LITURGICAL YEAR TODAY

Some Cautions

The foregoing sections have been an attempt to show that we need to think about justice and the liturgical year at a pop-

ular level. How is the assembly's ownership of the liturgy ever
to be experienced if we continue to work from the abstract and
elitist principles and not popular experience and needs? My
fear is that most attempts to make the celebration of the liturgical year an authentic experience of and challenge to social
justice will be perceived as the effort of an "enlightened" few
to impose progressive political views on an unsuspecting—or
perhaps increasingly suspicious—many. Such manipulation,
to call it by its proper name, will never be effective in the long
run, for it cannot appeal to the cultural experience of the people, nor can it help them to be counter-cultural in any confi-
dent fashion when the Gospel demands that they read the
signs of the times in a discriminating manner. This is not to
argue that liturgy and politics do not mix. Any manifestation
of Christianity will be political in one way or another. However, it would be a perversion to make the liturgy a platform for
a particular partisan political program. Such activity destroys
the liturgy's call to unity. On the other hand, to altogether
avoid social issues, which always include politics in the larger
sense, is irresponsible.

The second caution is that the liturgy cannot do everything.
It is unrealistic to imagine that an hour or so a week, and often
less than that, of involvement in the liturgical assembly is going to be able to attune people to the value system and way of
life to which the Gospel invites all Christians. The liturgy, supremely important as it is in the life of the Christian community, can only be the ritual highpoint of Christian life set in the
context of rich communal activity. To alert people to the need
to do something about world hunger, in a homily or in other
ways in the Sunday liturgy, and not to provide a means within
parish life to actually work against hunger is superficial if not
hypocritical; education about peace and justice issues from the
pulpit can only be part of a wider parochial catechesis on the
subject. The setting of the Sunday eucharist does not allow significant time or dialogue for people to get involved in complex
and sensitive issues like arms reduction, economic justice, ra-
cial and sexual discrimination, or the right to life, set in the
context of the seamless-garment approach advocated these
past years by Cardinal Bernardin and others. A parish with no
active, extra-liturgical, adult-education-and-action committee

is not likely to do much of substance in terms of addressing the many issues of justice.

How then can the liturgical year be an expression of the Christian vision of justice and peace celebrated in a community with an active commitment to these issues? Needless to say, there is a dialogical relation between the active commitment to justice issues and the impetus which the liturgy gives to working on them. In three areas, the celebration of the liturgical year can be improved as a calendar for a just community.

A Sharper Focus: The Sunday Eucharist

In the first place, social justice in the eucharistic assembly's weekly practice is a prerequisite for the expression of social justice. The celebration of the paschal mystery every Sunday and the weekly rhythm that this celebration provides is the fundamental building block of the liturgical year. Robert Hovda has written that we don't need specially designated peace liturgies since every celebration of the eucharist is, or *should* be, a peace liturgy.[12] To the extent that every liturgy manifests the same basic facts of our Christian existence, this is true. One needs, however, to add that we do choose specific motifs, reflected by variable readings and prayers, to emphasize different aspects of Christian faith at different times; this is why we have a liturgical year in the first place. At the same time, what Hovda claims about peace and the liturgy is true of social justice as well. Each community needs to ask itself some hard questions about the weekly assembly in terms of the fundamental equality of the baptized as well as the potential activity of God in all human beings. Is there anyone excluded from the assembly on the basis of political, economic, or social status, gender, sexual preference, or race? Is there concern manifested, by the offerings of the assembly, for the poor and needy? Do the common prayers of the assembly always manifest in one way or another a concern for the needs of the world as well as the church and individuals? Does the allocation of space and decoration reveal a community that has gathered as equals to praise and serve the Lord? Is the language employed in the liturgy inclusive?

One last question with regard to weekly practice is bound

to bring us up short. Are the ministerial functions of the liturgy distributed in a manner that reflects charism, not status, gender, or race? Assigning ministerial functions to the non-ordained should be a relatively simple problem to solve. However, when it comes to the ordained, one encounters a certain frustration, for women and married men may not be ordained to the presbyterate and episcopacy in the Roman Catholic Church. Among other considerations, this is a justice issue. Until people can be ordained to ministry on the basis of their charisms, there will always be a certain injustice present in our liturgical assemblies.

The point here is that the whole of the liturgical year must reflect a concern with social justice and not simply certain special occasions. The formative work of the liturgy is gradual and subtle; it inculcates Christian identity by the pattern of worship repeated ritually week after week. This means that the way that the liturgy is celebrated every Sunday is going to have more of an impact on the assembly's orientation toward justice than special peak moments. In a sense, the liturgical year will be successful as an agent of justice when that aspect of Christian communal existence is taken for granted—not ignored—as one of the attitudes that describe the assembly's existence. If the Seventeenth Sunday of Ordinary Time reveals a justice orientation of the community, then special occasions that focus on social justice will be all the more effective. The clue is to look at the activity of the whole assembly and not merely at its ministers. To neglect reflection on the assembly's activity is to fall into the trap of regarding the liturgy as entertainment instead of primarily as the common action of God's people responding in the Holy Spirit.

A specific example may help to flesh this out. At St. Francis de Sales Cathedral in Oakland, California, an assembly that includes a wide variety of Christian folk and has become fairly well-known throughout the United States, people do not sit after they have received holy communion. They remain standing until everyone has received and the post-communion prayer has been said. Then all the people sit for a period of meditation that more often than not includes a choral piece. There is liturgical genius operative in this practice. If one wants to express the idea that communion means not only vertical union with the Lord but also horizontal union with one another by the sharing of the bread and the cup, then this belief is demonstrated most powerfully not only by words but also by action? What better way than this relatively minor change in the assembly's physical disposition to imply that the eucharist makes the communicants one, commits them to one another, and therefore acts as a mirror to reflect the successes, struggles, and failures in treating each other with reverence and love in daily life as well? As with all important areas of life, in liturgy actions speak louder than words.

The Lectionary

In the second place, orientation toward justice in the liturgical year should be formed by the church's lectionary. In the present theological climate, given the interest in the socio-cultural interpretation of Scripture as well as the leanings of liberation and political theologies, it should not be too difficult for preachers and those who prepare for liturgy to makes use of these resources. Recent interpretation of the *Magnificat* (Lk 1:46-55) has concentrated on the socially subversive aspects of this canticle. The hungry are fed and the rich sent empty away; the mighty are cast down from their thrones and those of low degree have been exalted. Those who prepare liturgy should avoid spiritualizing a passage like this with its radical social implications. Strangely enough, this passage never serves as the gospel for a Sunday, but it is employed on 22 December in preparation for Christmas, on 31 May for the Visitation, and on 15 August for the Assumption, as well as daily in evening prayer. It is possible to see in this passage a new kind of Marian piety, stressing God's preferential option for the poor. As we have already seen, such piety is an aspect of the celebration of the Virgin of Guadalupe.

Another example of the correct use of the lectionary for promoting a social justice orientation to the liturgical year is an experience I had with the liturgical commission of the Diocese of Oakland. The diocesan office planning a Sunday liturgy focusing on AIDS-awareness had turned to the local Office of Worship for liturgical advice. Their response suggested choosing a Sunday on which the scriptural readings lent themselves readily to preaching on this theme. This was, of course, the correct instinct. Often one has the impression that themes are imposed on Sundays with no relation to the character of the Sunday liturgy itself. But there is no need to do this if liturgy planners are willing to accept the lectionary's lead in developing various motifs for different Sunday celebrations. Purists might object to this approach by claiming, correctly, that every Sunday is a celebration of the paschal mystery and that one of the major reforms of the current Roman calendar is a restoration of Sunday to its pride of place in the liturgical year.[13] Formerly, the celebration of Sunday was easily superceded by saints' feast and other commemorations. This much is true. However, calendars inevitably exhibit more growth than any other aspect of liturgy precisely because they have always responded to the concrete needs and piety of the people. Moreover, the fact that our weekly celebrations are variable with regard to the lectionary shows that the paschal mystery is always celebrated with one or another focus. As long as the lectionary is properly employed, it should be possible to recognize certain Sundays as particular occasions with special themes without abandoning the needed reform of the present calendar. It is the nature of calendars that such occasions come and go because cultures and needs change. One should expect that calendars need pruning from time to time. Therefore, designating certain Sundays in Ordinary Time for special observances should be a possibility even in the current calendar.

In addition to employing certain Sundays in Ordinary Time for the promotion of social justice, it is clear that the seasons of the liturgical year provide valuable opportunities as well. Certainly the lectionary for Advent, as well as the eschatological thrust of the season itself, offers the challenge to envision the world anew, encouraged by the hope of God's ultimate reconciliatory power. Here, the figure of John the Baptist and the selections from the prophets—in particular, Isaiah—can speak powerfully to the need to attend to justice in our own time. The Easter season also provides an opportunity for a more socially sensitive celebration of the Good News with its weekly readings from the experience of the early community in the Acts of the Apostles, the record of the church's outward mission to the world. Further, the second reading of this season in Cycle B is always taken from the Book of Revelation. No one reading contemporary commentaries on this biblical work can avoid the social implications of a community experiencing persecution and oppression.

One final comment needs to be made with regard to adapting the social justice themes to the lectionary. Music will be the key to effectively integrating these themes in communal worship. To employ lyrics and tunes that have a self-centered or sentimental effect, while emphasizing justice in the homily, is self-defeating. Here, as with the liturgical environment, the medium is the message. It is necessary for justice themes in the biblical readings and prayers to be matched with music that is mission oriented and expressive of a certain confidence in God's activity in the world as well as in individual lives.

The Saints of the Calendar

In the third place, the true promotion of justice in the liturgical year will result from attention to people, not causes. I have already asserted that a justice orientation to the liturgical year will not succeed if it is perceived as manipulation by an elite group imposing "radical" social, political, or economic ideas on the majority of the assembly. The best way to avoid this trap is to focus on individual examples of Christian lives that mirror a commitment to social justice. People relate to life stories in a way that they can never relate to abstract causes. This has always been the native genius of the calendar of the saints. I see this calendar as a resource for Christian worship rather than a series of commemorations consisting of variable prayers and an occasional special set of readings.[14] Certain saints like Martin de Porres, Peter Claver, and Francis and Clare of Assisi, appeal readily to the Christian social conscience. In addition, it seems opportune to commemorate unofficial contemporary saints, a few of whom I mention with their memorial days: Dorothy Day (29 November), Martin Luther King, Jr. (the third Monday of January), the Four Women Martyrs of El Salvador—Maura Clark, Jean Donovan, Ita Ford, and Dorothy Kazel (2 December), Archbishop Oscar Romero (24 March), Dietrich Bonhoeffer (9 April), Rutilio Grande (12

March), Dag Hammarskjold (18 September), and the Jesuit martyrs of El Salvador and their companions (16 November). Certain liturgical communities may want to celebrate these unofficial contemporary saints on their anniversaries, but an incorporation of these figures into the preaching and prayers of the Sunday assembly, especially if aspects of their lives and deaths can throw light on the lectionary readings, would be more likely. The greatest and most powerful source for Christian reflection on peace and justice in the liturgical year is Jesus of Nazareth. However, one should bear in mind that Christians have traditionally turned to holy individuals, those reflecting the truth of the Gospel in Jesus, with whom they could relate culturally as well.

Ember Days

A final note on specific occasions for the promotion of justice in the liturgical calendar concerns Ember Days, one aspect of the traditional Roman calendar whose observance has been left to the discretion of national conferences of bishops.[15] These celebrations on Wednesday, Fridays, and Saturdays in the spring, summer, fall, and winter of each year originally had a penitential—or better, supplicatory—flavor, asking God for favorable weather. Such celebrations obviously need to be remodeled in a post-agrarian society. Perhaps civic occasions that have also become relatively popular as liturgical observances in the American Church already meet this need. Certainly Thanksgiving, Labor, Memorial, and Independence Days are well suited to this effort to relate individual liturgical assemblies to wider social needs in the context of imploring God's aid.[16] The sacramentary already contains special prayers and prefaces for Thanksgiving and for the Fourth of July. In addition, votive Masses such as those provided for peace and for a blessing on human labor can be used creatively for such combined civic and religious celebrations. Much more can be done to relate the penitential focus of Lent to social needs, though to be sure it is not its only aspect. Fasting and asceticism can well be directed to consciousness of hunger and poverty as any number of movements have recently demonstrated.

* * * * * *

The many justice issues and concerns that face our contemporary world—the arms race, poverty, homelessness, famine, racism, discrimination because of gender or sexual preference, oppression in Latin America and elsewhere, health care, the rights of the disabled and the elderly, respect for life—can all be integrated into the liturgical year. But they must be integrated in a way that meets with popular acceptance and that respects the nature of the liturgical calendar itself. A religious faith is worthless if it has nothing to offer the needs that people experience. Those needs are reflected in the Scriptures that we read week after week in the rich Christian tradition. Although the challenge to justice in an affluent and self-centered society is great, great also is our confidence in the Spirit that empowers Christians. The struggle for justice and peace is not ours alone.

Notes

1. National Conference of Catholic Bishops, *Economic Justice for All* (Washington, D.C.: United States Catholic Conference, 1986) no. 56.
2. Ibid., no. 325.
3. James A. Sanders, "Canon and Calendar: An Alternative Lectionary Proposal," in *Social Themes of the Christian Year*, ed., Dieter T. Hessel (Philadelphia: Westminster Press, 1983) 258.
4. Richard Sennett, *The Fall of Public Man* (New York: Alfred A. Knopf, 1977).
5. Robert Bellah and others, *Habits of the Heart: Individualism and Commitment in American Life* (Berkeley: University of California Press, 1985) 219-249.
6. Aidan Kavanagh, *On Liturgical Theology* (New York: Pueblo Publishing Co., 1984) 45.
7. David N. Power, *Unsearchable Riches* (New York: Pueblo Publishing Co., 1984) see 172-210.
8. Thomas J. Talley, *The Origins of the Liturgical Year* (New York: Pueblo Publishing Co., 1986) 87-99.
9. John F. Baldovin, "The City as Church, the Church as City," *Liturgy* 3:4 (1983) 69-73. Reprinted as Chapter 1 of this volume.
10. See Peter Brown, *The Cult of the Saints* (Chicago: University of Chicago Press, 1981).

11. See Robert A. Orsi, *The Madonna of 115th Street* (New Haven: Yale University Press, 1986).

12. Robert Hovda, "The Amen Corner," *Worship* 57 (1983) 438-443.

13. General Norms for the Liturgical Year and Calendar, no. 4. Liturgy Documentary Series 6. (Washington, D.C.: United States Catholic Conference, 1984) 14.

14. John F. Baldovin, "On Feasting the Saints," *Worship* 55 (1980) 342-344. Reprinted as Chapter 4 in this volume.

15. General Norms for the Liturgical Year and Calendar, nos. 45-47.

16. See Richard Eslinger, "Civil Religion and the Year of Grace," *Worship* 58 (1984) 372-383.

CONTEMPORARY
LITURGY
AND LIFE

7

Concelebration:
A Problem of Symbolic Roles
in the Church

IT IS COMMONPLACE TO ARGUE THAT THE ENTIRE CHURCH HAS EXPE-
rienced a profound change in liturgical and sacramental life in
the past twenty years, and that a major part of this change has
included the manner in which we celebrate the eucharist. The
concelebration of presbyters has played a large part in this latter shift. Originally intended in Vatican II's Constitution on
the Liturgy as a rather limited extension of sacramental concelebration,[1] it has grown to be the regular practice of most
male religious communities in both the domestic and public
celebration of the eucharist.

Today, after more than twenty years of experiencing this
rite, the practice of eucharistic concelebration needs reexami-
nation. The thesis of this study is that it has proved to be a
mixed blessing, raising as many questions about the church
and the sacraments as it solves. There can be little doubt, I
think, that concelebration has signaled an advance over the
Roman Church's eucharistic practice for nearly a millennium,
especially since it is far preferable to the so-called "private
Mass." Nevertheless, we need to reflect seriously on the meaning and consequences of eucharistic concelebration for the
church and especially for situations in which a large number

of presbyters are present on a regular basis. The first area of concern will be the character of the worshiping community as a whole. Only in this context can we reflect adequately on the theology of the eucharist itself and the role of the ordained presbyters in the rite. Third, I will adduce some conclusions that can be reached from the history of concelebration. Finally, I will propose some general norms and practical suggestions for concelebration in the future.[2]

THE ASSEMBLY AT WORSHIP

It is fair to say that only rather recently have Catholics begun to recover in any significant way a sense of the enormous dignity associated with being a baptized member of the body of Christ. A certain priority to the church as the people of God and as the sacrament of the world's salvation is attributed to all the baptized in Vatican II's *Lumen Gentium*. This same priority of the gathered church is affirmed in the earlier document on the liturgy, *Sacrosanctum Concilium*, which calls the eucharist "the summit and source" of the church's life.[3] As a result of this shift in emphasis from an earlier and more institutional ecclesiology, a great deal of attention has lately been given to the nature of the eucharistic assembly itself and to the necessity of seeing the eucharist as a sign of the unity of the worshiping church.[4] As Aidan Kavanagh has put it: "The fundamental criterion against which all liturgical things, words, gestures, and persons are measured is the liturgical assembly."[5]

The ordained priesthood does not nullify baptism, for lay people cannot be robbed of their baptismal dignity.[6] Any theory of concelebration which begins with the ordained priesthood and ignores the central purpose of the eucharist as the unity of the gathered church will ultimately reach a dead end; it will remain extrinsic to the real nature of the eucharistic liturgy. The major question to be asked of *any* aspect of the celebration of the eucharist is: What will best express the unity of the assembly in its praise and adoration of God and in its growth as a community in the image of God? To be sure, there must be roles in any hierarchically ordered church, but roles in the Christian assembly are secondary and subservient to this primary goal of the eucharist.[7]

As the reenactment of the mystery of our salvation, of the

entire paschal mystery in ritual form, the goal of the eucharist is the building up of Christ's body. In view of this goal all participants in the eucharist share a fundamental equality. All the baptized, who have prepared themselves adequately, share in the same communion of the body and blood of the Lord. In this sense, all who celebrate from peasant to presbyter to pope are in a strict sense equal despite the necessary differentiation in roles. To be frank, our tradition has not adequately communicated this reality so fundamental to Paul's treatment of the eucharist and church in 1 Corinthians 10-12. One need only think of the use of large versus small wafers and of withholding the cup from the laity to realize that we have constantly communicated ritually and symbolically something contrary to the doctrinal reality of the eucharistic communion. A particularly striking example of this sort of symbolic communication in contemporary Roman Catholic parishes is the practice of commentators inviting the assembly to song with the phrase, "Let us all stand and greet our celebrant with the entrance hymn . . ." The function of the opening song is to act as a means of gathering the assembly. But in the frequent practice that I have noted, instead of gathering the people together in an act of worship, they are invited to pay attention to the special role and status of one of the members of the assembly. Thus differentiations are made in the assembly, not according to function (role) but according to rank (status). But role differentiation in the life of the church in general and in the liturgy in particular need not mean status differentiation. The only status that Christians ought to know is in terms of service of the assembly and of the church at large.

What then of the council's reasoning that the expansion of concelebration should manifest the "unity of the priesthood"?[8] Some twenty-five years later we can see that this is a misplaced emphasis, for what is at stake in the celebration of the eucharist is always the unity of the particular worshiping assembly, a factor which should always be kept in mind when considering the nature and function of presbyteral concelebration.

CONCELEBRATION AND THE THEOLOGY
OF THE EUCHARIST

In view of the priority of the worshiping assembly's unity in its praise of God and growth in God's image, we can now inquire into the meaning of concelebration in terms of the theology of the eucharist and ecclesiology. One of the most important shifts in contemporary sacramental theology (prompted by the liturgical movement) has been an emphasis on celebration as the locus of the sacraments. A sacrament is not some *thing* encased within the shell of liturgical celebration, but is rather the unfolding of the actual celebration itself. The sophisticated questions which Scholastic theology raised with regard to the matter and form of the sacraments tended to draw attention away from celebration itself and thus to make the nature of the sacraments seem abstract and extrinsic to their liturgical setting.[9] An example of this is the concentration on the moment of consecration, a question which focuses on the priest's power to pronounce consecratory words. Hence the textbook question of the renegade priest in the bakery—as if ecclesial power could possibly be exercised outside of an ecclesial context. The result was theology about the sacraments instead of theology of the sacraments, drawn from the liturgical data.[10] Such a theology draws attention away from the worshiping community and toward the ordained ministers who performed sacramental rites on behalf of the people. Today, however, we recognize that the nonordained are not passive spectators of a rite performed on their behalf, but rather active participants in accordance with their order in the church.[11]

This shift in the understanding of the sacraments has also begun to prompt a profound reevaluation of the meaning of the ordained ministry. In short, the celebrational focus of the sacraments implies that the church is ordered not for dominion but for service. Research into the ministerial ordering of the early church has shown that no one organizational form prevailed from the beginning.[12] Only gradually were presbyters commissioned to preach and preside at the eucharist as it were on their own. The primary concern of the early church in any case was the unity represented by the gathered community around the bishop.[13] This concern can still be clearly seen in the early fifth-century letter of Pope Innocent I to the Umbrian bishop, Decentius of Gubbio, in which the former insists that the Roman Church maintains the unity of the celebration of the eucharist despite the fact that on a given Sunday and feast there are a number of eucharistic celebrations in the city.[14] This unity is maintained by the use of the *fermentum* or consecrated particles of the eucharistized bread which are brought to the titular churches of the city from the pope's stational Mass.[15] The early medieval Roman celebration of the eucharist was above all a manifestation of ecclesial unity extended in time and space and centered on the bishop as the head of a community gathered about the table of the Lord.[16] Allegorical commentaries on the liturgy as well as Romanesque and Gothic church architecture tended to obscure this manifestation of ecclesial unity. The reformed Roman Catholic rite of the eucharist and contemporary church architecture have reversed this serious loss.

But what of the precise role of the presbyter in the assembly? Our theological tradition has seen this role in two ways: either *in persona Christi* or *in persona Ecclesiae*. The priest is viewed as the representative of Christ or as the representative of the church before the Triune God. The position adopted by Pius XII in *Mediator Dei* clearly followed the former school of thought.[17] In contemporary discussion, on the other hand, the priest is more often understood as acting *in persona Ecclesiae*. He is a representative offered only on the basis of Christ's activity in the church through the Holy Spirit. Therefore, the priest acts *in persona Christi* insofar as he acts *in persona Ecclesiae* and not vice versa. As Edward Kilmartin puts it:

> Christ's headship is fully manifested by the public display of the variety of charisms in the Church. In this respect the office bearer has the chief responsibility of representing the community insofar as ordering the charisms by which dependence of all on Christ is manifested and realized. In the liturgy the priest represents and acts *in persona Ecclesiae*. Since the Church is the sacrament of Christ, the priest also acts *in persona Christi* in liturgical activity.[18]

This difference of emphasis is by no means merely an abstract theological quibble over phraseology, for it reflects profoundly different attitudes about the actual circumstances of sacramental celebration. If indeed the priest acts primarily as a representative in the church, then he can never act simply over against the community even in serving it. The consequences of the shift in this understanding of the role of ordained ministry will be spelled out below.

Closely allied to the representative function of the priest is the question of the nature of the eucharistic sacrifice and the fruits of the Mass. As early as 1949 Karl Rahner attempted to show that since the Mass is no new sacrifice over and above the sacrificial act of Christ, the fruit of the eucharistic sacrifice is dependent upon the devotion of the actual offerers.[19] If Rahner is correct, as I think he is, then there is a real problem with Mass stipends. If the effect of the eucharistic sacrifice is directly linked with the existential circumstances of the celebration of the eucharist, then the Mass offered for an absent donor is an anomaly at best.[20]

We can be grateful that today discussion has begun on the reform of the system of Mass stipends.[21] Certainly one factor that seems to make individual Mass stipends superfluous is the reintroduction of the prayer of the faithful in the Roman Rite. The prayer of the faithful should make it clear that the object of the eucharistic sacrifice is the whole church offering itself in union with Christ's sacrifice. Individual needs and intentions fall within this offering of the whole church on its own behalf and for the life of the world. I suspect that any change in the practice of concelebration will have to be accompanied by a change in the system of Mass stipends, since offering the Mass for a stipend is so frequently given as reason for concelebration rather than attendance at the eucharist. The obvious economic ramifications of this shift will have to be worked out in concert with the whole church of course, but an economic issue should not ultimately determine the sacramental practice of the church.

A final issue with regard to concelebration and the theology of the eucharist is the manner in which Christ becomes present in the liturgical celebration. On this issue undue emphasis in past theology on "words of consecration" and the moment of consecration has helped to limit the perception of the eucharistic celebration as a symbolic ritual. The eucharistic prayer is a necessary but insufficient condition for the rendering of Christ present in the eucharist, for it is part of a fourfold action (taking, blessing, breaking, and sharing) which is in itself a mimet-

ic unfolding of the activity of the Lord not only at the Last
Supper but in the entire paschal mystery. For this reason activities like breaking the bread during the institution narrative
tend to draw all attention to the eucharistic prayer at the expense of the entire eucharistic action. Attention should be giv-
en first and foremost to the form of the eucharistic action rather than to an individual's devotion or "power" to consecrate.
Ideally the eucharist as a ritual action is formative of the
whole community in becoming what it celebrates, namely, in
being the body of Christ by conforming itself both in ritual
and in daily action to the reality of the paschal mystery.[22]

In terms of any theory of concelebration, therefore, contemporary theology of the eucharist suggests that while the presider has a most important role at the eucharist, he has by no
means a role that is extrinsic to the gathered community or in
any way denigrates the baptismal dignity of the assembled
faithful. On the other hand, concelebration often underlines
symbolically an inequality of status in the assembly.

CONCELEBRATION IN THE CHURCH'S TRADITION

At this point we can consider what can be learned from the
preconciliar debate on concelebration and from the nature of
presbyteral concelebration in the church's history. While historical investigation does not usually provide direct answers
to contemporary ecclesial questions, yet it can point to those
practices which are more in conformity with the nature of the
Christian community and its worship.

Let us begin with the preconciliar debate about concelebration.[23] The preconciliar discussion was framed by a series of
distinctions about the mode of concelebration. Pius XII distinguished sacramental concelebration, at which presbyters recited together the prayer of the eucharist proper, from the communal eucharist, at which priests assisted but did not verbally
co-consecrate. At the same time there were the so-called syn-
chronized Masses at which each priest consecrated the bread
and wine separately but as much as possible at the same time.
These distinctions led to a long debate among theologians and
liturgists over the nature of sacramental concelebration. Karl
Rahner argued that there could be true sacramental concele-

bration without verbal co-consecration, based on the affirmation that even in concelebration there is only one celebration of the eucharist.[24] Bernhard Schultze argued that as far as the historical question was concerned, whether or not the tradition required verbal consecration must remain an open issue.[25] The matter was settled in 1956 for the time being by Pius XII in his address to the Assisi Pastoral Liturgical Congress, in which he maintained the distinction between ceremonial (non-sacramental) and true concelebration.[26] In May 1957 the Holy Office further clarified the matter by stating that only priests who pronounce the consecratory words can be said to be concelebrating.[27] This was to remain the discipline of the Roman Church in the reform of the liturgy after Vatican II.[28]

However, Schultze was correct. It does remain an open question whether historically verbal co-consecration must be the norm for sacramental concelebration. In the first place, it is difficult to imagine that anyone could have verbally co-consecrated during the early centuries in which eucharistic prayers were extemporized by the presider.[29] Moreover, it is far from clear that all early eucharistic prayers contained what we could call a consecration, that is, the narrative of the institution of the eucharist at the Last Supper.[30] The early prayers were an outgrowth of the Jewish table blessing of the kind that Jesus himself must have used at the Last Supper. It is not certain that the institution narrative, which serves grammatically even in later prayers as a warrant for the rite and not as a consecration, was a part of each and every prayer from the very beginning. Indeed, had this been the case, Paul would probably not have had to remind the Corinthians of the narrative itself (1 Cor 11:23-25). Though the institution narrative does begin to appear in prayers that we have from the third century, it is only in the fourth century that the theological tradition begins to be concerned about a moment of consecration.[31] Such concern eventually led to a dispute between east and west as to whether it was the invocation of the Holy Spirit (epiclesis) or the institution narrative that was actually consecratory. The correct answer is both—and neither—for the whole prayer is a prayer of consecration. The unity of the eucharistic prayer has important consequences for the practice of concelebration, as we shall see below.

The question of sacramental concelebration also depends on how the eucharist was viewed from the beginning. We have already suggested that the main concern of the eucharist is the unity of the body of Christ. The early tradition of the church bears this out. Ecclesial unity is the governing concept of Clement's late first-century letter to the Corinthians, as it had been in Paul's first letter to the same community (especially chapters 1, 10, and 11). Concern for the eucharist as a manifestation of unity is most evident in Ignatius of Antioch's letters, especially when he exhorts the Philadelphians to observe one eucharist, one flesh, one cup, and one altar together with one bishop, the presbytery, and the deacons.[32] In the first three centuries we have no evidence at all to suggest what we know today as sacramental concelebration. Rather, the bishop presided at the one eucharist. He alone prayed aloud for the community, and all other orders in the church (laity, deacons, presbyters, widows, etc.) took their places in the assembly.

Robert Taft has pointed out that the custom of concelebration most likely originated not with the ordinary eucharistic celebrations of the early church, but rather as a sign of eucharistic hospitality. A visiting bishop would be invited to share in the eucharistic prayer by a host bishop in order to manifest ecclesial unity.[33] There are a number of examples of this mode of concelebration from the second century on.[34]

It is only from the end of the eighth century in the west that we begin to get references to concelebration by verbal co-consecration. The introduction to the *Ordo Romanus* III states that each bishop at the papal stational liturgy stands around the pope holding his own paten and that all recite the eucharistic prayer together.[35] On the other hand, the late seventh-century *Ordo Romanus* I had clearly stated that the pope alone "entered into the canon." Taft has shown that the earliest eastern evidence for the practice of verbal co-consecration dates from the tenth century.[36] Moreover, we find great variety in the manner of eucharistic concelebration in the various traditions of the Christian East even today.[37]

No need to repeat here was was said above about the concern for unity in the early medieval Roman stational liturgy. But we might add that the same concern for unity is evidenced by similar patterns of city-wide (stational) liturgy found at Jerusalem, Constantinople, Antioch, Milan, Ravenna, and a number of the larger towns of northern Europe.

All this historical investigation provides no sure answer to the theological question of sacramental concelebration. After all, there are advances in theology, and this theology is no mere recapitulation of the past. However, we can see clearly that no one arrangement of concelebration has been absolute in the Christian tradition. Moreover, the tradition does show us what a central part the unifying conception of the eucharist has played.

CONCELEBRATION TODAY

A useful example of a male religious order's adaptation of the liturgical reform may be found in the Jesuits. Following closely on the conclusion of Vatican II, the Thirty-first General Congregation of the Society of Jesus took up implementation of the conciliar decrees and the renewal of religious life. A vital part of this renewal was, of course, set in terms of prayer and worship. The Congregation's decree on prayer in relation to liturgy reads in part:

> Liturgical celebrations, especially those in which the community worships as a group, and above all the celebration of the Eucharist, should mean much to us . . . Concelebration, by which the unity of the priesthood is appropriately manifested, is encouraged in our houses when allowed by proper authority, while each priest shall always retain his right to celebrate Mass individually.[38]

Encouragement was obviously needed in order to foster concelebration. Any common liturgical celebration, aside from several devotions and apart from houses of formation, was quite foreign to the traditional practice of Jesuits. The council's Constitution on the Liturgy had insisted on the option of priests to celebrate individually,[39] and so did the Jesuits. There may have been some confusion here. While the council's decree stressed the retention of the right of a priest to celebrate individually, it was not referring to the idea of a "private Mass," that is, Mass without a server. The General Instruction on the Roman Missal, one of the major documents of the liturgical reform, made it clear that "Mass should never be celebrated without a server, except out of serious necessity."[40] The church simply does not sanction private Mass as many priests seem to understand it. At any rate, the Jesuits were in line with the rest of the church in encouraging a more communal vision of the liturgy.

It is not altogether clear today whether concelebration is the more popular form of eucharistic celebration among priests. Of course, we are concerned here with situations in which priests need not serve congregations on a day-to-day basis; that is, circumstances in which a number of priests live together without daily pastoral obligations, such as high schools, colleges, and universities. Given the nature of the eucharist as a communal act of symbolizing the church's unity, it seems to me that concelebration in such circumstances is far preferable to individual celebrations, with or without a server. Of course, scheduling can be a difficulty for a communal eucharist, especially where so many follow busy and different schedules, but surely every effort should be made to avoid fragmentation of liturgical celebration.

It does not take a social psychologist, however, to perceive that there are far more profound difficulties with concelebration than scheduling. To concelebrate is obviously not the same as to preside, and in normal circumstances the eucharist has only one presider. Some priests feel that their priesthood is thus denigrated and that, after all is said and done, they are no more than ceremonial appendages to the celebration.[41] They are certainly corrrect in feeling that they are not exercising presidential leadership in the assembly. One wonders if this awkwardness is not due to a poor understanding of the collegial nature of Christian ministry. Sacraments are not simply available for the personal devotion of the priest, nor is the priesthood a kind of possession that can ever be exercised independently of the church. Each presbyter must ask himself: Is it always necessary for me as an individual to function publicly as a priest? Are there not situations in which it is more appropriate to be ministered to than to minister? For many reasons a negative answer to the first position and an affirmative answer to the second may be a bitter pill to swallow.

On the other hand, awkwardness with the current practice of concelebration could well be a healthy sign among apostolic men yearning to preach the Gospel and minister the sacraments. It is hard to imagine presbyters always being content with concelebration and never presiding and preaching. Yet there are circumstances in which it is impossible for all presbyters present to preside, and it is also a sign of health when one who normally exercises leadership knows how to take a back seat.

Frankly, although I think that concelebration can be an effective sign of the unity of the church, there are circumstances in which priests should assist at the eucharist in the same manner as lay people[42] and that ritual concelebration should be extremely rare. These circumstances certainly include any occasions on which the priests outnumber the lay people present.[43] It has been my experience, as well as the experience of many lay people with whom I have spoken, that such occasions make the eucharist more a sign of the disunity and differentiation of the church than a sign of unity.[44] That such a circumstance might warrant priests assisting in the same way as the laity was not envisioned at the time of the recent liturgical reform, but is much clearer today when lay people have become much more conscious of their baptismal dignity and active role in the eucharistic assembly.

Another occasion which seems to warrant priests refraining from concelebration is the frequent or daily eucharist. Here no sacramental or ecclesial purpose is served by the outward manifestation of the unity of the priesthood, especially when there may be a very small minority of nonordained people present. Concelebration should be limited to those relatively few occasions on which the corporate ministry of the presbyterate ought to be made evident. It is never merely a sign of honor or dignity, since the highest dignity one can have in the assembly is the status of being a baptized member. Of course, eucharistic celebrations presided over by a bishop or great feasts do warrant concelebrants. It does not seem to me that one can legislate precisely on which occasions one should concelebrate or refrain from concelebrating. Ultimately, competent ecclesiastical authorities like bishops and major superiors can decide such matters, especially in limiting numbers of concelebrants, but usually this will be left up to the common sense of individual priests.

Finally, there remain several aspects of concelebration which require some comment: vesture; the eucharistic prayer; ecclesial space; communion.

Vesture

Since concelebration should clearly exhibit the unity of the church, the eucharistic sacrifice, and the priesthood,[45] those who concelebrate should be vested in the manner prescribed by the General Instruction on the Roman Missal. This includes albs, stoles, and chasubles, although chasubles may be omitted when there are not enough vestments.[46] Under no circumstances should stoles be worn over streetclothes in the celebration of the eucharist.

Liturgical vesture can often be a sign of great consternation, especially when concelebrants do not vest with care and an appropriate sense of the sacredness of liturgical activity. As a public act and a public symbol, the liturgy necessarily includes an aesthetic dimension. To ignore this dimension is not only to show disrespect for one's own role, but also to show disrespect for the assembly. Care in vesture is not fussiness, but attention to the sacredness and dignity of liturgical acts. Lack of care is often indicated by wearing vestments that do not fit properly as well as albs and stoles originally designed to be worn under chasubles.

The Eucharistic Prayer

With regard to those parts of the eucharistic prayer which are to be recited in common, the General Instruction on the Roman Missal reads: "The parts said by all the concelebrants are to be recited in such a way that the concelebrants say them in a softer voice (submissa voce) and the principal celebrant's voice stands out clearly. In this way the congregation should be able to hear the text without difficulty."[47] This instruction is often honored in the breach. Moreover, the result of the concelebrant's joining in the prayers in a full voice is that the presider has a tendency to drop his own voice, which makes for even greater unintelligibility.

As I have pointed out above, the eucharistic prayer is a unity, from the opening dialogue to the final doxology and Amen. It seems to me that this unity is broken in two ways in the current practice of concelebration. The first is by the practice of verbal co-consecration, which necessarily implies that there are some portions of the prayer which are more important than others and that, in a pinch, the praise and adoration aspects of the prayer are window dressing. It would seem best to limit participation of concelebrants during the eucharistic prayer to the gesture outlined in the General Instruction, that is, the outstretched hands at the invocation of the Holy Spirit and the right hand which may (optionally) be pointed toward the gifts at the recitation of the dominical words.[48] The second way of breaking the unity of the eucharistic prayer is to distribute portions of the prayer to one or more concelebrants. The practice can reach ludicrous proportions. All have witnessed occasions on which the prayer has been so apportioned that every concelebrant "gets a chance" to recite a part of the prayer no matter how brief. The eucharistic prayer is not an honorific; it is a prayer.

Ecclesial Space

The great majority of Roman Catholic churches and chapels are not arranged to accommodate large numbers of concelebrants. Likewise, most sanctuary spaces cannot accommodate a large number of concelebrants around the altar table. These factors should be taken into account when considering the number of concelebrants for a eucharistic celebration.

Concelebrants should never block off the view of the rest of the congregation.[49] In addition, placing them in the front pew of a church that is oriented on a longitudinal axis can be very distracting to the rest of the congregation, especially during the eucharistic prayer. Several times I have noticed that the congregation shifts its attention from the altar to concelebrants in the congregation throughout the verbally participated parts of the prayer. Surely this is not desirable and makes it all the more imperative that concelebrants recite the common parts of the eucharistic prayer *sotto voce*.

The final note on concelebration has to do with the reception of holy communion. Few actions during the liturgy can so highlight the disunity of the assembly, especially when all do not receive under both species. The idea of concelebrants taking communion for themselves is an anomaly.[50] It seems to me that instead of coming to the altar to take consecrated bread or the cup for themselves, concelebrants should receive communion from another's hands in their own places. In fact, in light of our renewed emphasis on the dignity of the worshiping assembly, I wonder if it is not time to begin consideration of the ordained and other ministers of communion receiving holy communion last instead of first, as a sign of hospitality. Every liturgical action is a symbolic communication fraught with power, and nothing communicates symbolically like "who gets to go first."

* * * * * *

The current practice of concelebration has raised a host of questions which were understandably not considered when the Second Vatican Council extended this practice for the whole church. The experience of celebration of the reformed rite, historical investigations, and further theological reflection have taught us that the unity of the church is a primary focus in any celebration of the eucharist. It is this unity which should always be the governing norm in the decision to concelebrate or not.

One last word on the underlying issue in the question of concelebration. It seems to me that when all is said and done, concelebration is about the exercise of power and symbolic roles in the church.[51] This is indeed a neuralgic issue. The manner in which ordained ministers exercise their power can and will have either good or ill effect on the people of God. For those who do hold the office of presbyter in the church, the issue of concelebration might serve as a reminder that leadership will never be truly effective unless it is practiced in terms of service. They might well come to the conclusion pointed to in this study: that those presbyters also serve who from time to time insist not on their office or rank but on their equality with the baptized and their dignified membership in the assembly of God's people.

Notes

1. Second Vatican Council, Constitution on the Sacred Liturgy, nos. 57, 58.

2. I owe a great debt to a number of people whom I consulted both formally and informally in the preparation of this study. I would like to thank especially the Board of the Loyola Pastoral Institute (New York), the Association of Jesuit Liturgists, and my colleagues at the Jesuit School of Theology at Berkeley.

3. Constitution on the Sacred Liturgy, no. 10; Dogmatic Constitution on the Church, nos. 1, 9-17.

4. In recent writing see for example: Eligius Dekkers, "Concelebration—Limitations of Current Practice," *Doctrine and Life* 22 (1972) 190-202; L. Leigssen, "La communauté eucharistique: communauté de personnes en action," *Questions liturgiques* (1983) 123-144; J.F. Lescrauwaet, "Concélébration," *Questions liturgiques* 64 (1983) 145-152.

5. Aidan Kavanagh, *Elements of Rite: A Handbook of Liturgical Style* (New York: Pueblo Publishing Co., 1982) 10; see also 13.

6. Ibid. 61.

7. Thomas Aquinas, *Summa Theologiae* 3, q. 82, a. 3, ad 2. Confer Jerome Murphy-O'Connor, "Eucharist and Community in First Corinthians," *Worship* 50 (1976) 370-385; 51 (1970) 56-69. Confer also Elisabeth Schüssler-Fiorenza's excellent study, "Tablesharing and the Celebration of the Eucharist," *Concilium* 152 (1982) 3-12.

8. Constitution on the Sacred Liturgy, no. 57. On the importance of the additional question of the eucharist and the unity of the church, especially in the conciliar debates and postconciliar documents, confer Stanislaw Madeja, "Analisi del concetto di concelebrazione eucaristica nel concilio Vatican II e nella riforma liturgica postconciliare," *Ephemerides Liturgicae* 96 (1982) 3-56, esp. 38-48; and Marcel Rooney, "Eucharistic Concelebration: Twenty-Five Years of Development," *Ecclesia Orans* 6 (1989) 117-129.

9. Alexander Gerken, *Theologie der Eucharistie* (Munich: Kösel, 1972) 299-300.

10. See Louis Bouyer, *Eucharist* (Notre Dame: University of Notre Dame Press, 1968) 9.

11. Constitution on the Sacred Liturgy, no. 14.

12. Raymond E. Brown, *Priest and Bishop* (New York: Paulist Press, 1970); Hans von Campenhausen, *Ecclesiastical Authority and Spiritual*

Power in the Early Church (Stanford, CA: Stanford University Press, 1969); Nathan Mitchell, *Mission and Ministry* (Wilmington, DE: Michael Glazier, 1982); and Chapter 11 in this volume.

13. As in the letters of Ignatius of Antioch, confer note 31 below.

14. Robert Cabié, ed., *La Lettre du Innocent Ier à Decentius de Gubbio* (Louvain: Publications Universitaires de Louvain, 1973)

15. See Pierre Nautin, "Le rite du 'Fermentum' dans les églises urbaines de Rome," *Ephemerides Liturgicae* 96 (1982) 510-522. Nautin argues that the *fermentum* meant that there was still only *one* eucharist in the early fifth century and that presbyters did not have the right to preside over the eucharist on their own.

16. See my "The City as Church and the Church as City," *Liturgy* 3 (1983) 69-73; reprinted as chapter 1 of this volume.

17. Pius XII, *Mediator Dei*, AAS 38 (1947) 555.

18. Edward J. Kilmartin, "Ecclesiastical Office, Power and Spirit," *Proceedings of the Catholic Theological Society of America* 37 (1982) 100-108; see also David N. Power, "Sacraments: Symbolizing God's Power in the Church," ibid. 66. For another approach to this discussion, see Peter Fink, "The Sacrament of Orders: Some Liturgical Reflections," *Worship* 56 (1982) 490-493, 498-502.

19. Karl Rahner, "Die vielen Messen und das eine Opfer," *Zeitschrift für katholischen Theologie* 71 (1949) 257-317. For an expanded treatment, see Karl Rahner and Angelus Häussling, *The Celebration of the Eucharist* (New York: Herder and Herder, 1968). For this discussion I am indebted to Edward J. Kilmartin, "The One Fruit and the Many Fruits of the Mass," *Proceedings of the Catholic Theological Society of America* 21 (1966) 37-69 and Paul deClerck, "La fréquences des messes," *La Maison-Dieu* 121 (1975) 151-158. On the Mass as sacrifice, see also David N. Power, "Words That Crack: The Uses of 'Sacrifice' in Eucharistic Discourse," *Worship* 53 (1979) 386-404; idem., *The Sacrifice We Offer: The Tridentine Dogma and Its Reinterpretation* (New York: Crossroad, 1987).

20. Kilmartin, "The One Fruit" 64.

21. See M. Francis Mannion, "Stipends and Eucharistic Praxis," *Worship* 57 (1983) 194-214; also John M. Huels, "Stipends in the New Code of Canon Law," *Worship* 57 (1983) 215-224.

22. See Augustine, Sermon 202.

23. The various positions are outlined and assessed in Katherine McGowan, *Concelebration* (New York: Herder and Herder, 1964) 72-109.

24. Karl Rahner, "Dogmatische Bemerkungen über die Frage der Konzelebration," *Münchener Theologische Zeitschrift* 16 (1955) 81-106.

On this issue, see also R. Kevin Seasoltz, *New Liturgy, New Laws* (Collegeville: The Liturgical Press, 1980) 87-90.

25. Bernhard Schultze, "Das theologische Problem der Konzelebration," *Gregorianum* 36 (1955) 212-271.

26. AAS 48 (1956) 711-725.

27. AAS 49 (1957) 370.

28. See the General Instruction on the Roman Missal (hereafter General Instruction), 1969, revised 1975, 170ff.

29. On extemporaneous eucharistic prayer in the early church, see Allan Bouley, *From Freedom to Formula: The Eucharistic Prayer from Oral Improvisation to Written Texts* (Washington, D.C.: Catholic University of America Press, 1981).

30. Among prayers which do not contain the institution narrative are: *Didache* 9-10, the Anaphora of Addai and Mari (E. Syrian tradition), Papyrus Strasbourg (Egyptian tradition). On this problem, see Louis Ligier, "The Origins of the Eucharistic Prayer," *Studia Liturgica* 9 (1973) 161-185; also Geoffrey J. Cuming, "The Anaphora of St. Mark: A Study in Development," *Le Muséon* 95 (1982) 115-129.

31. Confer Gregory Dix, *The Shape of the Liturgy* (London: A. and C. Black, 1945) 268-302.

32. Ignatius of Antioch, Letter to the Philadelphians 4; confer 6:2; Magnesians 6-7; Smyrnaeans 8 and Ephesians 20:2.

33. Robert F. Taft, "Ex Oriente Lux? Some Reflections on Eucharistic Celebration," *Worship* 54 (1980) 308-325; reprinted in *Living Bread, Saving Cup: Readings on the Eucharist*, ed., Kevin R. Seasoltz (Collegeville: The Liturgical Press, 1982) 242-259. References will be to the later edition, here confer 252.

34. See McGowan, *Concelebration* 24-30, 40-43. For similar treatments of the history of concelebration, see Archdale A. King, *Concelebration in the Christian Church* (London: Mowbray, 1966) 6-35, and Pierre Jounel, *The Rite of Concelebrating the Mass and Communion under Both Species* (New York: Desclée, 1967) 13-24.

35. See Michel Andrieu, *Les "Ordines Romani" du haut moyen-âge*, vol. 2 (Louvain: Spicilegium Sacrum Lovaniense, 1960) 131.

36. Taft, "Ex Oriente Lux?" 253.

37. Ibid. 242-247.

38. *Documents of the 31st and 32nd General Congregation of the Society of Jesus* (St. Louis: Institute of Jesuit Sources, 1977) 142-143.

39. Constitution on the Sacred Liturgy, no. 57.

40. General Instruction, no. 211. On the basis of the 1983 Code of Canon Law, this paragraph of the General Instruction has been revised to read: "Mass should not be celebrated without a server or the participation of at least one of the faithful, except for some legitimate

and reasonable cause." See *Emendations in the Liturgical Books Following upon the New Code of Canon Law* (Washington, D.C. ICEL, 1984).

41. See the treatment of this issue in J. Leo Klein, "American Jesuits and the Liturgy," *Studies in the Spirituality of Jesuits* 11:3 (1979) 17-21.

42. This is not the position taken by the Declaration of the Sacred Congregation on Divine Worship, *In Celebratione Missae* 7 August 1972, AAS 64 (1972) 561, cited in *Documents on the Liturgy 1963-1979* (Collegeville: The Liturgical Press, 1982) 563.

43. See the trenchant comments of Kavanagh, *Elements of Rite* 72.

44. See Dekkers, "Concelebration" 195.

45. Sacred Congregation of Rites, Decree *Ecclesiae Semper*, 7 March 1965, AAS 57 (1965) 410.

46. General Instruction, no. 161.

47. Ibid., no. 170.

48. Ibid., no. 174.

49. Ibid., no. 167.

50. See Robert F. Taft, "Receiving Communion—A Forgotten Symbol?", *Worship* 57 (1983) 412-418.

51. See the discussion of David Power in "Sacraments Symbolizing God's Power." The entire proceedings of the Catholic Theological Society of America for 1982 deal with a theological analysis of power. One issue that is not considered here, but is also an important aspect of the concelebration question, is that of the overwhelming maleness of presbyteral concelebration. An undue emphasis on male priesthood is, to say the least, insensitive with regard to an issue that many find painful.

8

Reflections on the Frequency of Eucharistic Celebration

THERE CAN BE LITTLE DOUBT THAT THE CELEBRATION OF THE EU-charist has improved in the course of the past twenty years in the wake of Vatican II's mandated liturgical reform. However, our new model for the celebration of the eucharist, the Sunday assembly, raises some questions as to the value and effectiveness of the practice of daily Mass. To be sure, ecclesiastical legislation is of two minds on the subject. While on the one hand a case can be made that the Sunday assembly as the image of the gathered church is the norm for all eucharistic celebration,[1] on the other, priests are urged to frequent and even daily celebration of the eucharist even if pastoral necessity does not warrant their individual presidency, that is, even if circumstances force them to celebrate without a congregation.[2] At the same time it can safely be said that in much Roman Catholic popular piety the ideal person is the one who presides at or attends Mass daily. Hence with glowing approbation we often hear that so-and-so is a daily communicant. While it is true that in many parts of the world this subject is rendered otiose by the shortage of priests, the image of the daily Mass attender or presider as ideal must still be dealt with. No doubt this is a most sensitive issue and it may well be, as one author has put it, that "the attempt to convince those who want it that they really shouldn't is plain foolishness."[3] The ramifications of this issue with regard to the meaning of the eucharist and the quality of Sunday celebration are too important not to be discussed.

Therefore, on the basis of historical, theological, and pastoral observations, I intend to discuss some avenues of approach to this thorny topic in the context of parochial life. I have chosen to focus on the parish because it seems to me that different ecclesial situations might determine particular norms for eucharistic frequency. What might be a proper norm for a parish or university campus chapel might not be appropriate in a monastery or religious house. Another reason for concentrating on parochial life is that this is the situation in which the issue of daily Mass is likely to be raised, if only because of the lack of ordained presbyters. However, it is my hope that all things being equal, some of the conclusions reached in this study might be applied to nonparochial situations as well.

What then constitutes an appropriate avenue of approach to this sensitive topic? Is it correct to focus attention on the history of eucharistic frequency? Will doctrinal theology provide the most convincing solutions? Should pastoral considerations alone govern our conclusions? None of these approaches is sufficient unto itself. All three—historical, doctrinal, and pastoral—must be studied in concert, for if contemporary theology in the form of the liberation thought of Gustavo Gutierrez, Leonardo Boff, Jon Sobrino, and others has taught us anything, it is that all true theology is a dialogue between our tradition and our individual and communal experience of the world and of God. Therefore, what follows will deal with the issue of eucharistic frequency in all three realms, but with an emphasis on the doctrinal questions that arise, since these seem to be the most difficult.

HISTORICAL CONSIDERATIONS

It is very important to state the reason for historical investigation of a topic such as ours from the outset. We should not look for the earliest practice merely to imitate it. Such a procedure leads to the so-called genetic fallacy, that is, what is earliest is best, the notion that the entire meaning of an activity can be discerned in its most pristine form.[4] Historical investigation is enlightening because it reveals the development of forms in their context, not in that it discovers absolutes which must be (re)instituted. With this in mind, let us turn to the results of recent investigations into the history of eucharistic frequency.

The New Testament offers no clear pattern of how often the eucharist was celebrated in the primitive church. The Acts of the Apostles refers to what seems to be a daily domestic form of celebration ("breaking bread," Acts 2:46),[5] but at the same time Acts 20:7 refers to a special communal meeting of Christians for the same purpose on the first day of the week, Sunday. At any rate, by the second century the link between Sunday and the eucharist is indisputable.[6] Up to the Reformation of the sixteenth century, Sunday is the common denominator for frequency of celebration in the whole church.

However, Sunday was not the only day designated for eucharistic celebration in the church of the first centuries. Even prior to Constantine's fourth-century legitimation of the church there were feasts like Epiphany that obviously included such celebration.[7] In addition, from the second century on it was customary to celebrate the eucharist at the tombs of the martyrs on the anniversary of their death.[8] From at least the middle of the third century it was also the custom to hold a eucharistic celebration at tombs of all loved ones on their anniversaries. This is why Cyprian can refer to a daily celebration at Carthage.[9] Finally, in some places it was the practice to celebrate at the end of the traditional station days (Wednesday and Friday) by the beginning of the third century.[10]

What is notable about the growth in eucharistic frequency in the pre-Constantinian period is that different motives governed celebration. While eucharists may have been celebrated on a larger or smaller scale, and the forms of celebration may even have differed,[11] still there was always a specific reason for celebrating more frequently than Sunday. There seems to have been no such thing as daily eucharistic celebration as a matter of course.[12]

By the end of the fourth century there are a number of references to daily eucharist, at least for Milan and North Africa. Daniel Callam has argued that the increase in frequency during this period can be linked to the practice of daily communion being elevated to daily celebration by bishops of ascetic bent like Ambrose of Milan and Augustine of Hippo.[13] Greater frequency may also be related to the growing calendar of feasts in this period, as Robert Taft has pointed out.[14] Writing of the early medieval period, Angelus Häussling has noted that daily Mass (especially private Mass) was inspired by the imitation of the stational system of the city of Rome, that is, the monastic church multiplied its altars to form a miniature city representative of the Roman model and hence provided the opportunity for the multiplication of Masses.[15] While the various churches of the Christian east have never settled on daily eucharist as an ideal,[16] such was the norm for the west from the early medieval period on.

Of course all this changed with the sixteenth-century Protestant Reformation. A recovery of the meaning of eucharistic communion in the new churches coupled with an abhorrence of an over-crowded Roman calendar and the reluctance of people of a late medieval mentality to receive communion, all led to a decrease in the frequency of celebration. Thus, even Sunday was disassociated from eucharistic celebration, a loss which the churches of the Reformation have only been making good in this century. On the Roman Catholic side, the norm remained daily Mass, while up until the current century, the majority of daily Mass attenders were not daily communicants.

What then can we make of this varied historical development, albeit treated in only the briefest fashion here? The most important conclusion is that history offers no easy solution to our question. It presents no clear norm for eucharistic frequency, but does reveal a strong connection between Sunday and eucharistic assembly for the first millennium and a half of Christianity's existence. At the same time, it would be a simplistic error, as Taft has pointed out, merely to dismiss greater frequency as aberrant or to tag it with the supposedly perjorative terms like "medieval" or even "modern."[17] That there have been numerous appropriate occasions for the celebration of the eucharist throughout the centuries has been demonstrated by Gregory Dix in a truly lyrical passage in his classic, *The Shape of the Liturgy*.[18] However, it seems to me that some historical developments lack sufficient justification. They happen more or less accidentally. Such is the leap from celebrating the eucharist from various motivations to the practice of daily Mass as a matter of course. To assess this development, which is tied to the very idea of the eucharist, we must now turn to doctrinal considerations.

THEOLOGICAL CONSIDERATIONS

Finding proper norms for the frequency of eucharistic celebration raises a host of problems with regard to sacramental theology, and, while none of these problems can be dealt with thoroughly here, they need at least to be mentioned in order to arrive at a reasonable solution.

I will begin with my own reworking of the traditional definition of a sacrament, employing this as a basis for further reflection. I maintain that sacraments are those symbolic activities which mediate Christian identity by reactualizing the paschal mystery in the context of the church as the assembly of God's people. Key to this definition is an understanding of the seven traditional sacraments as *ecclesial* activities. Although individuals participate in their celebration, sacraments always have a communal dimension; individuals take part in them as members of the church. This is true even of reconciliation celebrated individually.[19] In addition, the reality of Christ (or what I have called here the reactualization of the paschal mystery) is communicated in a symbolic manner, that is, in a multivalent way that conceals as well as reveals. As such, no symbolic activity, even a religious one (or perhaps one must say especially a religious one) ever discloses its referent without surplus; in other words, Christ is never present in sacramental celebration purely and simply.[20] This, I would maintain, is an appropriate stance before the God of mystery who can never be captured by us or held prisoner by our categories. In this sense, although the tradition has firmly maintained a confidence in God's efficacious presence in sacramental celebrations rightly enacted, Christian worship can never manipulate God. A valuable expression of this sovereign freedom of God can be found in the need for an epicletic moment, calling down or calling forth the power of the Holy Spirit, as a safeguard against thinking that the actualization of the paschal mystery were wholly within our power. It is on this pneumatological level that western theology has traditionally been weakest. Such reflection on the symbolic and dialectical presence and absence of Christ in sacramental celebration should encourage in us a healthy reticence about taking sacramental effectiveness for granted. It provides as well a way to understand the significant critique of sacramental worship offered today by liberation theologians.[21] We must be aware that sacraments can be badly misused, as when they subtly canonize a *status quo* system of exploitation and domination and when they imply a subconscious manipulation of God.

The celebration of the eucharist is supremely vulnerable to this critique. What ought to be happening is that the assembly of the baptized recognizes its true identity as called into union with Christ's sacrifice in a mimetic representation of the paschal mystery around the table of the Lord. However, it seems to me that this common action has often been perceived as the action of a special class of persons endowed with supernatural powers and controlling an activity over which the nonordained members of the assembly have no power. Such a cultic understanding of sacramental activity runs counter to the prophetic critique of worship engaged in by Jesus himself.[22] It turns the church as the assembly of a baptized priestly people into a two-tiered system of those who hold power and those who benefit from power, ignoring the New Testament insight that there is only one priest in whose priesthood all baptized Christians participate, especially by leading lives that are sacrificial (Rom 12:1).[23]

The result of what I call "the cultification of a sacramental activity" is both reification and absolutizing. The eucharist is reified by being perceived as an object which is produced instead of a celebration, hence the increasing attention paid to the ontological nature of the consecrated bread and wine themselves in medieval sacramental theology.[24] The eucharist is absolutized in that such a cultic celebration takes on an absolute value distinct from the participation of the assembly. In other words, the eucharist becomes one thing and the people's participation in it something else.[25] Such a conceptualization vitiates the very reason for celebrating the eucharist in the first place, that is, the gradual growth and transformation of the baptized into the body of Christ. Consequently, if the eucharist is absolutized, the principle of "the more the better" or "daily Mass as a matter of course" can hardly be criticized.

However, if the eucharist is to be the act of an assembly becoming itself in this most focused activity of Christian life, then it is appropriate to ask in which situations this particular symbolic activity is appropriate. In other words, the value of the celebration of the Mass is always relative and never absolute.

These conclusions are similar to those reached by Karl Rahner in his classic study on the one sacrifice and the many Masses.[26] Rahner analyzes eucharistic celebration in the context of neoscholastic theology and its concern with the fruits of the Mass. His conclusion is that the eucharist should be celebrated as often as it increases the faith and devotion (*fides et devotio*) of those who participate.[27] What he failed to do, however, was to provide a way to think about the eucharistic celebration as a truly ecclesial act and to articulate the inherent connection between the sacrifice of the Mass and the celebrating assembly.[28]

More recently, Angelus Häussling, perceiving that a sacramental celebration ought always to be received as a gift and never as a kind of product, has argued that the appropriate reason for celebrating the eucharist is always an occasion (*Anlass*) and not simply a motive. The occasion arises from some "change of situation" in the life of Christians.[29] I take it that he means here the frequency of eucharistic celebration over and above the meeting of the Sunday assembly. From his basic principle of occasionality, there follow three norms for frequency: (1) That worship takes place as often as there are changes in the life situation of the local church. Clearly weddings, baptisms, funerals, ordinations, and major events all call for the celebration of the eucharist. (2) The frequency of liturgical celebration diminishes with the increasing worth of each form of worship. When it is occasional, the eucharist can be perceived as special and its meaning as the preeminent form of Christian worship can be appreciated. (3) Worship is inadmissible when there is no proportion between the form and the basic activity of ecclesial self-realization.[30] This suggests that even small group eucharistic celebrations for special occasions must somehow be perceptibly linked to the worship of the wider church. These norms are an important safeguard of the dignity of the eucharist against the trivialization that can occur when it is celebrated merely as a matter of course.

These theological issues remain to be discussed within this framework: the status of the presider, the question of stipends, and the identification of an authentic worshiping assembly. As to the first, it should be clear that the ordained presbyter should not be viewed as presiding in abstraction from the worshiping assembly.[31] Though it is clear from the tradition of theology that the priest has been understood to preside in the person of Christ, he does not do this apart from the fact that he presides in the name of the church. Here we can detect that the same kind of absolutizing that occurred with regard to the eucharistic elements was characteristic of the understanding of those ordained to the presbyterate.[32] The question of exactly what kind of power is given to the ordained is an extremely thorny one and will not be treated extensively here. However, at the very least it should be said that whatever this power is, it is never to be exercised outside of the context of the community, as if the priest were granted a kind of control over the eucharist over and above the situation of the worshiping assembly.[33] If the priest is conceived in such an absolutized fashion that he has totally free control over the frequency of celebration, then it is difficult to see why he should not celebrate as often as possible, as the current code of canon law recommends.[34] Here even Rahner's principle of an increase of faith and devotion is not persuasive for it can conceivably be presumed that such an increase would result from the daily celebration of Mass. In any case, the whole conceptuality of the eucharist as an act which the priest performs must be called into question. Surely the presider is both servant and leader of the community in a primary role, but he is always doing something with, as well as for, the community. This makes the celebration of private Mass, even when the priest considers himself in union with the whole church in a spiritual manner, an anomaly at best. It seems to me that a correct understanding of the nature of the eucharistic act can no longer sustain the inherent contradiction between private Mass and the celebration of a worshiping assembly. A return to the practice of the first Christian millennium in which, according to the sixth canon of the Council of Chalcedon, presbyters were ordained to a title, that is, the service of a local church, would indeed be a welcome development.[35]

The second theological issue that needs to be addressed with regard to frequency is the issue of stipends. This matter is made all the more sensitive because of its economic implications. However, here we have another problem in which the Gordian knot must be cut. In addition to de-absolutizing the role of the presider at the eucharist, the reintroduction of the general intercessions on the part of the assembly as their priestly prayer has made it obvious that the Mass cannot be offered for the sake of one special intention, especially when the donor is absent.[36] Stipends should simply be abandoned, especially since they promote a reified understanding and practice of eucharistic celebration.

A final issue is the most complex of all, namely, what constitutes an authentic worshiping assembly. Since numbers alone will not suffice as a norm here, let me propose three criteria. First, the worshiping assembly is a group of baptized individuals honestly struggling to incarnate the Gospel in their lives. This criterion might all too often be passed over lightly as it is so difficult to reach a judgment on the intentions of the people that make up an assembly. However, it is not possible to imagine an authentic celebration of the eucharist, that is, only truly effective of unity in Christ, in an assembly which consists of groups of people who are manifestly practicing injustice and have no intention of changing.[37] While on this side of the parousia all of our eucharistic celebrations will be relatively defective, whether because of unjust social situations, the split between the churches, injustice to women, or the ordinary sinfulness of the members of the assembly, yet relative judgments can be made in this matter, similar to the interdicts of the Middle Ages.

The second and third criteria have more to do with the reasons that bring Christians together to celebrate. One of these is the weekly meeting or synaxis of Christians on Sunday, the day of resurrection, when the community celebrates the paschal mystery in its fullness. The last is the feast day, a day that calls forth festivity and exuberance connecting the people and their social and cultural roots with some important religious event as a focus for the meaning of the paschal mystery. Here one might identify feasts like Christmas, the Assumption of Mary, a patronal feast of a church, diocese, or nation, for example, Our Lady of Guadalupe.[38] In addition, one would want to include significant moments in the life of parts of the community which affect the community as a whole, like weddings and funerals.

These theological conclusions are admittedly somewhat abstract and correctly so, for they must be tempered by considerations from the realm of pastoral practice.

PASTORAL CONSIDERATIONS

We have seen that the eucharist ought to be celebrated when and if it builds up the church as the body of Christ. On the pastoral level it seems to me that this means that it cannot be celebrated adequately every day. Several observations lead me to this conclusion. In the first place, the eucharist is a fairly complex ritual action. As described in the General Instruction of the Roman Missal, it calls forth diverse roles of service from the community and images the whole community as the body of Christ. As a true celebration, it also implies music and singing.[39] This full image of the eucharist is truncated and short-circuited in all but a few daily celebrations. Needless to say, it is difficult to plan a well-thought-out eucharistic liturgy each Sunday, let alone every day. The result of daily Mass is usually that people settle for a kind of watered down version of the eucharist, a least common denominator or the equivalent of the old low Mass.

If the daily low Mass stood by itself and did not affect other celebrations, we could perhaps make our peace with it. However, such liturgies have a deleterious effect on the community at large. On the one hand, they encourage people who attend (even with the best of motives) to perceive the eucharist not as a gift, a true high point of ecclesial life, but rather as a duty. Moreover, such truncated celebrations have a tendency to focus on the elements of communion rather than the activity of communion in the Lord, which is both a vertical and horizontal reality. Hence daily Masses tend to individualize what ought to be the primary and privileged sign of our common unity. On the other hand, for presbyters who are entrusted with daily eucharist as a matter of course, such frequent celebration inevitably leads to a rather minimalistic concern with observing the legal conditions for proper liturgical celebration. The upshot is that Sunday celebrations suffer because after all "the Mass is the Mass." In this way the majority of the people of God suffer because those who have the duty of presiding cannot adequately perceive the difference between daily Mass and the gathering of the assembly which ought to be the crown of the week.

One alternative which has been offered is to provide a different order of service for daily Masses.[40] Clearly there is a healthy Christian instinct for daily services, at least among a minority of Catholics.[41] There is ample evidence for such frequency of celebration in the tradition of the liturgy of the hours as the prayer of the people, a tradition just now beginning to be recovered on a parochial level.[42] We must also take into account the long-standing tradition of daily communion (as opposed to daily Mass) in the early church. This last practice, however, may run the risk of continuing to reify the eucharist, focusing attention on the elements to the exclusion of the activity of communion. A better solution for daily services than a different order of Mass might be to construct daily liturgies which correspond more closely to the prayer needs of the assembly in question. Then, when it is celebrated, the eucharist could be experienced as a true occasion, imaging the reality that it symbolizes. According to this principle, it is entirely possible that pastors might end up celebrating a daily eucharist, but for specific pastoral needs and never simply as a matter of course. Needless to say, dropping daily Mass and not replacing it with some opportunity for daily public liturgical prayer would be irresponsible pastoral practice. In fact, celebration of the liturgy of the hours or word services might be helpful in encouraging people to realize the true presence of Christ in their midst by the very fact that they are a praying community.

Another pastoral issue is pertinent to the discussion of daily Mass, namely, the decline of priests and the growing number of lay ministers. I did not treat this issue under doctrinal considerations because in the Roman Catholic Church we have clearly failed to understand that the need for ordained ministers of word and sacrament obviates the current discipline that prevents women and noncelibate men from being ordained. In

other words, Schillebeeckx's principle that the local community has the right to the eucharist and hence the *right* to a presbyter should overrule our current discipline.[43] However, on a
pastoral level, since the current state of affairs is not likely to
change within the immediate future, it is necessary to envision
other forms of the ministry of liturgical presidency in the
church. Encouraging lay ministers to preside at the liturgy of
the hours and other services may well be of great benefit especially to many women who increasingly find it difficult to participate in eucharistic celebrations perceived as male dominated. If the eucharist is the climactic moment in ecclesial life, it is
not the only true liturgy. The employment of noneucharistic
forms of worship might well help us to understand a point alluded to above: Christ is truly and really present in the assembly of the faithful as a praying community.

These reflections on the inadvisability of daily eucharist
should not be considered an attempt to denigrate the place of
the eucharist in Christian life. Surely the renewed interest in
celebrating the eucharist has been a tremendous achievement
of the Second Vatican Council, and it would be wrong to gainsay the enrichment it has brought to the church as well as the
inspiration it has given to other Christian Churches in their
own ongoing liturgical renewal. The same must be said for the
recovery of frequent communion in the twentieth century.
However, we risk neglecting the genius for popular devotion
as well as other forms of liturgical prayer when we become
mono-eucharistic, convinced that only the best will do in every situation. Human beings experience reality in a modulated
fashion; if every day is expected to be a feast, which the eucharist is, then no day will be truly festal. It is just such a modulation which in my opinion is lacking in the continuance of
the practice of daily Mass. In other words, daily Mass as a
matter of course is too much of a good thing.

Notes

1. The General Instruction of the Roman Missal, Introduction 5;
ch. 1, nos. 1, 3, 4; ch. 2, nos. 7, 14, 15; ch. 4, no. 75, in *Documents of the
Liturgy 1963-1975: Conciliar, Papal, and Curial Texts*, International
Commission on English in the Liturgy (Collegeville: The Liturgical
Press, 1982) 1380, 1391, 1393, 1394, 1404, 1465 (hereafter DOL). See

also Aidan Kavanagh, *The Shape of Baptism: The Rite of Christian Initiation* (New York: Pueblo Publishing Co., 1978) 106-109.

2. Paul VI, "Mysterium Fidei," 3 September 1965 (DOL 1177); Sacred Congregation for Catholic Education, "Instruction on Liturgical Formation in Seminaries," 3 June 1979 (DOL 2805); John Paul II, "On the Mystery and Worship of the Eucharist (*Dominicae Coenae*)" in A. Flannery, ed., *Vatican II: More Postconciliar Documents* (Northport, NY: Costello, 1982) no. 9.

3. Robert F. Taft, *The Liturgy of the Hours in East and West: The Origins of the Divine Office and Its Meaning for Today* (Collegeville: The Liturgical Press, 1986) 317.

4. See Susanne K. Langer, *Philosophy in a New Key*, 3rd ed. (Cambridge: Harvard University Press, 1957) 248. This dictum runs into some difficulty in a religion that holds its earliest writings as sacred, but in any case we shall see that the New Testament does not offer clear guidance as to eucharistic frequency.

5. This verse could possibly refer to daily temple worship with less frequent meetings for the breaking of the bread. This is Taft's reading in "The Frequency of the Eucharist throughout History," in *Beyond East and West: Problems in Liturgical Understanding* (Washington, D.C.: The Pastoral Press, 1984) 61. However, it seems to me that grammatically the *kath'hemeran* (daily) of the first phrase of the sentence governs the whole.

6. See Willy Rordorf, *Sunday* (Philadelphia: Westminster, 1986) 294-307; also Aimé-Georges Martimort, ed., *The Church at Prayer*, vol. 4: *The Liturgy and Time* (Collegeville: The Liturgical Press, 1986) 13-15; Taft, "Frequency," 62.

7. See Thomas J. Talley, *The Origins of the Liturgical Year* (New York: Pueblo Publishing Co., 1986) 112-124.

8. See *Martyrdom of Polycarp* 18:2-3, in Cyril C. Richardson, ed., *The Early Christian Fathers* (New York: Macmillan, 1970) 156; also John F. Baldovin, "On Feasting the Saints," *Worship* 54 (1980) 338. Reprinted as Chapter 4 in this volume.

9. Cyprian, *Ep 57:3*, CSEL 3:652; see Taft "Frequency" 62.

10. Tertullian *De Oratione* 19, CCL 1:267-268); see Taft, "Frequency" 62.

11. See Innocent I's letter to Decentius of Gubbio (A.D. 416) where there are three kinds of Sunday celebration within the city of Rome and its environs. For the differences between the papal stational liturgy and that of the titular presbyteral churches, see *La Lettre du pape Innocent Ier à Decentius de Gubbio*, ed., Robert Cabié (Louvain: Publications Universitaires de Louvain, 1973) 26-28, and Geoffrey G. Willis, *Further Essays in Roman Liturgy* (London: SPCK, 1968) 7-9.

12. Taft, "Frequency," 62-63 sets this out rather clearly. On the

question of daily communion as opposed to daily worship, see A. de Vogüé, "Eucharist and Monastic Life," *Worship* 59 (1985) 498-510.

13. D. Callam, "The Frequency of the Mass in the Latin Church ca. 400," *Theological Studies* 45 (1985) 615-626.

14. Taft, "Frequency" 66.

15. A. Häussling, *Mönchskonvent und Eucharistiefeier* (Münster: Aschendorff, 1973) 298-330; see also his "Motives for the Frequency of the Eucharist," *Concilium* 152 (1982) 27.

16. Taft, "Frequency," 71-73.

17. Taft, "Frequency," 74.

18. Gregory Dix, *The Shape of the Liturgy* (London: A. and C. Black, 1945); rpt. with additional notes by Paul V. Marshall (New York: Seabury, 1982) 744; see also the important social analysis of the late medieval Mass in John Bossy, *Christianity in the West 1400-1700* (New York: Oxford University Press, 1985) 57-75.

19. Karl Rahner, "Penance as an Additional Act of Reconciliation with the Church," *Theological Investigations* X (New York: Herder and Herder, 1973) 125-149. I am prescinding in this definition from Rahner's theology of the church as the primary sacrament as well as Schillebeeckx's approach which designates Christ as the primary sacrament, because the main focus of my definition aims at understanding why these particular seven actions are sacramental.

20. For a contemporary discussion of the nature of symbol, see Louis Dupré, *The Other Dimension* (New York: Seabury, 1979) 105-153; David N. Power, *Unsearchable Riches: The Symbolic Nature of Liturgy* (New York: Pueblo Publishing Co., 1984) 61-82; Louis Marie Chauvet, *Du Symbolique au symbole: Essai sur les sacrements* (Paris: Cerf, 1979).

21. See Juan Luis Segundo, *The Sacraments Today* (Maryknoll: Orbis, 1974); Leonardo Boff, *Church: Charism and Power* (New York: Crossroad, 1975). On penumatology and the sacraments, see Edward Kilmartin, *Christian Liturgy*, vol 1: *Theology* (Kansas City, MO: Sheed & Ward, 1988).

22. See Ferdinand Hahn, *The Worship of the Early Church* (Philadelphia: Fortress Press, 1973) 12-31.

23. See my critique of this development with regard to concelebration, "Concelebration: A Problem of Symbolic Roles in the Church," *Worship* 59 (1985) 33-34.

24. See J.M. Powers, *Eucharistic Theology* (New York: Herder and Herder, 1967) 22-31.

25. This attitude is still discernible in documents as recent as John Paul II's *Dominicae Coenae* (see note 2 above) nos. 8-9, where the priest is seen as in some sense doing something parallel to the assembly.

26. Karl Rahner and Angelus Häussling, *The Celebration of the Eucharist* (New York: Herder and Herder, 1968) esp. 88ff.

27. Rahner, *Celebration* 91-92. A similar conclusion but with greater regard for the ecclesial dimensions is reached by J.M. Powers, "A Symposium on the Place of Daily Mass in the Life of a Jesuit," *Worship* 44 (1970) 280-281. Different approaches are taken in the same symposium by J.H. Wright, 282-288, and J.L. Boyle, 289-291.

28. Here I agree with the assessment made in a review article of Rahner's work by P. DeClerck, "La fréquence des messes," *La Maison-Dieu*, no. 121 (1975) 158; see also Robert Ledogar, "The Question of Daily Mass," *Worship* 43 (1969) 273.

29. Angelus Häussling, "Normen der Häufigkeit liturgischen Feiern," *Archiv für Liturgiewissenschaft* 20 (1978) 88.

30. Häussling, "Normen" 89-90, 93.

31. See my comments in "Concelebration" 36-38.

32. Nathan Mitchell, *Mission and Ministry* (Wilmington: Michael Glazier, 1982) 239-250; Bernard Cooke, *Ministry to Word and Sacrament* (Philadelphia: Fortress Press, 1976) 564.

33. See the important critique of *Dominicae Coenae* in these terms by Edward J. Kilmartin, *Church, Eucharist and Priesthood* (New York: Paulist Press, 1981) 21-22, 37-39.

34. Code of Canon Law (1985) 276:3; 904.

35. Edward Schillebeeckx, *Ministry* (New York: Crossroad, 1981) 38-41; *The Church with a Human Face* (New York: Crossroad, 1985) 154-156. On private Mass, see Thomas P. Rausch, "Is the Private Mass Traditional?", *Worship* 64 (1990) 237-242

36. See T. Fitzgerald, "The Story of the Stipend," *Liturgy '80* (October 1985) 2-5; (November-December 1985) 7-9; (January 1986) 2-4.

37. See R. Kevin Seasoltz, "Justice and the Eucharist," *Worship* 58 (1984) 508-509.

38. The criteria of "meeting" and "festivity" are drawn from Juan Mateos, *Beyond Conventional Christianity* (Manila: East Asian Pastoral Institute, 1974) 279-282.

39. On the importance of singing in the liturgy, see Don Saliers, "The Integrity of Sung Prayer," *Worship* 55 (1981) 290-303.

40. See A. Tegels, "Chronicle," *Worship* 59 (1985) 154-155.

41. See F. Kolschein, "Den täglichen Gottesdienst der Gemeinden retten," *Liturgisches Jahrbuch* 34 (1984) 195-234, esp. 213.

42. Patrick Regan, "Encountering Christ in Common Prayer," *Worship* 59 (1985) 48-59.

43. Schillebeeckx, *Ministry* 37, 72-73.

9

Liturgical Presidency: The Sacramental Question

IN HIS 1971 NOVEL, *LOVE IN THE RUINS,* SUBTITLED *THE ADVENTURES OF a Bad Catholic at a Time Near the End of the World,* the late Southern Catholic novelist Walker Percy painted a grim but also comic picture of the church of the future. Near the beginning of the novel, the hero, Dr. Tom More, says:

> Our Catholic Church here split into three pieces:
> (1) the American Catholic Church whose new Rome is Cicero, Illinois; (2) The Dutch schismatics who believe in relevance but not God; (3) The Roman Catholic remnant, a tiny scattered flock with no place to go.

> The American Catholic Church, which emphasizes property rights and the integrity of neighborhoods, retained the Latin Mass and plays the *Star-Spangled Banner* at the elevation.

> The Dutch schismatics in this area comprise several priests and nuns who left Rome to get married. They threw in with the Dutch schismatic Catholics. Now several divorced priests and nuns are importuning the Dutch cardinal to allow them to re-marry.

> The Roman Catholics hereabouts are scattered and demoralized. The one priest, an obscure curate, who remained faithful to Rome, could not support himself and had to hire out as a fire-watcher.[1]

We begin with Percy's vision not because it has been realized but because, as only a creative artist could do, he imagined even twenty years ago the possibilities and the perils of a church experiencing a new and dizzying sense of freedom. But while Percy's vision may not have come true today, it would be naive to imagine that the forces which Percy describes are not at work in the church. I want to set my reflections within this somewhat apocalyptic context in order to highlight the seriousness of the question before us. If the church is not to split asunder, then sane, balanced, and rigorous thinking must be applied to the question of liturgical leadership. Our question set is anything but simple. It includes: the nature of liturgical leadership in the context of the church's ministry, the question of who may exercise this leadership, and finally the double issue of (1) what happens in a eucharistic assembly when ordained leadership is not present and (2) what is one to say about communities which disregard the traditional notion of ordination.

I cannot begin directly with the question as a sacramental or liturgical issue. That is to say, our question must be situated within a contemporary understanding of church since liturgical leadership has everything to do with what it means for us to be a community of the Gospel. Therefore, before confronting the question of the relation between ordination and liturgical presidency, we need to lay a foundation with a few brief considerations regarding the purpose of the church and then regarding the nature of sacramental activity, in particular the eucharist.

MINISTRY AND THE CHURCH

One of the main reasons that liturgical presidency has become a pressing issue for us is the radical shift in the notion of the church confirmed in doctrine at the Second Vatican Council and in the experience of the grassroots church in subsequent years. We have experienced a major transformation from the image or model of the church as a perfectly ordained hierarchical society, in which grace and divine power flow from the top down as in a pyramid, to one in which the assembly of baptized believers as the people of God stands at the

center. Although our subject does not permit me to nuance
this rather global statement sufficiently, let me suggest that although a number of models of the church are held in tension
in Vatican II's Dogmatic Constitution on the Church, the more
communitarian notion of the people of God, buttressed signifi-
cantly by an insistence on conscious and active liturgical participation especially as this has been expressed in the Rite of
Christian Initiation of Adults, has inspired a radical shift in
perception of what it means to be a Catholic Christian.[2] We
have recovered a sense of what I like to call "baptismal dignity," the respect and honor due to each and every member of
the church. And although, as I shall argue, there is room and
even necessity for differentiated roles in the church (with the
inevitable differentiation of power), there is no basis for differ-
entiating according to status in the Christian community. That
is to say, all ministries exist for service, not as mere human
honors. Throughout its history the church has struggled, often
unsuccessfully, with the temptation to accommodate itself to
purely secular notions of leadership and power, despite the
rather clear evangelical injunction of Mark 10:43-44, "Whoever
would be great among you must be your servant, and whoever would be first among you must be slave of all"[3] and the
Pauline principle of baptismal equality in Galatians 3:28 where
there is no room for distinctions based on ethnicity, social status, or gender. To put the matter plainly: one can no longer
argue that God's Spirit is communicated to all the members of
the church *solely* through the channels of an official or hierarchical ministry, that is, one can no longer mount such an argument without entering into considerable theological debate. In
other words, the revolution of thinking about the Catholic
Church in the years after Vatican II centers on the insight that
the Spirit works throughout the church.

Without this move to a more biblical and communally
based ecclesiology, contemporary trends in Catholic thought,
such as the various political and liberation theologies as well
as theologies of inculturation and the feminist critiques of the
church, would have no starting point. Here it is impossible to
over-emphasize the importance of the liturgical renewal in
this process, which is of course what makes the liturgy such a
point of contention. As the most clearly expressed symbol of
the church's experience and belief, the liturgy serves as the fo-

cus of every significant element in Christian faith: from the very idea of God to ethical behavior. When one connects the idea of active liturgical participation with the concept of the church itself as a sacrament, that is, a vehicle for proclaiming God's activity in Christ rather than the "ark" of the saved,[4] one has a radically different approach both to church membership and to liturgical experience.

This notion of the sacramentality of the church relativizes any claim the church might have to being the sole realization of the Reign of God and therefore shows that the church is to serve as a symbol of the unity of the human race as well as of unity with God.[5] Little wonder, then, that unity has been a prime concern for Christians from the very beginning. One of the functions of the ordained ministry has been to symbolize that unity both through leadership of local communities and communication between communities, as the Faith and Order Commission of the World Council of Churches has pointed out in its landmark convergence document, *Baptism, Eucharist and Ministry*.[6] A major element in symbolizing the church's unity has been the ordained ministry's continuity with the apostolic witness, in other words, what is called apostolic succession. I have no doubt, as Edward Schillebeeckx has pointed out,[7] that in the past too much emphasis has been placed on a mechanical notion of continuity through the laying-on-of-hands to the neglect of the preservation of the faith of the *whole* community witnessed by its ordained ministers. Moreover, there has been a tendency in Catholic theology to identify the handing on of apostolic succession through the imposition of hands with an objectified definition of power and thus to see a direct transmission of power from Jesus to the apostles to their successors. The roots of such a concept can be traced as early as the second century in the attempt of Irenaeus of Lyons to safeguard orthodoxy (or the unity and authenticity of the church's faith) by naming the lists of bishops in important churches. The result, however, of the critical study of the New Testament and of primitive Christianity has been to question the presumption that Jesus intended to found a church in all of its organizational details and to show that up till the late second century the threefold ordering of the ordained ministry into bishop-presbyter-deacon was far from universal.[8] In fact, even the

church of Rome seems to have known a more collegial governance by a council of presbyters (i.e., without a single bishop as
its head) until the middle of the second century.

There are two ways that one can understand the development of the forms of ordained ministry: first, as the gradual
unfolding of the divine will, such that "by divine institution"
the threefold ministery of bishop-presbyter-deacon was always what Christ intended; second, that although the church
has always been served by office bearers, the shape taken by
ministry has conformed to the need of the church at any given
time and in any given culture. Because of the shifting interpretations given even to the three forms of ordained ministry I
have mentioned, it seems to me that the latter understanding
is the more probable.

I draw the following conclusions with regard to the nature
of the church. The ordained ministry is one of the basic ways
in which the church's unity is expressed. The forms that such
ministry takes should be related to the culture and historical
situation in which the church finds itself. Finally, the role of
ordained ministry must be related to the role of the church as
a sacrament or symbol of salvation of the entire human race,
and the church itself is best understood in terms of the Spirit-
filled people of God. The ramifications of these conclusions
will become clear in the following section.

MINISTRY AND SACRAMENT

But before we turn to any further consideration of the relation between ordained ministry and liturgical leadership, we
must clarify some presuppositions about the nature of our sacramental activity and, in particular, the eucharist. Here again
we must distinguish between two theological approaches in
thinking about the sacraments. In one approach the sacraments are channels of grace from God to a fundamentally un-
graced world. They are vehicles of God's condescending mercy by which the faith of the church and of individuals within it
is strengthened. In another view, however, sacramental activity arises out of a world that has already received God's self-
communication or grace. There sacraments act not, as it were,
from above but from within the world and the church as the

sacrament of the world's salvation. This is what I take to be Karl Rahner's lasting contribution to the contemporary theology of liturgy.[9]

These approaches signify nothing less than a chasm which exists in Catholic theology today—a chasm which runs from the doctrine of God to the theology of the church and sacraments, extending to moral theology as well. Bernard Lonergan has named this the difference between the classical and modern worldviews.[10] I maintain that the first (or classical) approach is not tenable in a world which we experience as filled with with divine activity outside as well as within the church. In the latter (or modern) approach, then, sacramental activity serves as a focus of God's activity as everyday life. This approach by no means minimizes the importance and even necessity of liturgy but rather situates it within the wider compass of divine activity. In fact, far from denigrating the importance of liturgy, sacramental activity as focus highlights the role of liturgy as the clearest communal expression of Christian faith and the existential response of faith in ritual activity. Let me make this as clear as possible. Liturgy or sacramental activity "works" not so much by transfering a grace (understood as some kind of quantity) to those who do not have it as by enlivening or, if you wish, fermenting the grace-filled faith that exists in the baptized. One's attitude toward the nature and function of ministry, both the ministry of the ordained and all other forms of Christian ministry, is profoundly affected by how one conceives God operating in the world. If one sees the divine activity as an intrusion from outside the world, then ministry will inevitably be the communication of grace to the great mass of the "unwashed" (with the pun on baptism intended). If, on the other hand, God is already at work in people's lives in the "profane" world, then ministry will serve to encourage and enable the gifts of the Spirit that are already present. As far as I can tell, in the pastoral arena much ministry is still predicated on the classic assumption that ministers are giving the rest of the community something the community's members do not already have or tell them something they do not already know.

When we understand the nature of sacramentality as arising out of the lived faith experience of Christian people, the eucharist is no longer a sacred rite performed by some (the ordained) on behalf of others who are powerless. Rather, it is the self-expression of the Body of Christ, head and members, made visible in a ritual manner. Though I risk digressing here, I must add that this understanding of the symbolic importance of ritual action, namely, bringing to visible expression (and furthering) the communal life of faith, shows why Catholic theology took such a disastrous turn in the medieval period by separating the theology of the sacraments from commentary on the liturgy, as though the liturgical "envelope" were unimportant relative to the "essential elements" of the sacraments. Any contemporary theology of the sacraments, therefore, must take into account the way that the ritual activity symbolizes the presence and activity of God in the faith of the church. Once again I must refer to the Rite of Christian Initiation of Adults, because there in the clearest fashion we have been able to understand that sacramental activity is a process rather than the mechanical communication of grace, conceived as some sort of quantity.

The consistent and traditional Catholic insight has been that the community gathers on the Lord's Day to celebrate the Lord's Supper because in the eucharist the community experiences itself in the most heightened ritual fashion as the Body of Christ. This is by no means a purely external or arbitrary obligation but rather flows from the nature of the church itself—to ritually and symbolically express its union in faith by the sacred sacrificial meal which it understands to be the Lord's most precious heritage. The climax of this sacramental realization of being the Body of Christ is the act of communion, but today we risk divorcing that communion from the enactment of the body of Christ in eucharist. This is an understandable development, given the concentration of our piety and our theology on the sacred elements of transformed bread and wine. In the process of defining and adoring the real presence of Christ in the sacred elements, however, we have, at least in the past, lost track of the intimate connection between the elements and the church which consumes them. We have forgotten that Body of Christ is as accurate a designation of the church as it is of the transformed elements.[11] After all, we speak of a transformation of the eucharistic elements primarily because the eucharist is concerned with our ongoing transformation as the Body of Christ. Furthermore, overemphasis on the act of communion represents an imbalance with regard to our other important aspects or meanings of the eucharist so well treated in the World Council of Churches document *Baptism, Eucharist and Ministry*: namely, thanksgiving to the Father, memorial of the Son, invocation of the Spirit, and meal of the kingdom.[12]

The reason for this potential divorce today stems not only from an overemphasis on communion, which is after all related to a happy recovery since the time of Pius X, but also to the situation of churches which lack an ordained presbyter at the Sunday celebration, the question of so-called "priestless Sundays." Our acquiescence to the theology and practice of Sunday services in the absence of a priest which include communion has, in my opinion, nothing less than potentially disastrous consequences. As others have well pointed out,[13] divorcing the Sunday service from eucharistic celebration is thoroughly untraditional and breaks the inherent connection between Sunday, assembly, and eucharist. William Marravee puts the matter very well:

> What in fact appears to be most characteristic of the present situation is that less importance is being ascribed to the integrity of the eucharist and to the eucharistic dimension of the local community than to the maintaining of a male celibate ordained ministry.[14]

Marravee's point is no exaggeration. He is referring to the same priority of eucharist over ordained ministry that Edward Schillebeeckx has insisted upon when he writes that the community has more of a right to the eucharist than the church has a right to impose being a male celibate as a condition for ordination to the presbyterate.[15] It is, of course, the insistence on limiting presbyteral ordination to male celibates that has created the anomalous situation of Christian communities without ordained ministers to preside at the eucharist. Therefore at this point we must turn to the relation between ordination and liturgical presidency. But first let me stress that Sunday communion services in the absence of a presbyter are not making the best of a bad situation. On the contrary, they capitalize on a communion-centered piety to weaken the relation between eucharist and assembly; in other words, eventually they will considerably weaken the Body of Christ.

ORDINATION AND LITURGICAL PRESIDENCY

In beginning this section I am keenly aware of the need to be self-critical. If we have been able to learn anything from contemporary liberation and feminist theologies, it is that systems of thought always have a tendency to be ideological or, to put it simply, self-serving. Since I and many other theologians like me (not to mention those who exercise official teaching authority in the church) are male, celibate, and ordained, we must always be wary of arguing in such a way that our conclusions serve some perceived or implicit interest in the *status quo*. I will try to point out where I think this exists in the current theological situation of reflection upon ordained ministry, but it may of course unconsciously be operative in my own treatment of the question. It is my hope, however, than an honest reading of tradition, in which I include the Scriptures as foundational, can liberate even male, celibate, ordained theologians like myself from our most cherished ideological presuppositions.

I intend here to situate the relation between ordained ministry and liturgical presidency within the context of the theology of the presbyterate. Subsequently I shall deal with the theological problems as I see them, and finally I shall treat some practical or pastoral problems in our liturgical experience vis-à-vis presidency of the assembly.

I have thus far deliberately refrained from using the term "priesthood" for the ordained presbyterate. I do this on the basis of the complete absence of sacerdotal or priestly vocabulary in the New Testament itself—at least as far as Christian ministry is concerned. In the New Testament only Christ is priest of the New Covenant, and the Body of Christ— Christians—is a priestly people.[16] Moreover, nowhere does the New Testament link presidency over the eucharist to any specific minister, with the exception of Acts 13:1ff where prophets and teachers preside and Acts 20:7ff where Paul presides over the breaking of bread.[17] In fact, it seems to me that employing the term priesthood for ordained presbyters clouds the issue, as Joyce Zimmermann has recently argued.[18] At least as far as the New Testament is concerned, the entirety of the Christian people exercises a sacerdotal or priestly role in light of its unity in Christ. There can be no question of certain Christians bestowing blessings upon others simply in virtue of their office.

On the other hand, it is misleading to think of the earliest Christian communities as pure democracies of the Spirit or, as is often argued in some feminist theologies today, as a discipleship of equals.[19] Certainly the primitive Christians were equals when it came to being members of the Body of Christ, but at least in Pauline thought they were differentiated when it came to charisms or gifts of the Spirit, as in 1 Corinthians 12. This is to say that it is highly unlikely that leadership in worship devolved upon just anyone at all. Rather, it seems that the most fundamental meaning of ordination points to the community's designation of leaders who were found to be possessed of the Spirit of leadership. Such leadership was not primarily cultic or liturgical but rather communal. Seeing the origins of Christian ministry in this way has two results: it places liturgical leadership within the context of communal or ecclesial leadership, and at the same time it considerably relativizes notions of purely cultic ordination, as in the mistaken notion that Jesus ordained his apostles at the Last Supper, which is based on what Kenan Osborne has called a (faulty) ecclesiological presupposition.[20] I understand the distinction between the two ecclesiological presuppositions that Osborne outlines: namely, (1) the direct foundation and organization of the church by Jesus himself, or (2) the birth of the church in the Easter experience of the disciples, who are filled with the Spirit, as similar to the classic and modern approaches to God's activity in the world that I outlined above. The first model (direct foundation by Christ) has been labelled Christomonistic in contemporary theological vocabulary, whereas the second has been called pneumatological.[21] It is the pneumatological model which understands the ongoing role of the Spirit in the organization of the church and its ministry. To sum up, then, the churches represented by the New Testament documents knew a number of forms of leadership and charism, but they do not witness to a cultic priesthood. In fact, strictly cultic (i.e., liturgical) forms seem to be radically questioned by the true form of worship which Paul sees as sacrifice of self in Romans 12:2 or indeed in John's Gospel where Jesus claims that true worship will take place "in Spirit and truth" (Jn 4:23).

It did not take long, however, for roles within the leadership of worship to be stabilized. By the end of the first century we have glimmers in the document known as the *Didache* of a transition from the itinerant ministry of prophets and teachers to that of overseers (or bishops) and presbyters in the presidency of the eucharist. As Paul Bradshaw points out, at the outset such leadership of the community at worship was conceived of collegially. If a bishop presided, he did so as a member of a kind of governing board of the community.[22] As far as I can tell, this move toward stable structures was not problematic in and of itself—it is natural for a community of any longevity to establish structures and rules, in our case what is called "ecclesiastical office." But even as late as the early third century the first Latin theologian, Tertullian, was able to argue that the nonordained could preside at the eucharist by virtue of their baptism.[23] What does become problematic is the radical distinction drawn between clergy and laity that we can observe in the fourth and fifth centuries.[24] Of particular importance in this development is the gradual adoption or re-adoption of ideas of purity with regard to worship, ideas developed on the basis of typology from the religious faith of Israel. In other words, the Christian "priesthood" is likened to that of Israel, a radical departure, as I see it, from the New Testament notion of the priestly Body of Christ.

In the adaptation of Jewish ideas of purity related to worship we can find the beginnings of clerical celibacy. Whereas married men could become presbyters, they could no longer engage in sexual relations with their wives before they celebrated the eucharist.[25] Doubtless this regulation mirrored the increasing Christian concern with sex and sexual abstinence that has been so well described by Peter Brown in *Body and Society*.[26] Ultimately, of course, celibacy became mandatory for the ordained in the Western Church with the Second Lateran Council in 1139. When we combine this attitude toward purity with the shift away from a symbolic to a more objectively realist concept of worship in the early Middle Ages (i.e., an approach in which the symbol and reality could not mean the same thing), we arrive at what has essentially become the classic Roman Catholic approach to priesthood in which this office is "ordered" primarily to the celebration of the eucharist rather than to communal or pastoral leadership.[27] It is in part this sacralization of Christian life to which the sixteenth-century Reformers objected.

Today the approach of Catholic theology to the presbyterate has shifted considerably. While at the same time affirming an essential difference between the priesthood of the faithful and the ministerial priesthood,[28] the council documents place ordained ministry within the context of the threefold office of Christ as prophet, priest, and king. In other words, the council stressed the preaching and leadership roles of the presbyter in addition to the cultic role, even though the priesthood is ordered to the eucharist as its culmination. In other words, ministerial leadership is exercised in the church not only through the expression of a kind of cultic power, but even primarily through the preaching of the word.[29] In my opinion this is the correct model for ordained ministry in that it places the liturgical role of the presbyter within the wider context of whole-hearted service of the faith and of the faithful.

No doubt a tension will continue to be felt between what I have called the baptismal dignity of the people of God and the need for the leadership of those who have been called in a special way to devote their lives to the service of the community. What is most important, it seems to me, is that ordained ministry must be conceived as the church's recognition of the charism of leadership, which for the Christian must always be expressed as service, and consequently the community's empowerment of leaders through ordination. As with any charism, such empowerment is to be recognized as God's gift, not the creation of the community or of the individual who is called, but at the same time this empowerment takes place on the basis of the preceived talent (another word for "charism") and preparation of the candidate for ministry. I am trying to avoid here any idea of the granting of some kind of metaphysical power to the ordained through the rite of ordination, loosed as it were from its moorings in the faith life of the community and the individual who arises within it as a leader.

To make myself clear, let me give a practical example. It is commonplace to "import" presbyters into parishes and other assemblies to which they do not really belong in order to preside at liturgical celebrations. Or, from time to time one sees a presbyter visiting a parish to which he does not belong insisting on his right to concelebrate by virtue of his status as someone who happens to be ordained. There are aberrations as far as the model I have been describing is concerned. Though it would be foolish not to allow exceptions, for example, a presbyter invited to preside or to preach in another community for some good reason, at the same time this should be considered as normal practice.[30]

This brings us to the question of presidency today. I have argued on the basis of consistent Christian tradition that the church needs ministers who are designated for service, but that this office can and has taken different forms throughout church history. I have also argued that distinguishing too sharply between the status of the ordained and that of the baptismal priesthood has been an unhelpful direction in Catholic theology and needs to be corrected. On the other hand, it seems to me that today we run the risk of blurring the distinction of roles within the community and therefore within the liturgy—and this for several reasons, namely, the question of who can be ordained and the proper model for exercising leadership, particularly in liturgy.

I will treat these questions one by one. First, who should be candidates for ordination to the presbyterate? It seems to me that today the position that only male celibates are apt candidates for ordination in the Latin Church is indefensible. There are absolutely no doctrinal grounds for denying ordination to married men. Certainly the experience of the primitive church, not to mention our sisters and brothers in the Protestant and Eastern Christian Churches, attests to this. The prohibition on married clergy only makes sense if sexual activity is perceived as somehow marring one's ability to pray. I should add that this has been precisely the pious and theological attitude of Catholics since at least the fourth century and will not easily be transformed into a positive and healthy valuing of sexual activity without a great deal of effort. On the other hand, relaxation of the rule of clerical celibacy is essential if we are ever to communicate in any persuasive way the true baptismal dignity of all Christ's people. Moreover, as Schillebeeckx has argued,[31] the useful and valuable charism of celibacy will fail to be truly credible until it is made optional.

What then of the other side of this question about candidates—the admission of women to the presbyterate? Here we cannot argue so clearly from tradition, but we can see that the present position of the magisterium is based on certain ideological (or self-serving) presuppositions. Let me quote a paper, by Joseph Fessio, circulated at the last synod of bishops as a fair representation of the approach currently being taken by the Roman authorities:

> In the sacrament of holy orders God, through the instrumentality of those whom he has authorized to speak in the name of Christ, confers upon the sacred ministers the power to act in the name of Christ and in certain sacramental acts to act in fact as extension of the one mediator, Christ. While the entire church is feminine and maternal, the clerical ministry within the church is by nature masculine and paternal. Because the bishop, the priest (and by participation, the deacon) not only represent Christ, but act as Christ in the eucharistic sacrifice of sacrament and word, only the masculine sex can represent sacramentally in an adequate way the male Christ who himself as male represents God facing creation and the bridegroom facing his bride the church.
>
> The church only becomes the body of Christ in the mystery of the two in one flesh by which, initially bride, by being joined to her groom, she becomes one body with the head. The eucharist, the center and summit of the sacraments, involves a sacred place, a sacred time and a sacred person both symbolically setting apart the orders of grace and redemption from the order of creation and sacrament. For this reason, many theologians (e.g., DeLubac, von Balthasar, Bouyer) hold in keeping with a long and unbroken ecclesiastical tradition, that there is an absolute prohibition of women as recipients of the sacrament of holy orders.[32]

Here one finds essentially the same argument as in the Congregation for the Faith's "Declaration on the Admission of Women to the Ministerial Priesthood."[33] I will point out several flaws in Fessio's argument. First, he bases himself clearly on an understanding of Christianity which I have called "classical," that is, in which the sacred confronts the profane and transforms it, where grace is not to be found in the act of creation itself. Second, and this always seems to follow from the first, he upholds the "ecclesiological presupposition" that Christ founded the church and its organization in an explicit and conscious mnanner, which we have seen to be extremely doubtful today. Third, he raises the lovely Pauline metaphor of the relation of Christ to the church as one between bride and bridegroom to the status of a doctrinal position. And fourth, on the basis of this abuse of metaphorical language, he argues that women are incapable of representing Christ. The language of representing Christ (or *in persona Christi*) has become commonplace in recent documents of the magisterium. I would contend first that the fundamental ability to represent Christ is given in baptism to all Christians and not limited by gender; second, the very idea of such representation must always be contextualized within the church (*in persona Christi*) which acts as one with its head as one Spirit-filled Body.[34] On the basis of talent in leadership and ability to preach and to pray publicly, I can see no good reason to refuse women as candidates to the presbyterate. I assume that on a profound level what is at stake here is both a deep and abiding fear of the feminine, especially in relation to the sacred, and an effort to maintain control over the sacramental system, a system that would inevitably change if women were ordained because the imaging of human beings in relation to the sacred would be completely transformed.[35] It seems to me that we currently suffer not so much from a lack of ordained ministers as a lack of courage to allow the Spirit to guide us into a truly contemporary form of Christian life and worship.

What then of the appropriate model for liturgical leadership in the contemporary church? It would be not only untraditional but naive to suppose that the Christian community could do without structure and leadership. Demythologizing or desacralizing this leadership and placing it within the context of the baptismal priesthood is not the same as doing away with it altogether. The real question is: how can liturgical presidency be "strong, loving, and wise" (to quote the title of Robert Hovda's excellent handbook on presiding) and at the same time be more representative of the church in contemporary culture? It seems to me that what is being called co-presidency or shared presidency may well be a solution to the problem of a perceived (even if unintended) domination over the liturgy by the presider. Such sharing of presidency is by no means untraditional. It occurred when bishops in the early church ceded the eucharistic prayer as a sign of hospitality to visting bishops;[36] it occurs within the framework of the Roman Rite today when a bishop presides at the liturgy of the word, while a presbyter is designated to preside at the liturgy of the eucharist proper. It occurs as a matter of course when one presbyter presides in the eucharistic or other liturgical celebration and another presbyter or deacon preaches. Perhaps shared leadership today can effectively symbolize that liturgical presidency does not mean domination but rather service.

There are several practical or pastoral corollaries to what I have been saying. The first relates to the current construction of the eucharist in the Roman Rite. As Ralph Keifer insightfully pointed out some time ago, a major weakness of the eucharist in the current Roman Rite is that it is priest-centered rather than prayer- or ritual-centered.[37] This is an unfortunate by-product of the change to intelligible language, the stance of the presider facing the people, and the liberties for more personalized expression at different points in the rite itself. The difficulty arises when presiders personalize the rite so much that they make it their own show. Even if their words are inclusive and progressive, the very activity succeeds only in drawing attention to themselves and away from the communal activity of prayer. Thus every introduction becomes a mini-homily, not an invitation to prayer, and the eucharist becomes a supreme means of self-expression—for the presider, that is. One of the major reasons that liturgical presidency appears as problematic today is that it has become so important. If the liturgy must stand or fall on the personality of the presider (no matter how "with-it"), then all we have accomplished is to exchange an old form of clericalism for a new form of clericalism.

This leads me to what I call the paradox of liturgical presidency. Presiders cannot "hide" in the new rite, that is, they must be themselves, and they must do this with considerable skill, especially insofar as they affect the whole flow and mood of worship. So, at the same time they must be their authentic selves *and* avoid pointing to themselves. Many presiders confuse their real selves with talking about themselves. Inability to hold authenticity and the rite itself, which after all is the possession of the whole assembly, in balance has led to the "star syndrome." As Robert Hovda put it:

> Any practice which communicates the notion that leaders in public worship are "stars" is basically and desperately unproductive, whether the leaders in question are clergy or musicians or any other ministers. Desirable gifts in the leader are no excuse. If her or his style in the particular role fails to communicate a sense of prayerful performance, of being (first of all) a worshiper and a member of the worshiping assembly, then he or she is not a leader but an intruder. And the gifts of such a one or such a group damage rather than enhance worship.[38]

To put the matter another way, the most appropriate question that liturgical ministers should ask themselves after a celebration is not "how did I do?" but rather "did we pray?" If one is looking for stardom, then one should enter the entertainment industry rather than Christian ministry. I would submit that genuine human qualities and the prayerfulness of the assembly are best respected when presiders attend to the rite that the community has come to expect—which leaves room of course for necessary local adaptations of the Roman Rite— rather than seeming to make up the whole, or to comment on it, as it goes along.

We do indeed suffer from a number of difficulties with regard to liturgical presidency. Two major causes are the undue appropriation of the rite by presiders or other ministers for their own purposes, and the perceived domination of the liturgy by a male celibate clerical establishment. The first cause can be redressed with relative ease (i.e., by ministers respecting the dignity of the assembly by respecting the rite which is the common possession of all); the other, namely, the question of who can be ordained, cannot. Since the very unity of the church is at stake, it would be my hope that local communities not take matters into their own hands, thus potentially causing the kind of split that Walker Percy foresaw in his dark vision of the future.[39] As far as I can tell, schism has never really accomplished much lasting good. In an ecumenical era like our own, dialogue is a much more productive approach. But short of provoking schism, it seems to me that Roman Catholics must use every effort at their disposal to force the issue of opening up admission to candidacy for ordination to women and to married men. Only when that issue is resolved can we get on with the business of our common call—our full vocation to baptismal dignity and to the awesome power of the Gospel at work in us and in our liturgical assemblies.

Notes

1. Walker Percy, *Love in the Ruins: The Adventures of a Bad Catholic at a Time near the End of the World* (New York: Farrar, Straus & Giroux, 1971) 5.

2. The necessary nuance would have to explore the tension between chapter 2 of the Constitution on the Church ("The People of God") and chapter 3 ("The Church Is Hierarchical"). See Joseph A. Komonchak, "The Local Realization of the Church," in *The Reception of Vatican II*, eds., G. Albergio, J.-P. Jossua, and J.A. Komonchak (Washington, D.C.: Catholic University of America Press, 1987) 77-90.

3. See also Luke 22:24-27 where the debate about who is greatest is set within the context of the Last Supper.

4. In this see Karl Rahner, "Considerations on the Active Role of the Person in the Sacramental Event," *Theological Investigations* XIV (New York: Herder and Herder, 1976) 169-170.

5. Dogmatic Constitution on the Church, no. 1.

6. *Baptism, Eucharist and Ministry*, Faith and Order Paper 111 (Geneva: World Council of Churches, 1982): Eucharist 29; Ministry 23.

7. Edward Schillebeeckx, *The Church with a Human Face: A New and Expanded Theology of Ministry* (New York: Crossroad, 1985) 116.

8. See, for example, Hans von Campenhausen, *Ecclesiastical Authority and Spiritual Power in the Church of the First Three Centuries* (Stanford: Standford University Press, 1969); also Raymond E. Brown, *The Churches the Apostles Left Behind* (New York: Paulist, 1984).

9. See Rahner, "Considerations"; also his "On the Theology of Worship," *Theological Investigations* XIX, 141-149.

10. Bernard J. Lonergan, *Method in Theology* (New York: Herder and Herder, 1972) 300-302.

11. On the Pauline notion of the Body of Christ, see Jerome Murphy-O'Connor, "Eucharist and Community in First Corinthians" in

Living Bread, Saving Cup: Essays on the Eucharist, ed., R. Kevin Seasoltz, 2d edition (Collegeville: The Liturgical Press, 1987) 1-30. On the changing concept of the Body of Christ in the Middle Ages, see the classic treatment by Henri de Lubac, *Corpus Mysticum: Eucharistie et l'église au moyen-âge* (Paris: Aubier, 1944).

12. See *Baptism, Eucharist and Ministry;* Eucharist 2-26.

13. See Robert Hovda, "Priestless Sundays Reconsidered," *Worship* 62 (1988) 154-159; also Gabe Huck, "Why Settle for Communion?" *Commonweal* 37 (1989) 37-39; and especially William Marravee, "'Priestless Masses' - At What Cost?" *Eglise et théologie* 19 (1988) 207-222. For further bibliography see this last article.

14. Marravee, "'Priestless Masses'" 220.

15. Schillebeeckx, *Church* 256-257; also his *Ministry: Leadership in the Community of Jesus Christ* (New York: Crossroad, 1981) 72-74.

16. On the question of the terminology used of ministers in the New Testament, see Raymond E. Brown, *Priest and Bishop: Biblical Reflections* (New York: Paulist Press, 1970); Nathan Mitchell, *Mission and Ministry: History and Theology in the Sacrament of Order* (Wilmington, DE: Michael Glazier, Inc., 1982) 107-109; Kenan Osborne, *Priesthood: A History of Ordained Ministry in the Roman Catholic Church* (New York: Paulist Press, 1988) 40-85.

17. See Schillebeeckx, *Church* 119-120; Hervé-Marie Legrand, "The Priesthood of the Eucharist according to the Ancient Tradition" in Seasoltz, *Living Bread* 197; Paul F. Bradshaw, *Liturgical Presidency in the Early Church* (Bramcote, Notts: Grove Books, 1983) 6-8.

18. Joyce Zimmermann, "Priesthood through the Eyes of a Non-Ordained Priest," *Eglise et théologie* 19 (1988) 223-229.

19. For example, Elisabeth Schüssler Fiorenza, *In Memory of Her: A Feminist Theological Reconstruction of Christian Origins* (New York: Crossroad, 1983) esp. 97-235.

20. See Osborne, *Priesthood* 30-39.

21. See, for example, Edward Kilmartin, *Church, Eucharist and Priesthood* (New York: Paulist Press, 1981) 37-39.

22. Bradshaw, *Liturgical Presidency* 28.

23. Tertullian, *De Exhortatione Castitatis* 7:2-6; see Cyrille Vogel, "Is the Presbyteral Ordination of the Celebrant a Condition for the Celebration of the Eucharist?" in *Roles in the Christian Assembly,* ed., A. Triacca (New York: Pueblo Publishing Co., 1981) 253-263.

24. See Schillebeeckx, *Church* 152.

25. See Schillebeeckx, *Church* 240-244.

26. Peter Brown, *Body and Society: Men, Women, and Sexual Renunciation in Early Christianity* (New York: Columbia University Press, 1988).

27. On the transformation from symbolic to "realist" thinking, see William R. Crockett, *Eucharist: Symbol of Transformation* (New York: Pueblo Publishing Co., 1989) 78ff.; in the medieval relation between eucharist and priesthood, see Osborne, *Priesthood* 204ff.

28. *Lumen Gentium*, no. 10; *Presbyterorum Ordinis*, no. 2.

29. On this development, see Walter Kasper, "The Priest's Nature and Mission" in his *Faith and the Future* (New York: Crossroad, 1982) 64-85.

30. I do not mean to argue that ordained presbyters might not be associated as liturgical presidents in communities at which they are not full-time ministers, but it seems to me that they should have some ongoing relation with the assembly.

31. Schillebeeckx, *Church* 211-234.

32. Joseph Fessio, "Reasons Given against Women Acolytes and Lectors," *Origins* 17:22 (1987) 399.

33. Of 1976, in A. Flannery, ed., *Vatican Council II: More Postconciliar Documents* (Northport, NY: Costello, 1982) 331-345.

34. On the history of the terminology, see Bernard Marliangeas, *Clés pour une théologie du ministère: In Persona Christi, In Persona Ecclesiae* (Paris: Beauchesne, 1978); for a recent theological discussion, see David N. Power, *The Sacrifice We Offer: The Tridentine Dogma and Its Reinterpretation* (New York: Crossroad, 1987) 21-26; also his "Liturgy and Empowerment," in *Alternative Futures for Worship*, vol. 6, ed., Michael A. Cowan *Leadership Ministry in Community* (Collegeville: The Liturgical Press, 1987) 81-104; also his "Sacraments: Symbolizing God's Power in the Church," *Proceedings of the Catholic Theological Society of America* (1982) 50-66; see also Edward Kilmartin, "Ecclesiastical Office, Power and Spirit," in the same volume, 98-108.

35. For further evaluation of the question of women and ordained ministry, see Leonardo Boff, *Ecclesiogenesis: The Base Communities Reinvent the Church* (Maryknoll: Orbis, 1986) 76-97.

36. See Bradshaw, *Liturgical Presidency* 25-26.

37. Ralph Keifer, *To Give Thanks and Praise* (Washington, D.C.: The Pastoral Press, 1980) 97-103.

38. Robert Hovda, "The Amen Corner: Liturgy's Many Roles: Ministers? . . . or Intruders?" *Worship* 64 (1990) 173.

39. On this issue, see my further reflections (with Don Timmermann and Gordon Zahn) in "The Eucharist: Who May Preside?" *Commonweal* (9 Sept. 1988) 460-466.

10

Kyrie Eleison
and the Entrance Rite
of the Roman Eucharist

IT IS COMMONLY ACKNOWLEDGED THAT THE RITE OF ENTRANCE IS one of the more unwieldy elements of the reformed Roman Catholic rite of eucharistic celebration. The concatenation of entrance song, greeting, penitential rite, *Gloria in excelsis*, and opening prayer make for an awkward and confusing act of assembling God's people to hear the word of God and to share the eucharistic banquet; in short, to be and to become more intensely the Body of Christ. The purpose of this essay is to analyze the historical development and function of the most refractory element in the entrance rite, namely, the acclamation *Kyrie eleison, Christe eleison* (Lord, have mercy, Christ, have mercy) which accompanies the penitential rite employed in almost every eucharistic celebration.[1] To do this we shall turn first to the role of the *Kyrie eleison* in the contemporary Roman rite, next to the historical development of this acclamation vis-à-vis another classic Christian liturgical expression, and finally to a constructive proposal for the Roman entrance rite in general.

MISSAL OF PAUL VI

In the 1969 Missal of Paul VI, *Kyrie eleison* takes the form of an acclamation which "praises the Lord and implores his mercy."[2] It can take one of two forms, either as an independent piece of chant sung or recited alternately after the penitential rite (when rite 1, the *Confiteor*, is used) or as part of a penitential litany (in rites 2 and 3). Thus, three forms of the penitential rite may be chosen, but there are occasions when no penitential rite at all is called for, namely, weddings, funerals, and those Sunday celebrations in which it is replaced by the rite of blessing and sprinkling with holy water to recall the assembly's common baptism.

Moreover, the General Instruction of the Roman Missal allows for much flexibility in the use of this acclamation. It may be spoken or sung either in the language employed in the eucharistic celebration or in the original Greek, and it need not be sung only six times but may be repeated as many times as needed. The sacramentary provides only models of the invocations employed in the third form of the penitential rite.[3]

The difficulty with the *Kyrie eleison* as a ritual expression of an entrance or gathering rite arises because it seems to fulfill two functions, namely, an acclamation of praise and an expression of penitence. If the *Kyrie* is merely the former, then it duplicates the *Gloria in excelsis*. If the *Kyrie* is only a petition for forgiveness of sin, one may legitimately ask why such a penitential aspect should be placed after what is usually a positive ritual experience of assembling.[4] One answer given to this quandry is that the *Kyrie* traditionally has no place in the penitential rite because it is not a penitential expression at all, and that, moreover, a common penitential rite in the eucharistic liturgy is absolutely an innovation in the Missal of Paul VI.[5] There is some merit to this argument in that the Roman Rite never contained a public penitential rite at the beginning of the eucharist. The apologetic prayers at the foot of the altar were a private devotion of the presider. However, it is going too far to consider the *Kyrie* as merely a purely joyful acclamation of praise and to eliminate all penitential and intercessory connotations.

HISTORY IN THE ROMAN RITE

Kyrie eleison, roughly translated "Lord, have mercy," is not originally a Christian prayer at all but rather an acclamation employed in pagan worship, adopted in the cult of the Roman emperor, who was called *Kyrios* or Lord.[6] It is, however, not surprising that Christians could use this acclamation to call upon Jesus, the *Kyrios* of New Testament faith.

We do not find liturgical evidence for the usage of *Kyrie eleison* as an acclamation until the end of the fourth century, in the travel diary of Egeria, who reports that at the end of the intercessory prayers at vespers a choir of boys sings *Kyrie eleison* repeatedly.[7] Roughly contemporary with Egeria's account of the liturgy in Jerusalem is the liturgy of the eighth book of the *Apostolic Constitutions*, a church order from the neighborhood of Antioch. Here *Kyrie eleison* is employed in a eucharistic setting as the response sung at the end of the prayers for the catechumens and most probably at the prayers for the energumens (mentally disturbed) and the penitents, and at the prayers of the faithful.[8] All these prayers are located in the classic position between the gospel and the beginning of the eucharist proper with the presentation of gifts. Therefore, the earliest use of the acclamation *Kyrie eleison* took place during intercessory prayers, in the course of the eucharist (*Apostolic Constitutions*) or the liturgy of the hours (Egeria).

Although on the basis of the written evidence alone, it is not possible to argue that the use of this acclamation was an innovation of the late fourth century, we can perceive in the litany form a shift from what seems to have been an earlier form of intercessory prayer, namely, that form which is still found today in the solemn prayers on Good Friday in the Roman Rite. This latter form is characterized by a bidding to prayer by the deacon, along with a directive to kneel, silent prayer by all for the stated intentions, a directive to rise, and a concluding spoken prayer by the presider. As Robert Taft has shown, litanies represent a developed form of this kind of prayer with acclamations or responses substituting for the silent prayer and the presider's collect postponed until the end of all the intercessions.[9] It was precisely this litany form that was better suited to large congregations, larger churches, and outdoor processions. This is the situation in which the Christian assemblies found themselves at the end of the fourth century. This easier form of liturgical prayer was increasingly employed in the churches, for example in the eucharistic liturgy presided over by John Chrysostom both at Antioch and Constantinople.[10]

Up to this point there has been little reason to suspect a relation between the *Kyrie eleison* as we know it today in the eucharistic entrance rite and the type of intercessory prayers where we first find it evidenced at the end of the fourth century. After all, the intercessions we have been considering took place either toward the end of vespers or in the middle of the eucharistic liturgy. It was Edmund Bishop who first made a connection between the old prayer of the faithful, which disappeared from the Roman Rite after the fifth century, and the *Kyrie eleison* inserted between the Introit and *Gloria* in the entrance rite of the classic form of the Roman eucharist between the sixth century and the late twentieth. Bishop pointed out that *Kyrie eleison* was employed in litanies similar to the prayer of the faithful and perhaps had an origin in the liturgical processions of the Christian East.[11] Some thirty years later the same question was taken up by Bernard Capelle in a series of articles. Capelle contended that since the solemn prayers were not mentioned at all after the pontificate of Felix III (484-492), it was Gelasius (492-496) who replaced them with the litany that bears his name and situated this litany in the Roman entrance rite. The old solemn prayers, he hypothesized, were replaced by a prayer similar to the Milanese *Oratio super sindonem* (prayer over the altar cloth). This theory would explain the presence of multiple collects before the prayer over the gifts in the Verona collection of Mass prayers and the Old Gelasian Sacramentary. Finally, Capelle argued, Gregory the Great (in a text we shall consider thoroughly below) omitted the litany biddings of the *Deprecatio Gelasii* in favor of chanting only a series of *Kyrie* and *Christe eleisons* on weekdays. It was this form of the *Kyrie* which became the common usage of the Roman Rite.[12]

Capelle's hypothesis was later modified by Antoine Chavasse, who argued that the *Oratio super sindonem* or its equivalent in the sixth-century Roman liturgy witnessed by the Old Gelasian Sacramentary did not replace the *Deprecatio Gelasii* but rather concluded it in the presbyteral or titular churches of the city of Rome, while in the papal or stational liturgy of the city the litany was included in the entrance rite.[13]

Lacking in the theories of both Capelle and Chavasse is, first of all, sufficient evidence to make them more than conjectural, and second, the likely motivation for transferring the prayer of the faithful in its litany form to the entrance rite of the eucharist. However, in his recent work on the prayer of the faithful or universal prayer in the western churches, Paul DeClerck has done much to clarify the history of the introduction of the *Kyrie* into the Roman Mass. His interpretation of two crucial texts is important for the solution that I will elucidate below.

The first text is the third canon of the Synod of Vaison (529) in southern France:

> Since the sweet and salutary custom of singing *Kyrie eleison* frequently and with great feeling has been introduced in the Apostolic See as well as throughout the Orient and the province of Italy, it is also our pleasure that this holy custom be introduced in all of our churches at matins, Mass, and vespers. And, in addition, it will not cause aversion to sing the "Holy, Holy" (a holy, sweet, and desirable sound both by day and by night) at all Masses whether in the morning, or during Lent, or in those Masses which are performed for the commemoration of the dead in the same manner as is done at public Masses.[14]

The second text is from a letter of Pope Gregory the Great to Bishop John of Syracuse in 598:

> Someone coming from Sicily has told me that some friend of his, whether Greek or Latin I do not know, but having great zeal for the Holy Roman Church, has grumbled about my changes, saying: "Why do you wish to amalgamate with the church of Constantinople by following its customs in all things?" But to him I say: "Which of its customs do we follow?" They respond: "Because the *Kyrie eleison* is sung." But we have not sung nor do we sing the *Kyrie eleison* as the Greeks do, for among the Greeks all sing it at the same time, whereas among us the clergy sing it and the people respond. We all sing *Christe eleison* as many times [as *Kyrie eleison*], and the Greeks do not. Finally, in daily Masses we omit the other things which are usually sung and sing only *Kyrie* and *Christe eleison*, so that we might spend a little more time in this prayer of supplication.[15]

In light of these two texts DeClerck has argued from the fact that the Rule of Benedict distinguishes between a litany at lauds and vespers and simple repetition of the *Kyrie* at other hours,[16] and from his thorough study of various forms of the prayer of the faithful in the west, that both Capelle and Chavasse were mistaken in their interpretation of the manner in which the *Kyrie* became part of the entrance rite of the Roman eucharist. In the first place he found that *Kyrie eleison* was not the original response to the *Deprecatio Gelasii*. The original response was *Domine exaudi et miserere.*[17] Second, the *Kyrie eleison* first appeared in the west, not in Rome, but in the Milanese *Litania divinae pacis*, where it is repeated three times in a row at the end of the litany.[18] Moreover, this Milanese litany, probably dating from the first half of the fifth century, seems to have been modeled on a particular litany from the Byzantine tradition, a point to which we shall return. Third, DeClerck notes that the third canon of the Synod of Vaison says nothing about the introduction of the litany into the churches of southern Gaul, but merely states that *Kyrie eleison* is to be sung at matins, Mass, and vespers. Fourth, Gregory the Great's comments on the *Kyrie* have usually been interpreted to mean that on ferial days the invocations of a litany similar to the *Deprecatio Gelasii* were omitted, leaving only a supplicatory *Kyrie* and *Christe eleison*. However, given the existence of the threefold *Kyrie* as an independent piece of chant in the Milanese litany, DeClerck argues that Gregory was not referring to dropping the biddings of the entrance litany but rather to the entire litany in favor of a (transformed) independent piece of chant at the end.

On the basis of these observations DeClerck has concluded that the primary reason the *Kyrie eleison* was placed at the entrance rite of the Roman eucharist was not so much to replace the solemn prayers after the homily as to provide a piece of chant for every eucharistic celebration that had been attached to only the processional liturgy of the Roman Church.[19] DeClerck's analysis is correct as far as it goes, but it leaves unanswered two questions: first, why did processional practice alter the shape of the eucharistic rite and, second, why was the *Kyrie* chant placed after the entrance chant (Introit) instead of before it if it was related to processional practice? For answers to these unsolved problems we must turn to the comparative study of liturgical development.

It is fairly certain that up to the end of the fourth century the eucharist began with a simple greeting followed by the readings. For example, both Augustine in the west and John

Chrysostom in the east (Antioch and Constantinople) refer to the service beginning with a silent entrance, greeting, and readings.[20] However, it was very shortly after this that psalms were sung in entrance processions, at least in Rome. A notice from the *Liber Pontificalis* for the pontificate of Celestine I (422-432) reads that this pope arranged the psalms of David as entrance songs to be sung antiphonally.[21] Later Roman sources suggest that the normal practice was for the entrance psalm to be sung after the people had all taken their places and during the entrance of the bishop and his ministers.

In the east, however, the eucharistic entrance rite had a different shape, at least in the stational liturgy of the city of Constantinople, which was to prove so influential for all Byzantine churches. At Constantinople the clergy and people entered the church at the same time. This is borne out architecturally by the great number of doors in early Byzantine churches, for example, in Justinian's Hagia Sophia.[22] The reason for this simultaneous entrance of clergy and people is in the processional practice of the urban liturgy. Here it would be a mistake to think that for the inhabitant of the eastern Mediterranean of the late antique period "going to church" had the same meaning it has for us. In late antique Christian culture "going to church" meant participation in a public event which spanned the city both in terms of time and of space. Processions were an essential aspect of this urban liturgical repertoire.[23]

Fifth-century Greek historians inform us that in the time of Chrysostom the various Christian parties held processions on the streets prior to every public celebration of the eucharist, that is, one every Sunday, Saturday, and feast day.[24] The tenth-century *Typikon* of the Great Church, which refers in the main to much earlier practice, prescribes sixty-eight public processions in the course of the liturgical year.[25] Moreover, more than half of these processions included an intermediate prayer service at the Forum of Constantine on the way to the stational church of the day. A litany of some form was always sung at these services. This sung litany took two forms in the Byzantine rite. In the *synapte* (or "series") form the people's response, *Kyrie eleison*, completed the diaconal biddings, which were addressed to them. The *ektene* (or "insistent" litany) was characterized by three other factors. The deacon's biddings

were addressed directly to God, intercessory verbs were multiplied at the end of each prayer, and (the most significant for
our purposes) the people repeated *Kyrie eleison* a number of
times in a row at the end of the last petition.[26]

The *synapte* was associated with the *trisagion*, often considered an independent piece of chant but really a *troparion* or antiphon sung in outdoor processions prior to the celebration of
the eucharist. In fact, Pope Felix III, writing to the Emperor
Zeno in the late fifth century, referred to the supplicatory procession of the *trisagion* (*tēn trisagion litēn*).[27] In the course of the
sixth century at Constantinople the *trisagion* together with its
psalm became the ordinary entrance chant at the beginning of
the Byzantine eucharist. It was preceded by a litany, the *synapte*. In the seventh century yet another entrance psalm, most
likely Psalm 95, was added to the entrance rite and preceded
the *synapte*. Byzantine liturgical practice therefore confirms
that a parallel exists for the development of the supplicatory
use of *Kyrie eleison* at the beginning of the eucharist. Note,
however, that the *Kyrie* here is always associated, not only
with a litany, but with a litany of the *synapte* type.

This development would provide a simple enough explanation for the creation of the Roman eucharistic entrance rite
were it not that we can find no association of the *synapte* type
of litany with the Roman or other western rites at this point in
the liturgy. However, the multiple repetition of the *Kyrie* at the
end of the *ektene* type litany provides us with a solution to a
number of problems. As DeClerck noted, the *Kyrie* appears as
an independent piece of chant in the Roman Rite. The *litania
divinae pacis* of the early fifth century, which is the first example of the use of Greek terminology in Latin litanies, is precisely of the *ektene* type, characterized by the deacon's addressing
of the prayers directly to God and by a multiple repetition of
the *Kyrie* at the end of the entire litany.[28] Therefore, the Byzantine litany which had direct influence in the inclusion of the
Kyrie eleison into the Roman Rite was the *ektene*, associated in
Constantinople originally with outdoor processions and not
with the entrance into the church as was the *synapte*.[29]

At this point we have enough information to sketch out the
steps of the addition of the *Kyrie* to the Roman entrance rite.
The expanded scale and highly public style of eucharistic cele-

bration in the large Roman basilicas from the mid-fourth century on demanded something other than an entrance rite consisting of silent entrance and greeting, for as Taft has pointed out, it is precisely the action points of the liturgy which are most susceptible to ritual expansion.[30] The vacuum at the beginning of the eucharistic liturgy was filled in by the addition of an entrance psalm. At the latest this would have taken place in the pontificate of Celestine I (422-432). The liturgical development did not stop there. Although the Roman liturgy was very rarely innovative of its own accord,[31] it did adopt liturgical patterns from other churches, especially, Jerusalem, Constantinople, and Milan. One of the patterns it must have adopted was the practice of processional liturgy, replete with litanies, especially on penitential Lenten weekdays when stational processions made their way to different churches in the city. One of the proofs that Rome adopted its processional practice either directly or indirectly from the Christian East is that all of the processional terminology—*antiphona, litania, Kyrie eleison*—is taken from the Greek.

What is confusing in this whole development, however, is that the Roman Rite did not develop exactly as the Byzantine Rite did, for it employed a different kind of litany, one associated with the intermediate services in Constantinople's urban liturgy. This latter litany, the *ektene*, was sung after the reading of the gospel or after the initial processional psalmody. It was probably during the fifth century that the Roman liturgy adopted this litany, as it is taken for granted in the Synod of Vaison (529). In addition, it seems that the Synod of Vaison must somehow have confused the *ektene* and *synapte* types of litany as it associated the *Kyrie* as an independent piece of chant (if DeClerck is correct in his analysis) with the *trisagion*, which was combined as we have seen with the *synapte* in the Byzantine Rite.[32] The Roman Rite never adopted the *trisagion* as part of its entrance rite, for two reasons: the *Gloria in excelsis* (another eastern import, but from the daily office) functioned as a hymn at the entrance rite, and the litany combined with the Roman entrance rite was the *ektene*.

The next step in the development of the use of the *Kyrie eleison* came at the end of the sixth century when Gregory the Great simplified the rite for nonfestal days by dropping the litany as such and keeping the multiple repetition of *Kyrie* and *Christe eleison*. Subsequently the litany was eliminated on Sundays and feasts as well. This is the situation in the sacramentaries of the eighth and ninth centuries and the early *Ordines Romani* which gave the first ritual descriptions of the Roman eucharist. But even in these sources one clue that formerly the *Kyrie* was associated with a processional litany can be found in the fact that when the litany is sung in procession the *Kyrie* is dropped after the Introit.[33]

Regarding the number of *Kyrie* and *Christe eleisons* which were sung, it appears from the late seventh-century *Ordo Romanus Primus* that the choir repeated the chant as often as necessary until the bishop arrived at his throne after reverencing the altar.[34] Shortly thereafter, however, we begin to find witnesses to the situation as it obtained throughout most of the medieval and Tridentine periods, that is, the ninefold repetition of *Kyrie* and *Christe eleison* combined. Jungmann suspected that this regularization of the chant is attributable to the anti-Arianism of the Gallican region.[35]

From this rather complex historical development we can understand that the *Kyrie's* addition to the Roman liturgy as an independent piece of chant was something of an anomaly. As a cry of supplication in the processional liturgies of the city of Constantinople, the *Kyrie* was apparently so popular as to have been attracted to the Roman liturgy even after processions were no longer used in the latter liturgy on a regular basis and after the litany had been eliminated from the entrance rite. Just as we find scraps of liturgical debris in the Byzantine liturgy, so too the entrance rite of the Roman eucharist contains such a scrap in the employment of the *Kyrie eleison*.

SOME SUGGESTIONS

We have seen the historical roots of the use of the *Kyrie eleison* in the Roman Rite, roots which point primarily to a processional origin with the *Kyrie* as an independent piece of chant relating to the procession of the bishop from the altar to his throne in the apse of a church. This usage has, of course, been transformed in the contemporary Roman Rite. Far from being processional, the *Kyrie* now seems to intrude into the movement of the liturgy itself as a kind of penitential afterthought between the greeting and opening prayer. Therefore this chant either independently or as a litany—to give two of its forms in the current Roman Rite—fails to aid the very purpose of the entrance rite, which is to gather the people of God in prayer. It runs the risk of individualizing them in a penitential mode after they have been gathered precisely as an assembly.

This is not to argue against the use of the *Kyrie* as an acclamation. In fact, the repetition of brief sung acclamations like *Kyrie eleison* is one of the major contributions of the Taizé monks to contemporary liturgical practice. Sung acclamations and responses are without a doubt a key to truly participatory worship. Nor do I mean to argue against a processional use of the *Kyrie*. However, it will be necessary to rethink this kind of processional use in light of the fact that the cultural conditions which facilitated the use of the *Kyrie* litany as an entrance chant no longer obtain. That is, we no longer live in a culture in which most of the people will process into the church together. [36]

The possible usefulness of the *Kyrie* as an element of Roman liturgical practice lies in allowing it to become an element of supplication, when penitential or supplicatory litanies are called for. This raises the question of having a penitential rite in every celebration of the eucharist. Such a penitential rite does act as an intrusion into the rhythm of worship established by gathering song and greeting. Moreover, on the rational level it contributes to the notion that the assembly consists of unworthy individuals. While no doubt this is a theologically correct statement, at this precise point in the eucharistic liturgy there is no need to emphasize either individuality or unworthiness. It is better to consider participation in the eucharist itself as the ordinary reconciliatory act of Christians, as was traditional in the patristic period.[37] Surely in the early work of the Consilium on the liturgy, the proposed *Missa Normativa* made no provision for a penitential rite but provided the option of *either* the *Kyrie* (as an independent chant) or the *Gloria* as a hymn prior to the opening prayer.[38] On the other hand, for occasions when there is good reason for a penitential focus in the eucharistic liturgy, the current penitential rite is too brief and inconsequential, especially when it is recited and not sung.

Before proceeding to some suggestions with regard to the relation between the *Kyrie* and the entrance rite, we should be aware of one danger in the kind of historical argumentation which I have been proposing. The danger lies in the all too commonly uncritical appropriation of paragraph 34 of the Constitution on the Liturgy, which directs that liturgical rites should be characterized by a noble simplicity and unencumbered by useless repetition.[39] In terms of the actual unfolding of ritual, this statement lacks sufficient nuance, for it seems to insinuate that ritual works primarily on a rational level, when in fact the effect of ritual is far more subtle. It is by means of repetition and rhythm that rituals are effective,[40] and any proposal to simplify the entrance rite of the eucharist should come not from a rationalist desire to simplify or clarify the rite, but rather as an effort to highlight those aspects of the rite which are most important, in this case the gathering of the assembly for worship. Moreover, the liturgy of the word often suffers when the entrance rite is overblown or too heavy. Very often we give lip service to the importance of the ritual proclamation of the word and then undermine it by an overpowering entrance rite.

In conclusion, I would propose that any future revision of the entrance rite of the Roman eucharist be modulated according to the liturgical seasons.[41] There is no need for a penitential rite in every celebration of the eucharist. However, a penitential aspect for some celebrations, for example, in the season of Lent or on days like the equivalent of the old Ember Days that call for more attention to supplication or penitence, might be enhanced by replacing the entrance psalm or song by a *Kyrie* litany on the model of the Milanese *Litania divinae pacis*. In similar fashion the *Gloria in excelsis* might replace the entrance song on more festive occasions, and the rite of baptismal renewal by sprinkling might be better incorporated into the procession or the gathering of the assembly. On all other occasions, for example, the ordinary Sundays during the year, the entrance rite might best consist of opening psalm or song, greeting, and opening prayer. Modulation in ritual, like modulation in color and decoration, is a nonverbal way of alerting people to the particular character of a given liturgical celebration. This may be one way both to restore the *Kyrie* litany as a precious element in our common liturgical tradition and at the same time to unburden our awkward entrance rite.

Notes

1. That is, except for baptisms, funerals, and the occasions when the eucharist has been preceded by a part of the liturgy of the hours.

2. General Instruction of the Roman Missal, no. 30.

3. See Ralph A. Keifer, To Give Thanks and Praise: General Instruction on the Roman Missal with Commentary for Musicians and Priests (Washington, D.C.: The Pastoral Press, 1980) 111.

4. Ibid. 112.

5. Ibid.

6. See Franz J.Dölger, Sol Solutis: Gebet und Gesang im christlichen Altertum. Liturgiewissenschaftliche Quellen und Forschungen, vols. 4 and 5 (Münster: Aschendorff, 1925) 77-82. The idea, of course, is not foreign to the New Testament. See passages which read: "Jesus, Son of David, have mercy on me," e.g., Mk 10:47; Mt 9:27, 15:22; Lk 18:38.

7. John Wilkinson, ed., Egeria's Travels, 2d ed. (Warminster, England: Aris and Phillips, 1981) 124.

8. Apostolic Constitutions 8, in Frank E. Brightman, Liturgies Easter and Western, vol. 1: Eastern Liturgies (Oxford: Clarendon, 1896) 4-13. The directions for the liturgy refer specifically to Kyrie eleison only in the case of prayer for the catechumens. However, since the structure of prayers for energumens, the elect, penitents, and prayers of the faithful is precisely the same, it seems to me that the response Kyrie eleison is understood in these latter cases. For the same opinion, see Josef A. Jungmann, The Mass of the Roman Rite, F.A. Brunner, trans. (New York: Benziger, 1951) 335, n. 10.

9. Robert F. Taft, "The Structural Analysis of Liturgical Units: An Essay in Methodology," Beyond East and West: Essays in Liturgical Understanding (Washington, D.C.: The Pastoral Press, 1984) 154-156.

10. Frans van de Paverd, Zur Geschichte der Messliturgie in Antiocheia und Konstantinopel gegen Ende des vierten Jahrhunderts, Orientalia Christiana Analecta, vol. 187 (Rome: Pontificium Institutum Orientalium Studiorum, 1970) 83, 425.

11. Edmund Bishop, "Kyrie Eleison," Liturgica Historica (Oxford: Clarendon Press, 1918) 116-136.

12. Bernard Capelle, "Le Kyrie de la messe et le pape Gélase," Travaux liturgiques, vol. 2 (Louvain: Abbaye du Mont César, 1962) 116-134; "Le Pape Gélase et la messe romaine," ibid. 135-145; "L'oeuvre liturgique de S. Gélase," ibid. 146-160. For an excellent résumé of the

state of the question, see Paul DeClerck, *La Prière universelle dans les liturgies latines anciennes*, Liturgiewissenschaftliche Quellen und Forschungen, vol. 62 (Münster: Aschendorff, 1977) 282-284.

13. Antoine Chavasse, "L'oraison 'super sindonem' dans la liturgie romaine," *Revue bénédictine* 70 (1960) 313-323.

14. Mansi, *Sacrorum Conciliorum Nova et Amplissima Collectio* (Florence, 1795) 8:727. On the basis of the Byzantine evidence dealt with below, it is important to note that the threefold "Holy" referred to here is the *Trisagion*, not the *Sanctus* of the eucharistic prayer. Almost all commentators have understood the Synod of Vaison incorrectly to be dealing with the introduction of the *Sanctus* into the West.

15. Gregory the Great, *Epistola* 9:26 in Hartmann, ed., *Monumenta Germaniae Historica, Epistolae*, vol. 2 (Berlin, 1899).

16. Timothy Fry, ed., *The Rule of St. Benedict in Latin and English with Notes* (Collegeville: The Liturgical Press, 1980) chs. 9, 12, 13, 17.

17. *Pace* Jungmann, who thought that the response was originally in Greek, see *Mass of the Roman Rite*, vol. 1, 336; the same opinion is often repeated today, see Louis Weil, "The History of Christian Litanies," *Liturgy* 5:2 (1985) 37.

18. DeClerck, *Prière universelle* 155-158, 163-164. For another view, see C. Callewaert, "Les étapes de l'histoire de Kyrie," *Revue de l'histoire écclésiastique* 38 (1942) 25-26.

19. DeClerck, *Prière universelle* 292.

20. Augustine, *City of God* 22:8:22; John Chrysostom, *Homily on Matthew* 12:6 (PG 50:384-385); see Robert Cabié, "L'eucharistie" in A.G. Martimort, ed., *L'église en prière*, 2, 2d ed. (Paris: Desclée, 1983) 65-67 [English translation: *The Church at Prayer* 2, 2d ed. (Collegeville: The Liturgical Press, 1986) 50-51].

21. Louis Duchesne, ed., *Le Liber Pontificalis*, vol. 1 (Paris: E. Thorin, 1886) 230. The notice reads: "Hic constituit ut psalmi David CL ante sacrificium psalli antephanatim ex omnibus" ("Celestine arranged that the one hundred and fifty psalms of David be sung antiphonally by all before the sacrifice"). The passage could be interpreted to mean that the entire psalter was sung prior to each celebration of the eucharist, but this is most unlikely. A much more reasonable interpretation is that the Introit psalms are referred to here. On this issue, see Peter Jeffery, "The Introduction of Psalmody into the Roman Mass by Pope Celestine I (422-432)," *Archiv für Liturgiewissenschaft* 26 (1984) 147-165. Jeffery argues that the *Liber Pontificalis* is referring to the chants between the readings instead of the entrance rite.

22. See Thomas F. Mathews, *The Early Churches of Constantinople: Architecture and Liturgy* (University Park: Pennsylvania State Univer-

sity Press, 1971). See also Juan Mateos, *La Célébration de la parole dans la liturgie byzantine*, Orientalia Christiana Analecta, vol. 191 (Rome: Pontificium Institutum Studiorum Orientalium, 1971) 123-125; and Robert F. Taft, "How Liturgies Grow," *Beyond East and West* 169.

23. On this point, see my reflections on "The City as Church, the Church as City," *Liturgy* 4:1 (1983) 71-72. Reprinted as Chapter 1 in this volume.

24. Socrates, *Church History* 6:8 (PG 76:688-689); Sozomen, *Church History* 8:8 (PG 67:1536).

25. See John F. Baldovin, "La liturgie stationnale à Constantinople," *La Maison-Dieu* 147 (1981) 85-94; also Taft, *Beyond East and West* 174.

26. See Mateos, *La Célébration de la parole* 149-150, 155-156.

27. Ibid 98-102.

28. DeClerck recognizes here a litany of the *ektene* type, *Prière universelle* 158-159; Jungmann, *Mass of the Roman Rite* 1, 334 had already make this connection without elaborating any of the significance of this litany as an *ektene* rather than a *synapte*.

29. From the ninth century on, the *ektene* is found in the texts of the Byzantine liturgy of St. John Chrysostom after the gospel reading, but as Taft has pointed out, this cannot be its original position in the liturgy since it involves prayers addressed to God prior to the dismissal of the catechumens. The original position of the *ektene* was as a litany chanted after the gospel or psalmody at the intermediate services during stational processions. See *Beyond East and West* 177.

30. Taft, *Beyond East and West* 168.

31. See Edmund Bishop, "The Genius of the Roman Rite," *Liturgica Historica* 1-20.

32. See, for example, Klaus Gamber, *Ordo Antiquus Gallicanus: Der gallikanische Messritus des 6. Jahrhunderts*, Textus Patristici et Liturgici, vol. 3 (Regensburg: F. Pustet, 1965) 24-25, where a threefold *Kyrie* is sung between the Trisagion (*Aius*) and the Benedictus.

33. See Michel Andrieu, *Les Ordines Romani du haut moyen-âge*, vol. 3 (Louvain: Sacrum Lovaniense, 1953) 260: Nam quando letania agitur, nec Gloria in excelsis Deo, nec Cyrieleison post introitum nec Alleluia cantur, excepto letania majore. ("For when it is a question of the litany, neither the Gloria nor the Kyrie after the Introit nor the Alleluia is sung, except at the major litany.")

34. Andrieu, *Les Ordines Romani*, vol. 2, 83.

35. Jungmann, *Mass of the Roman Rite*, vol. 1, 341. Jungmann argues that originally the *Kyrie* was addressed solely to Christ, as it is in the Missal of Paul VI, a fact rarely adverted to.

36. This is not to gainsay the valuable insight of Alexander Schme-

mann (*For the Life of the World: Sacraments and Orthodoxy* [Crestwood, NY: St. Vladimir's Seminary, 1973] 27) that the divine liturgy begins with a kind of procession of individuals even from their homes. Surely we need a study of the phenomenology of processions. Some places to begin are: Herman Wegman, "Procedere und Prozession: eine Typologie," *Liturgisches Jahrbuch* 27 (1977) 28-39; I.H. Dalmais, "Note sur la sociologie des processions," *La Maison-Dieu* 43 (1955) 37-43; John F Baldovin, *The Urban Character of Christian Worship*, Orientalia Christiana Analecta, vol. 228 (Rome: Pontificium Institutum Orientalium Studiorum, 1987) 234-238.

37. See John Quinn, "The Lord's Supper and the Forgiveness of Sin," *Worship* 42 (1968) 281-291.

38. See Frederick R. McManus, "The Berakah Award for 1980: Response: The Genius of the Roman Rite Revisited," *Worship* 54 (1980) 370-371.

39. *Sacrosanctum Concilium*, no. 34.

40. Aidan Kavanagh, *Elements of Rite: A Handbook of Liturgical Style* (New York: Pueblo Publishing Co., 1982) 28.

41. This is similar to Ralph Keifer's suggestion in *To Give Thanks and Praise* 115, although he places a penitential litany after the greeting during Lent. One question, which I do not raise here, deals with whether it is always appropriate to have an entrance procession of ministers. Some occasions (e.g., weekday eucharists) or worship spaces do not seem to call for processions.

11

The Development of
the Monarchical Bishop
to 250 A.D.

FEW RESULTS OF THE SECOND VATICAN COUNCIL HAVE BEEN AS IM-
portant for the life of the Catholic Church as the council's
stress on the role of the diocesan bishop. In this regard Vatican
II was able to complete the work of Vatican I, which defined
papal primacy and infallibility but was unable to deal with the
role of the bishop because external political pressures forced
an early adjournment of its work. Happily, Vatican II was able
to balance the ecclesiology of the previous council by paying
due attention to the function of bishops and by emphasizing
the importance of the local church (diocese).

Among the gains of Vatican II were the resolution of the
problem of the sacramentality of episcopal orders[1] and the assessment of the bishop as the "visible principle and foundation of the unity of his particular church, fashioned after the
model of the universal church."[2] *Lumen Gentium* also makes
several claims about the historical origins of the episcopate as
instituted by Christ, claims to which I shall return below.[3]

Even more remarkable is the fact that a recent ecumenical
consensus document, *Baptism, Eucharist and Ministry,* of the
Faith and Order Commission of the World Council of Churches has supported episcopacy as an important role in the

church. On the matter of the institution of the episcopate, the ecumenical document is somewhat more careful than *Lumen Gentium* in stating that: "During the second and third centuries, a threefold pattern of bishop, presbyter, and deacon became established as the pattern of ordained ministry throughout the church."[4] The ministry document proceeds to argue that *episcope*, the function of episcopal ministry as "oversight" or "supervision," is an essential aspect of the constitution of the church.

> The Church as the body of Christ and the eschatological people of God is constituted by the Holy Spirit through a diversity of gifts or ministries. *Among these gifts a ministry of episcope is necessary* to safeguard the unity of the body. Every church needs this ministry of unity in some form in order to be the Church of God, the one body of Christ, a sign of unity of all in the kingdom.[5]

The task of this study is to investigate the rise of the monarchical or single bishop as leader of a local church from ca. 100 to ca. 250. If episcopacy is essential to the constitution of the church, we need to be as clear as possible about how it became so. *Lumen Gentium* provides a rather direct and traditional explanation of the institution of the episcopate by Christ—an explanation which in turn serves as the basis for doctrinal claims about the nature of episcopacy. The argument runs as follows: Christ instituted ministries in his church for the nurturing and growth of the people of God. That church is established by the mission of the apostles, and Christ (consciously) willed that their successors, namely, the bishops, should carry on the same mission.[6]

Lumen Gentium goes on to state that the apostles explicitly appointed bishops as their successors, thus passing on the "apostolic seed" in an unbroken succession down to our own day.[7] Thus, the council document claims a direct, explicit, and conscious connection between apostles and bishops. The question we raise, however, deals with the second and third century evidence for this claim. Surely one could raise questions with regard to Jesus' conscious institution of apostles as guardians of the message of the kingdom in the sense that he intended them to "found a church" in our sense of the word, but that is beyond the compass of this study.[8] We will confine ourselves here to asking to what extent the bishop of the second and third centuries looks like the bishop that we know today. For the beginning of our period the answer will be quite sketchy and tend toward a negative response. By the end of our period, however, and even by the end of the second century, the single or monarchical bishop as the leader of the church is well in place. How then did the kind of theory about apostolic succession that we find in *Lumen Gentium* arise? Is it a valid claim to talk about continuity in the role of apostle and bishop, and, if so, on what historical basis can one make that claim? Are there other valid historical reasons for judging the role of bishop to be essential to the constitution of the church?

In order to get at the evidence, I have decided to focus on three topics out of the ample Christian literature of the second and third centuries. First, I will ask how, where, when, and why the monarchical episcopate arose. Second, I will focus on the concept of apostolic succession as it developed in the second half of the second century. Third, I will examine two portraits of the bishop that come from the first half of the third century: that given in the ordination prayer for a bishop in the *Apostolic Tradition* of Hippolytus of Rome and the picture given in the Syrian *Didascalia Apostolorum*. Finally, I will raise some questions with regard to the theological consequences of our investigation.

ORIGINS OF THE MONARCHICAL EPISCOPATE

As we begin this part of our investigation, we should point out that the term "monarchical bishop" might be regarded as somewhat misleading. "Monarchical" here has nothing to do with a style of leadership, but rather with the fact that the term *episcopos* originally referred to a collegial leadership of the primitive Christian community and was equated with presbyters or elders. The development we are concerned with is the governance of a local church by a single leader. Perhaps the term *monepiskopos* would be more accurate. Given the common use of the phrase "monarchical bishop," however, I will use both terms.

The general argument of this section is that the monarchical episcopate is the gradual consolidation of an office in the church as the result of factors that threatened orthodox Christianity in the early second century. This is not to argue that there was no concern for office in the church prior to the beginning of the second century. The Pastoral Epistles (commonly dated to the 80s of the first century) clearly manifest such a concern.[9] But with these epistles we are still at the stage of collegial leadership of the community by presbyter-bishops.

Another suggestion that would date the origin of the monarchical episcopate far earlier than the first part of the second century is that James, the brother of the Lord—not one of the Twelve—was a *monepiscopos* in Jerusalem.[10] No source earlier than the middle of the second century, however, names James as bishop of the Jerusalem church. No doubt he held a special office in that church, one that rivaled Peter himself, but the leap to calling him a bishop is unwarranted and anachronistic.

The first indisputable witness to the monarchical episcopate is Ignatius of Antioch, whose seven authentic letters can be dated with some confidence to ca. 110, as he was being led to martyrdom in Rome.[11] Thus Ignatius is a representative of what R.E. Brown would call the third Christian generation or the post-apostolic period.[12] The overwhelming focus of Ignatius' letters is the concept of unity. He writes, for example, to the Magnesians:

> As, then, the Lord did nothing without the Father—being united with him—neither by himself nor through the apostles, so you too do nothing without the bishop and presbyters, nor try to have anything appear right by yourselves; but let there be one prayer in common, one petition, one mind, one hope in love, in blameless joy which is Jesus Christ, than whom nothing is better. All of you hurry together as to one altar, to one Jesus Christ, who proceeded from the one Father and was with the one and returned to him.[13]

Within this concern for unity, the threefold order of bishop-presbytery-deacons receives special attention from Ignatius. The bishop is the sole official leader of the local church. This is evident in Ignatius' mention of the names of the monarchical bishops of the churches with which he is corresponding, for example, Onesimus at Ephesus and Polybius at Tralles. The bishop is assisted, or "surrounded" to use Ignatius' term, by a council of elders or presbyterium. He is also assisted by deacons. It seems to me, as I shall argue below, that the bishop arose out of a collegial body of the presbyters and not independently. An argument against this position, however, could be made from the office of *mebaqqer* (overseer) at the Qumran community. [14]

What are the roles exercised by the monarchical bishop in the church?[15] According to Ignatius he is in charge of the community's works of charity,[16] and he regulates Christian marriage.[17] He is certainly due the obedience of the community, since he is the type (*typos*) of God the Father, whereas the presbyters are compared to the apostles and the deacons to Jesus Christ. Note that Ignatius does not make the equation "apostles=bishops." Christians must be subject to the bishop as in the following classic passage:

> You must all follow the bishop as Jesus Christ [followed] the Father, and [follow] the presbyters as the apostles; respect the deacons as the commandment of God. Let no one do anything apart from the bishop that has anything to do with the church. Let that be regarded as a valid eucharist which is held under the bishop or to whomever he entrusts it. Wherever the bishop appears, there let the congregation be; just as wherever Jesus Christ is, there is the whole church. It is not permissible apart from the bishop either to baptize or to celebrate the *agape* but whatever he approves is also pleasing to God, that everything you do may be sure and valid.[18]

This is strong language. It may well represent a reiteration of the importance of the bishop's role in the church. On the other hand, Ignatius' insistence might also be accounted for if the monepiscopacy is a recent innovation. To be a member of the church for Ignatius meant to be with the bishop, especially to submit to his liturgical leadership or the leadership of those appointed by him. This is the first time that we hear of the bishop delegating others to exercise liturgical leadership, a practice which becomes common later on by sheer necessity.

An index of the confidence that Ignatius puts in the office of bishop can be found in his comment on written tradition. Of course this cannot refer to the New Testament as such for it was not canonized till the latter part of the second century, but may well refer to the writings that went to make it up as well as the Hebrew Scriptures. Ignatius does not rely on written tradition, but rather on living authority, so intent is he on emphasizing the role of the bishop.

Given this evidence, we can turn to the questions of how, where, when, and why the monarchical episcopate arose. The first question is rather difficult to answer. John Meier has suggested that Antioch was the venue of the Gospel of Matthew in the second Christian generation. There the "officers" of the church seem to have been prophets and teachers (Mt 13:52; 23:34; Acts 13:2) only some twenty or so years prior to Ignatius. How the transition was made to the threefold structure of the office in so short a period of time will most likely depend on the answer as to why the shift took place.

As to where and when the shift to monarchical episcopacy took place, it seems safe to say that this office arose in the eastern Mediterranean, since our sources for monarchical episcopacy for Rome, Alexandria, Greece, and North Africa are all considerably later than for Syria and Asia Minor. Given the state of the evidence, it is impossible to know with any certainty whether this office originated in Asia Minor or in Syria. Certainly Ignatius seems to suppose that *monepiscopoi* have been established in the towns of Asia Minor to which he is writing. Interestingly enough, there is no appeal to the authority of the bishop and no mention of ecclesiastical office in his Letter to the Romans, which makes us suppose that Rome had no *monepiskopos* at this time.

When did the office of monarchical bishop arise? Given the fairly secure (although still disputed) dating of the letters of Ignatius to ca. 110, it would seem that this institution cannot have been much older. Therefore I would put it in the last decade of the first century or the first decade of the second. Much depends on whether one views the situation that Ignatius is describing as settled or in transition. It seems to me that the latter is more probable and accounts for the virulence of Ignatius' appeal to the authority and central position of the bishop in the church. Walter Bauer suggested that Ignatius represented a minority party in a divided community, a party that was trying to take control of the church.[19] One need not suppose that his was a minority party to recognize that what we mean by church in any large city of the first or second century is not all that simple. After all, conditions made it necessary for Christians to be divided into house churches and these various communities might have taken on very different characteristics. If one abandons the model of a golden age of the church in its first generation and presupposes rather that various approaches to Christianity were encountering one another from the very beginning, one has a better grasp on why not only doctrines but offices in the church were very much in the process of formation in the early Christian generations. Therefore it seems to me that Ignatius may well have been arguing for an office which was not readily accepted and was actually an innovation.[20] Ignatius himself alludes to the fact that there was some kind of strife or confusion at Antioch in his absence when he claims that the church at Antioch is *now* at peace.[21] Earlier, when writing to Rome, he claimed that the church at Antioch had God as its bishop in his stead.[22] Perhaps it was internal strife among the factions of the church at Antioch that led to Ignatius' martyrdom. It could very well be that his party was not in control when he was placed under arrest[23] and only gained supremacy afterwards. Monepiscopacy was a relatively recent innovation.

The final question is, of course, the most important. Why did such an office arise in the church? Can purely sociological reasons account for it? It would certainly be naive to think that some kind of office or governance was not a concern for Christians from the very beginning. Moreover, the New Testament evidence does not warrant it. The notion of religious faith itself requires it. But why a centralized office of such magnitude, one whose permanence was rivaled only by that of the emperor and whose social standing was quite unique for religious figures in the late Roman world?[24]

I think that the answer can be found in Christianity's need to find doctrinal self-definition. I have already alluded to the variety of approaches that primitive Christianity took, a variety which has been discerned more and more clearly in the New Testament itself. How were competing versions of Christianity to be reconciled? By what standard were they to be judged? Only living authority could do that and a strong living authority at that. Ignatius is very concerned about doctrinal matters in his letters. Two "heterodox" approaches stand out: Docetism on the one hand and Judaizing on the other.[25] Ignatius takes what ends up being the mainstream Christian position between the two. Just as with the Pastoral Letters, a major concern of the church has become the avoidance of "false teachers."[26] And again, as with the Pastorals, ecclesiastical office is required to deal with the problem, but in Ignatius and after him that authority has been vested in a single person, the bishop.

So the office of the monarchical bishop did not originate in the need for liturgical leadership nor because the monarchical leadership appealed to an oriental mentality accustomed to despotism,[27] nor simply for reasons of more efficient ecclesiastical administration, but rather specifically for the defense and determination of doctrine. This may give us some insight into how the office came into being. The governance of the community by a collegial board of presbyter-bishops did not offer enough "clout" in the fight against aberrant doctrinal positions.[28] Therefore, one among their number was chosen as the leader of all. I see the monepiscopal office as arising out of the presbyteral leadership of the church, not as a distinct principle.

At this point, we can turn to other churches which developed the monarchical episcopate more slowly than the communities of Antioch and Asia Minor. Just as the *Didache* manifests a transition in the late first century between the itinerant ministry of apostles and prophets and the residential ministry of bishops (presbyters) and deacons,[29] so also other churches must have experienced a transitional period between governance by the collegial presbyter-bishops and the *monepiscopos*.

Alexandria represents an interesting case in the development of the episcopacy. We can be sure that this church, whose primitive history has been notoriously difficult to uncover, had a bishop by at least the end of the second century. However, a number of scholars think that the bishop was chosen from among the "twelve presbyters" of the Alexandrian church and ordained by them right up to the selection of Athanasius in 328.[30]

Surprisingly enough, it is the church of Rome which seems to have been one of the slowest in developing this form of ecclesiastical order. *I Clement* (ca. 96) and the *Shepherd of Hermas* (ca. 140) are two Roman documents which show that the officers of the Roman community were presbyter-bishops.[31] We have already mentioned that Ignatius in writing to the Romans makes no reference to the offices in the community, even though he takes such great pains to promote the monarchical episcopacy in his other letters.

I Clement in particular has been the subject of a great deal of debate between Protestant and Catholic church historians, especially since, if Clement was not the *monepiscopos* of the Roman church, it is difficult to make him or his writing the basis of claims about the Roman primacy.[32] Today, however, very few if any scholars would argue that Clement was *the* bishop of Rome.[33] It seems rather that Clement (who does not name himself or his position in the letter to the Corinthians) may have been one of the presbyteral board of the Roman church. Rome did not have a monarchical bishop until the middle of the second century.[34]

I Clement does, however, represent an important step in the evolution of arguments for monarchical episcopacy, for he is concerned about succession and continuity in the church. The purpose of his letter to Corinth is to argue for the reinstatement of presbyters who have been ousted from their roles. Like Ignatius, he insists on the unity of the church. Part of his argument relies on a direct line between Christ, the apostles, and the presbyter-bishops. Christ himself sent the apostles, who in turn appointed bishops (plural) and arranged that the bishops themselves should have successors:

> And our apostles knew through our Lord Jesus Christ that there would be strife over the title of bishop. So for this reason because they had been given full fore-knowledge, they appointed those mentioned above and afterward added the stipulation that if these should die, other approved men should succeed to their ministry.[35]

Clement goes on to state that these are the very people now being thrust from their ministry, even though they are men who have offered the gifts (presided at the eucharist) blamelessly. This last statement links the ecclesiastical officers of the Christian community with the Jewish priesthood to which Clement referred previously in his argument for correct order in the church. This is, as far as I can tell, the first time that any individual Christians are alluded to as priests. Note, however, that Clement does not claim that bishops are the successors of the apostles, but rather that the apostles have arranged for an orderly succession of bishops. Von Campenhausen is probably correct in claiming that Clement is arguing not in sacramental but in juridical terms.[36]

APOSTOLIC SUCCESSION

If the foregoing analysis is accurate, what are we to make of the concept of an apostolic succession of bishops directly from the apostles, namely, in its traditional and most popular form as a chain of hands? It seems that historically speaking it must be regarded as somewhat dubious. Why, then, did the concept of apostolic succession arise?

We have already noted that the idea of succession (*diadoche*) was important to the second and third Christian generations. This should come as no surprise since any religious group would want to ensure that it held fast to its original tradition. It was not until the mid-to-late second century, however, that the technical concept of succession as transmitted by a chain of bishops beginning with the apostles saw the light of day.

This concept most probably originated not in mainline Christianity itself but among the Gnostics who *had* to appeal to secret traditions handed down through Gnostic teachers. In fact, the concept is originally not a religious one at all but rather stems from the succession of teachers in the Hellenistic schools. Von Campenhausen finds the first attestation of the use of this idea in Christian circles in the letter of the Gnostic Ptolemy to Flora (early second century).[37] Ptolemy supports his claim to possess the truth by naming a secret apostolic tradition (*paradosis*) over and above the canonically acceptable words of Jesus. Thus Ptolemy and other Gnostic teachers, like Valentinus and Basilides, claim to represent tradition and not innovation by supplying lists of witnesses extending from the apostles down to themselves. As von Campenhausen points out further, this kind of demonstration is likely to become necessary when a minority position is struggling to prove itself; otherwise the validity of a tradition tends to be taken for granted. [38]

Of course one already begins to find a critique of this idea of tradition in the Pastoral Epistles which appeal to Scripture rather than secret teachings (1 Tim 6:20; 3 Tim 3:16). This attitude toward tradition seems also to characterize the writers of the third Christian generation, with the possible exception of Ignatius who argued so strongly for living authority.[39] But it is only after the Gnostics have appealed to an apostolic succession of their own that Christian writers begin to fight fire with fire and make the same sort of appeal.

The first to do this seems to have been an obscure figure named Hegesippus, perhaps a converted Hellenistic Jew and an anti-gnostic, who travelled to Corinth and Rome in the mid-second century in an effort to compile the true doctrine.[40] Hegesippus' work has been lost, but fragments have been preserved in the *Church History* of Eusebius. To prove the claim to true doctrine, Hegesippus constructed lists of bishops from the time of the apostles for a number of major Christian sees, for example, Jerusalem, Corinth, and Rome. Since we already know that there were no such *monepiskopoi* in the second and third Christian generations, the early names on these lists were probably not monarchical bishops at all but rather well-known presbyter-bishops whose names had been preserved in the memory of the various churches.[41] One indication that this is the case is the comment of Hegesippus that he "*made* a succession [list] as far as Anicetus" for the church of Rome. Here he is probably describing the process of constructing a list, not merely reporting one that was already in existence.[42] A list of this kind was not necessary prior to Hegesippus and his concerns. This argument is further supported by the words of the Roman bishop, Anicetus himself, who referred to the "presbyters before him," according to Irenaeus.[43]

The classic example of Hegesippus' argument for apostolic succession is found in the *Adversus Haereses* of Irenaeus of Lyons toward the end of the second century. Irenaeus probably derived his succession lists from Hegesippus.[44] He writes primarily to defend the orthodox Christian truth contained in written traditions, that is, those writings which were in the process of being canonized as the New Testament. But to prove the truth of Scripture he must appeal to the unanimous witness of an unbroken chain of bishops, especially in the Roman church, unsullied by heresy.[45] He writes:

> It is within the power of all, therefore, in every church, who may wish to see the truth, to contemplate clearly the tradition of the apostles manifested throughout the whole world; and we

are in a position to reckon up those who were by the apostles instituted bishops in the churches, and the succession of these men to our own times; those who neither taught nor knew of anything like these [heretics] rave about.[46]

There is, to be sure, a certain circularity to Irenaeus' argument. The Scriptures are true because of the witness of the chain of bishops, and the chain of bishops is trustworthy because it is faithful to the Scriptures. The Gnostics could and did make the same kind of argument for their traditions. What concerns us, however, is not so much the form of the argument as the fact that it remained the acceptable proof for Christian orthodoxy and the demonstration of apostolic tradition as a chain of bishops down to Vatican II's *Lumen Gentium*.[47]

There are other ways of conceiving apostolic succession— for example in the faithfulness of the church as a whole to the apostles' teaching or its faithfulness as living witness to the truth of the Gospel, namely, by the ethical life and worship life of the community.[48] These do not have the appeal of a discernible chain of witnesses. Unfortunately the latter, though constructed with good reason (the refutation of heresy) rests on an apparently non-existent historical foundation. This notion of apostolic succession by a chain of hands from the apostles to bishops appointed by them and so forth amounts to what can be called an invented tradition.[49] It cannot be disproved beyond doubt, but we have shown that the late second-century defenders of orthodoxy had good reason to "construct" it. The transmission of the Gospel was a far more messy affair than the second-century defenders of orthodoxy made it out to be. There is merit in Irenaeus' theory, however, in that it shows that the bishops are only authentic teachers insofar as they hold fast to the truth of the Scriptures.[50] That is to say, they do not automatically possess the true tradition because of their office but rather demonstrate the validity of their office by their fidelity to the Gospel.

EARLY CHURCH ORDERS

We can conveniently conclude our study of the development of the monarchical episcopate until the end of the third century by reflecting on ordination in the *Apostolic Tradition* of

Hippolytus and the portrait of the bishop in the *Didascalia Apostolorum*.

The *Apostolic Tradition* of Hippolytus, most probably compiled by a recalcitrant Roman presbyter ca. 215, is the parent or grandparent of a number of later church orders and is therefore extremely important for the development of subsequent tradition in the church.[51] The section on the election and ordination of the bishop in *Apostolic Tradition* 2-4 is not without considerable textual problems.[52] For example, one scholar, E.C. Ratcliff, reconstructed the text, proposing that in the original directions on the election of the bishop it was the presbyters who imposed hands and prayed over the candidate. Only in a later recension did it become customary for other bishops to do the ordaining.[53] Thus when the received text claims that only the bishop says the prayer in the ordination of presbyters because he alone has the power to ordain,[54] this too may have been omitted in the original text of Hippolytus. In other words, the practice of the late second-century Roman church may have emphasized the role of the presbytery far more than the current text suggests.

In any case, the text of the *Apostolic Tradition* as we have it shows that other bishops were involved in the confirmation of a candidate for the episcopacy. It is the people who do the choosing.

> Let him be ordained bishop who has been chosen by all the people; and when he has been named and accepted by all, let the people assemble, together with the presbytery and those bishops who are present, on the Lord's day. When all [the bishops?] give consent, they shall lay hands on him, and the presbytery shall stand by and be still. And all shall keep silence, praying in their hearts for the descent of the Spirit; after which one of the bishops present, being asked by all, shall lay his hand on him who is being ordained bishop, and pray, saying . . .[55]

This text, as well as the prayer which follows, offers an interesting insight into the role of the bishop. In one sense he is chosen by popular suffrage. He is also joined to the other churches by the presence of other bishops at his ordination. But he receives his power, the "princely spirit" (*spiritus principalis*) not from the people or from other bishops but from God. In the prayer God is asked to bestow on the candidate the power to exercise the high priesthood, to offer the gifts, to bind and loose, to confer orders, and to pray before the Lord unceasingly. Strangely enough, not a word is said about the preservation of doctrine nor does the prayer imply apostolic succession in the sense of a chain of power. Rather, it emphasizes the fact that the power to exercise the episcopate comes from God. Clearly it is the bishop's cultic and disciplinary role which dominates in the prayer.

For another view which emphasizes a different dimension of the episcopacy, but one roughly contemporary with the *Apostolic Tradition*, we must turn to the *Didascalia Apostolorum*, an early third-century Syrian church order.[56] Although the *Didascalia* provides us with no evidence with regard to the selection and ordination of the bishop, it does present a rather full picture of what kind of person the bishop should be and what kind of functions he is to perform.

The bishop is to be blameless and physically unblemished man, not less than fifty years old. A small church may however choose a younger person if no older ones are available. He should be educated, but if uneducated, must be at least wise and capable in speech. He is to be married to one wife and is to be a good manager of his household and children (see 1 Tim 3:2). The bishop should be generous, discerning of those truly in need, patient and not given to anger, no respecter of persons, and a student of the Scriptures.

Further, the bishop stands as judge in the place of God (although his judgment can be false and badly motivated). He is to judge sinners strictly, but even greater emphasis is put on his quality of compassion with the repentant. He is to gather the presbyters and deacons around him when he sits in judgment—preferably on a Monday so that reconciliation can take place before the eucharist on the following Sunday. Since, as high priest, he offers up the sacrifice of the church to God, he deserves financial support from the community. But not even his offering is acceptable before God if he holds a grudge against someone. He is called "minister of the word." He appoints deacons and deaconesses in the church and regulates the order of widows.

We note that the bishop serves in a sense as a model Christian. How he functions and the kind of person he is are balanced in this document. Moreover, he exercises a great deal of direct pastoral ministry both liturgically and in terms of the governance of the church, especially with regard to the power of the keys.

Both the *Apostolic Tradition* and the *Didascalia Apostolorum* show that the role of the monepiscopate has been fairly well defined by the beginning of the third century. At this point it seems taken for granted that the bishops are the successors of the apostles and that they share the greatest part of responsibility for ecclesiastical governance as well as liturgical leadership. It must be stressed that this role grew out of the need for unified leadership in the face of doctrinal conflict. Perhaps by the end of the second century this need did not seem as pressing as at the century's beginning. Perhaps this role of the bishop could be taken for granted by the time of the writing of these church orders. It remains, however, the primary need that created the monepiscopacy and would be an important factor in the role of bishops as they gathered to face doctrinal crises in the fourth and fifth centuries.

CONCLUSION

What theological questions arise from the foregoing description of the development of the monarchical episcopate? It seems to me that three stand out.

First, given this "deconstruction" of the traditional picture of the development of the episcopacy, can one read the claims of *Lumen Gentium* (chapter 3) about the origins of the episcopate in an explicit and conscious dominical institution in a literal fashion? It seems obvious to me that one cannot. One can read the passage's *ex divina institutione* as referring to a decision of the early church rather than one made by Christ himself, as Rahner does.[57] Even if one asserts that the argument of *Lumen Gentium* is theological, if one were to take its claim about the historical institution of the episcopate literally as the will of Christ, it would rest finally upon an historical appeal which cannot be founded.

Would it not be better and more honest to construct an argument for the necessity of the episcopal role in the church not on institution by Christ but rather on the Holy Spirit's continual guidance of the community in the face of ever changing historical circumstances? Surely such an argument does not have the immediate appeal of the tangible picture of apostolic succession *via* a chain of hands. But, after all, that direct and simple theory when taken to a logical extreme has put us in the awkward position of recognizing the validity of episcopal orders when "conferred" by people like Msgr. Lefebvre, not to mention far shadier characters in the history of the church.[58] It seems to me that in more irenic times than those experienced by Ignatius of Antioch and Irenaeus of Lyons our doctrinal positions with regard to church order would better be characterized by modesty than by overkill. God works in the world, it seems to me, not through the unfolding of a plan predetermined in all its details, but providentially through the Holy Spirit guiding the faithful in the concrete vicissitudes of human history. This way of looking at the history and doctrine of church order enables us to take into account the social, political, and economic factors that helped to shape ecclesiastical office without our having to reduce historical developments to those factors alone. The drawback of this approach, of course, is that it is far more complex than claiming to discern the Lord's will for the constitution of the church for all time.[59]

A second question arises from considering the size of the communities in which the *monepiscopoi* originally ministered. No doubt by the middle of the third century a local church could be very large indeed. The church at Rome, ca. 250, had: one bishop, forty-six presbyters, seven deacons, seven subdeacons, forty-two acolytes, fifty-two exorcists, readers, and doorkeepers, and over fifteen-hundred widows and persons in distress.[60] But it is hard to conceive of the churches of the early second century, especially in out-of-the-way towns, as being larger than modest American parishes today. In fact, they would have been considerably smaller than some of our large parishes. The evidence we have reviewed seems to presuppose an intimate relation between the bishop and his church. Is the contemporary parish pastor more an equivalent of the early *monepiskopos* than the individuals we call bishops?

Finally, what is the essential charism of the bishop in the period of the formation of the monarchical episcopate? Is it liturgical leadership? administrative governance? teaching and guaranteeing the apostolic faith? the supervision of good works? probity of life? The evidence has suggested that all of these are legitimate and important aspects of the episcopacy. Doubtless when taken together, this presents a daunting picture. Can one person fulfill all these functions today, especially given the size and complexity of the contemporary Roman Catholic diocese? It would seem idealistic to suppose that any single bishop ever exercised all these charisms equally well, and it would seem unrealistic to expect that any single bishop could do so today. Perhaps that is why, although we can recognize the historical exigencies that created the monarchical episcopate, we should never imagine that any one class of persons in the church exercises charisms to the exclusion of the other baptized and that all ministries are performed in the power of the one who is finally *the* shepherd and bishop of our souls (1 Pt 2:25).

Notes

1. *Lumen Gentium*, no. 21.
2. Ibid., no. 23.
3. Ibid., nos. 18-30; see also *Christus Dominus*, no. 2.
4. *Baptism, Eucharist and Ministry*, Faith and Order Paper 111 (Geneva: World Council of Churches, 1982) Ministry 10. This consensus statement is more frequently called "The Lima Document."
5. Ibid., M-23 (emphasis mine). See also M-21.
6. *Lumen Gentium*, no. 18. I will leave aside the claims made there about the primacy of Peter and his successors.
7. Ibid., no. 20.
8. The very variety of structures in the primitive church makes it unlikely that Jesus had in mind a kind of blueprint for the organization of the church. On this topic, see Raymond E. Brown, *The Churches the Apostles Left Behind* (New York: Paulist Press, 1984); James D.J. Dunn, *Unity and Diversity in the New Testament* (Philadelphia: Westminster Press, 1977); Walter Bauer, *Orthodoxy and Heresy in Earliest Christianity*, English trans. of a 1934 work (Philadelphia: Fortress Press, 1971); and especially helpful with regard to a description of the first three Christian generations and a fourfold typology of Jewish-Gentile Christianity, Raymond E. Brown and John P. Meier, *Antioch and Rome: New Testament Cradles of Catholic Christianity* (New York: Paulist Press, 1983) 1-14.
9. Hans von Campenhausen, *Ecclesiastical Authority and Spiritual*

Power in the Church of the First Three Centuries (Stanford: Stanford University Press, 1969) 106-119 thinks that the Pastorals were written in the first half of the second century. But this is a minority opinion, as is his suggestion that these deutero-Pauline letters may refer to the monarchical episcopate. See Brown, *Churches* 31-46.

10. Thus William Telfer, *The Office of a Bishop* (London: Darton, Longmann & Todd, 1962) 1-23; also Jean Colson, *Les Fonctions écclésiales aux deux premiers siècles* (Paris: Desclée, De Brouwer, 1956) 240.

11. On the dating and authenticity of the seven letters, see William R. Schoedel, *Ignatius of Antioch* (Philadelphia: Fortress Press, 1985) 3-7; also Meier, *Antioch and Rome* 74-75.

12. On the three generations at Antioch—the first represented by Galatians and Acts, the second by the Gospel of Matthew, and the third by Ignatius—see Meier, *Antioch and Rome* 28-84.

13. Magnesians 7:1-2; see also Ephesians 4:1-2; 5:3; 6:2; Magnesians 6:1-2; 13:2; Trallians 11:1; 12:1; Philadelphians 2:1; 3:3; 4:1; 6:2; 8:1; Polycarp 1:2. In Polycarp Ignatius writes that the maintenance of unity is the office of the bishop.

14. On the *mebaqqer*, see Brown, *Churches* 33.

15. Ephesians 5:2; Smyrnaeans 8:1-2.

16. Polycarp 4:1-3.

17. Ibid. 5:1-2.

18. Smyrnaeans 8:1-2.

19. Bauer, *Orthodoxy and Heresy* 62.

20. As against the opinion of von Campenhausen, *Ecclesiastical Authority* 97.

21. Philadelphians 10:1; Smyrnaeans 11:2.

22. Romans 9:1.

24. On the social role of the bishop, see the response of P.R. Brown in Henry Chadwick, *The Role of the Christian Bishop in Ancient Society*, Protocol of the Center for Hermeneutical Studies, 35th Colloquy (Berkeley, CA: Center for Hermeneutical Studies, 1980) 16.

25. Against Docetism, see Trallians 9:1-2; Smyrnaeans 4-6; against Judaizing, see Philadelphians 8:2-9:2; Magnesians 9-10.

26. See Trallians 6:1-2.

27. As against Joseph B. Lightfoot, *St. Paul's Epistle to the Phillippians* (London: Macmillan, 1869); also K.A. Strand, "The Rise of the Monarchical Episcopate," *Andrews University Seminary Studies* 4 (1966) 81-82.

28. An alternative model for the relation between bishops, presbyters, and deacons in the primitive church has been proposed by D. Powell, "Ordo Presbyterii," *Journal of Theological Studies* n.s. 26 (1975). Powell argues, pp. 301-311, 321, that the designation *presbyter*

stood for those in the church who were considered the "first fruits" of conversion, first by chronological precedence and later by the quality of their lives. Thus *presbyter* according to him was a status designation. Bishops and deacons, on the other hand, referred to certain ministries within the community and thus these terms served as designations of functions.

29. On apostles and prophets, *Didache* 11-13; on bishops and deacons, *Didache* 15:1-2.

30. See the response of M.H. Shepherd in Chadwick, *The Role of the Christian Bishop* 32.

31. Bishops mentioned in the plural: *I Clement* 42:4; *Hermas Vis.* III:5:1; Sim IX; presbyters: *I Clement* 1:3; 21:6; 44:5; 47:6; 54:2; 57:1; *Hermas Vis.* II:4:3; III:1:8.

32. For a full account and assessment of this debate, see J. Fuellenbach, *Ecclesiastical Office and Primacy of Rome: An Evaluation of Recent Theological Discussion of First Clement* (Washington, D.C.: Catholic University of America Press, 1980).

33. See Brown, *Antioch and Rome* 173-174.

34. See Von Campenhausen, *Ecclesiastical Authority* 164-165.

35. *I Clement* 44. For the beginning of the argument, *I Clement* 42.

36. Von Campenhausen, *Ecclesiastical Authority* 157.

37. Ibid. 158. Ptolemy's letter is quoted in Epiphanius, *Panarion* 33:7.

38. Ibid. 158.

39. See Philadelphians 8:2. Ignatius, though by no means a Docetist, does seem attracted to a number of Gnostic ideas, for example, secret revelations.

40. On Hegesippus, see Johannes Quasten, *Patrology*, vol. 1 (Westminster, MD: Newman Press, 1962) 285.

41. See Telfer, *Office of a Bishop* 109.

42. Von Campenhausen, *Ecclesiastical Authority* 164-165. For the comment of Hegesippus, see Eusebius, *History of the Church* IV:22:3.

43. Reported in Eusebius, *History of the Church* V:24:16.

44. Von Campenhausen, *Ecclesiastical Authority* 169.

45. I am here summarizing the whole of the argument of *Adversus Haereses* III:1-3.

46. Irenaeus, *Adversus Haereses* III:3:1.

47. For example, the theory is quickly adopted by Tertullian at the turn of the third century. See Tertullian, *On the Prescription of Heretics* 32.

48. For a judicious treatment of apostolic succession with the broader context of apostolic continuity, see J.M.R. Tillard, "The Eucharist in Apostolic Continuity," *Worship* 62 (1988) 45-57.

49. See E. Hobsbawm, "Inventing Traditions," in *The Invention of Tradition*, eds., Eric J. Hobsbawm and Terrence Ranger Tanger (Cambridge: Cambridge University Press, 1983). Hobsbawm's definition runs: "'Invented tradition' is taken to mean a set of practices, normally goverened by overtly or tacitly accepted rules and of a ritual or symbolic nature, which seeks to inculcate certain values and norms of behaviour by repetition, which automatically implies continuity with the past. In fact, where possible, they normally attempt to establish continuity with a suitable historic past." The fact that the examples used in the essays of the study referred to are drawn from eighteenth- and nineteenth-century Europe only confirms the suspicion that when it comes to social identity communal memory can be both short and selective.

50. See von Campenhausen, *Ecclesiastical Authority* 173, citing Irenaeus, *Adversus Haereses* IV:26:3.

51. There is no need to go into the difficulties of authority and place of origin here. I have merely repeated the most commonly held scholarly opinion as to these questions. For details, see Geoffrey J. Cuming, *Hippolytus: A Text for Students* (Bramcote, Notts: Grove Books, 1976) 3-7.

52. See Paul Bradshaw, "Ordination," in Geoffrey H. Cuming, *Essays on Hippolytus* (Bramcote, Notts: Grove Books, 1978) 33-38, especially 34-35.

53. E.C. Ratcliff, "Apostolic Tradition: Questions Concerning the Apppointment of a Bishop," *Studia Patristica* (1966) 269.

54. *Apostolic Tradition* 7-8.

55. Ibid. 2.

56. See M. Vasey and S.P. Brock, eds., *The Liturgical Portions of the Didascalia* (Bramcote, Notts: Grove Books, 1982).

57. See Karl Rahner in *Commentary on the Documents of Vatican II*, ed., Herbert Vorgrimler, vol. 1 (New York: Herder and Herder, 1967) 191.

58. For a marvelous (and hilarious) exposition of the problem of *episcopi vagantes*, see Peter F. Anson, *Bishops at Large* (New York: October House, 1964).

59. As with so many important theological questions, this issue of ecclesiology comes down finally to how we understand the role and consciousness of Christ.

60. See the Letter of Cornelius (bishop of Rome) to Fabius (bishop of Antioch) in Eusebius, *History of the Church* VI:43:11.

12

The Sacraments
and the Paschal Presence
of the Bishop

THE BISHOP IS THE PRIMARY IMAGE OF THE PRAYING CHURCH GATH-
ered to worship its Lord. That is the simple thesis which I intend to expound.[1] The thesis is simply stated but complex and
profound in its application when it comes to the celebration of
the sacraments. I mean to explicate this thesis by way of commentary on Part V of the new *Ceremonial of Bishops*.

I do not intend so much to comment on the specific rubrics
of the sacramental celebrations in Part V—they are readable
and self-explanatory—as to reflect on the theological foundations and liturgical consequences of those foundations for the
participation of the bishop in the church's sacramental worship. As several commentators have pointed out, the importance of the new ceremonial lies not so much in specific rubrics as in the fact that it is a pastoral book.[2] If there were any
doubt about this, it would be sufficient to note the number of
times that the phrases "as circumstances suggest" or "unless
he decides otherwise" are used. Therefore, to appreciate the
theological and liturgical function of the bishop as a paschal
presence in sacramental celebration, I propose to do the following. In the first part I will discuss our renewed appreciation of the relation of liturgy to sacramental reality with par-

ticular reference to the importance of images. In the second part I will treat more specifically of the bishop as an image of the paschal presence. Finally, in the third part I will deal with the image and role of the bishop in a number of specific sacramental celebrations.

SACRAMENT, IMAGE AND SYMBOL

In a recent book entitled *Amusing Ourselves to Death: Public Discourse in the Age of Show Business*,[3] communications theorist Neil Postman argues persuasively that we are often unaware of the power of the means of communication as the major determinant of the content of what is to be communicated. I will not pursue the line of his thesis, namely, that television as a medium of entertainment has radically altered our public discourse (including the discourse of religion in a biting chapter entitled "Shuffle off to Bethlehem") and that television is ill-suited to serious discourse. It is of critical import, however, that we realize the accuracy of his argument that "the concept of truth is intimately linked to the biases of forms of expression. Truth does not," he continues, "and never has, come unadorned. It must appear in its proper clothing or it is not acknowledged . . ."[4]

What Postman argues philosophically in terms of communications media corresponds of course to the heart of the gospel message: that God has chosen to communicate Godself to the human race by the medium of a person, Jesus of Nazareth. This incarnational principle is at the heart of what so many recent theologians have named the root-metaphor of Christianity, namely, the paschal mystery or the passion, death, and resurrection of Jesus, a metaphor that governs not only liturgical celebration but the whole of Christian life itself.[5] I would go further to propose that it is by the medium of our personal and communal appropriation of that death and rising with Christ in faith and by grace that we become authentic embodiments of the truth of Christianity. In other words, this truth of Christianity is not primarily a matter of statements or propositions or doctrines but rather a way of life.[6] More clearly—what is most sacramental about our celebrations is our personal witness by means of our growth into the image of Christ.

In some ways in theory, but not always in practice, this has been a lost truth for sacramental theology—a truth that has been recovered only in the not-too-distant past. I have no intention here of reviewing the whole history of sacramental theology and doctrine.[7] It is, however, crucial for our understanding of the power of the sacramental/liturgical image that we recognize a discernible shift in western theology around the eighth and ninth centuries. This shift consisted in abandoning the Platonic sacramental worldview of the early church, a worldview in which symbols could truly represent the realities to which they referred, to a more reified or objectified Germanic mentality in which the concept "symbolic reality" became a contradiction in terms.[8] Such a dramatic shift is evident in the first eucharistic controversy between Ratramnus of Corbie and his fellow-monk, Paschasius Radbertus in the ninth century.

Subsequent western theology and doctrine did the best it could with sacraments, given the common intellectual ground-rules of the debate. It never lost sight of the fact that sacraments were effective because they were signs (today we would say "symbols") because this was so ingrained in its common Augustinian heritage. This tradition reaches the heighth of sophistication in St. Thomas Aquinas. At the same time, however, once a worldview in which symbol and reality could be intrinsically connected was lost, the relation between sacramental realities and liturgical celebration was weakened, with the result that liturgical celebration could be viewed mainly as a matter of canon law and not as a primary theological datum. Eastern Christian theology never quite lost the connection between liturgy and sacrament, and so retained a consistent relation between the two that lasts to this day.[9]

In addition, further reflection on the sacraments led theologians more and more to be concerned with specific questions that related to validity, a necessary concern but after the lowest common denominator and, in a way, the least interesting question about sacraments. The more specific the concerns, the more it seemed that sacraments could be treated like things. In other words, we find that sacraments (at least in terms of theology) lost their intrinsic connection with living communities of Christians.

Sacramental theology in the twentieth century has gone a long way in redressing this tendency. A great deal of credit for the rediscovery of the connection between sacraments and their liturgical celebration must go to the biblical and patristic revival of the first part of this century and among individual authors to Dom Odo Casel. It was Casel who, on the basis of his study of the early Fathers, recognized that the ritual (i.e., liturgy) and sacramental presence were intimately connected.[10] Whether or not he was right about the details of his theory of "Mystery-Presence," Casel struck a chord that resounded not only in Catholic sacramental theology but also in landmark ecclesiastical documents like Pius XII's 1947 encyclical *Mediator Dei* and the Second Vatican Council's Constitution on the Sacred Liturgy. The theology of the sacraments and the study of the liturgy can no longer be considered as if they were wholly distinct enterprises. That the medium (ritual) is determinative of the shape of the truth (of the Gospel) is valid not only for communications theory but for theology as well. And so, it is important to note that sacraments are more fruitfully considered as "actions" and not as "things," as "verbs" and not "nouns." This attitude in no way minimizes the indispensability of things (material elements) in sacramental celebration. Rather, it puts the material elements within their proper context, the ritual aspect of the growth of the community into the image of Christ—in other words, the liturgical action of Christ in his Body, the assembled church. Of course Catholic sacramental theology has always attended not only to the gestures and things but also to their verbal determination by the word of God and by sacramental prayers and formulas. Among contemporary sacramental theologians David Power has expressed the dialectic between word and sacrament particularly well in his insistence that sacraments are not automatically manifestations of the sacred in virtue of symbols and gestures but are always determined by the word.[11]

Hence the importance today of the use of anthropology and the other social sciences in the understanding of sacramental/liturgical celebrations.[12] All this work depends on the accuracy of insisting that sacramental reality is not some hidden quantity that happens to be lodged within liturgical celebration, but is rather conveyed by the ritual (liturgical action) itself. Symbols are not mere covers for realities. As Louis-Marie Chauvet put it: "To analyze the symbol to find there a hidden truth is like peeling an onion to find an onion."[13] This is why traditionalists are so opposed to the reformed Roman Catholic liturgy. Traditionalists understand very well that the transformation of symbolic-liturgical experience is a profound theological change.

Therefore, it will no longer do to consider sacramental realities as distinct from liturgical celebrations. They are embodied, both literally and figuratively, in the shape and quality of liturgical celebrations. In a sense, all of the foregoing is thus but a gloss on the succinct but suggestive lines from the Bishops' Committee on the Liturgy document, *Music in Catholic Worship*: "Good celebrations foster and nourish faith. Poor celebrations may weaken and destroy it."[14]

Consistent with this developing theological consciousness of the importance of liturgical celebration for the effectiveness of sacramental realities has been the parallel recognition of what one might call the "wider sacramentality," in other words, the realization that the realities of human life as well as the church and indeed Christ himself can be fruitfully understood on the basis of a theology of the symbol. In particular, Edward Schillebeeckx and Karl Rahner must be singled out as contributing to this tendency in contemporary Roman Catholic theology.[15] Rahner sums up what I have been reviewing quite well in his essay "Considerations on the Active Role of the Person in the Sacramental Event"[16] when he writes:

> The world and its history are the terrible and sublime liturgy, breathing of death and sacrifice, which God celebrates and causes to be celebrated in and through human history in its freedom, this being something which he in turn sustains in grace by his sovereign disposition . . . This liturgy therefore must, if the individual is really to share in the celebration of it in all freedom and self-commitment unto death, be interpreted, "reflected upon" in its ultimate depths in the celebration of that which we are accustomed to call liturgy in the more usual sense.

Thus I would summarize by saying that (1) a liturgical celebration serves as the vehicle of a sacramental reality, and not merely its occasion or envelope; and (2) that the celebration itself must be consistent and congruent with the experience of a wider sacramentality, God's gift of self (grace) in daily life. Thus (3) sacramental/liturgical celebrations serve to focus the activity that God is working in us. And (4) in the context of the contemporary Roman Catholic liturgical reform we can see why the bishop who images the local church has a role which must be appreciated with renewed attention and intensity.

SACRAMENTAL IMAGE OF THE BISHOP

One of the fruits of the theology leading up to, enshrined in, and inspired by the Second Vatican Council has been a renewed appreciation of the role of the bishop in the church, a role whose sacramentality is now assured.[17] It is important here to be clear about what constitutes the sacramentality of orders. While in baptism, confirmation, the eucharist, penance, and anointing, sacramentality is constituted by liturgical celebration, in the case of marriage and holy orders it is human beings themselves who become sacraments. Though weddings and ordinations are the public recognition and empowerment of this sacramentality, of themselves as liturgical celebrations they do not constitute it. Each of these two latter sacraments, therefore, are manifestations of the self-sacrificial or paschal love of Christ in the living witnesses of those who have received them. In fact, it is better to speak of people living these sacraments than receiving them. We are more concerned here, of course, with holy orders, and specifically with the liturgical role of the bishop.

If the bishop is to be a sacrament, namely, a symbolic mediator of God's self-gift in Christ to the world, then he must be so in all of the aspects of his life. Because of his symbolic position as the head of the local church, he does this in a heightened way in those situations in which the church is most focused—in which the church enacts itself by its imitation of the paschal mystery, which is true of all sacramental celebration, but in a most important manner in baptism and the eucharist. What may be most crucial then about the role of the bishop as a liturgist is the quality of his personal presentation as a witness to the paschal mystery.

Pseudo-Dionysius the Areopagite was well aware of this when he gave the bishop as priest pride of place among human beings for the transmission of the heavenly mysteries.[18] Not that we would proceed to argue on the basis of his neoplatonic hierarchy today, but I do want to suggest that the bishop does have a significant role as a human mirror of the saving realities of Christ. Before proceeding to the image of the bishop in specific sacramental celebration, I want to comment on three important aspects of the bishop's role in liturgical celebration.

Personal Witness to the Gospel

It seems to me that the bishop's role as a liturgical presider will be enhanced or diminished by the quality of his personal witness to the Gospel in other areas of his life.

As several fellow priests have remarked to me, they never feel as exposed as when they are presiding at a liturgy. In a sense this is a weakness of the reformed Roman Catholic liturgy, namely, that it depends so heavily on the presider and not as much on the rite itself as did the previous liturgical arrangement. If the bishop is a man of faith and commitment to the Gospel, this will be evident in his leadership of the community in sacramental celebration, even should he lack some of the communication skills requisite for our reformed worship. (I am presuming that bishops are chosen on the basis of a number of qualities and gifts, of which liturgical presidency may not be the highest in a particular situation.) If there is anything that stands out in the reformed Catholic liturgy, it is that individual rubrics are secondary to the presider's leadership of prayer.

Moreover, since bishops are members of a college, it seem to me that the credibility of our bishops in the United States has been enhanced by the public corporate stance taken by the National Conference of Catholic Bishops on a number of topics, chief among them the pastorals on peace and on the economy. Bishops are by definition public witnesses to the church and to its values—the local church, the universal church, and increasingly the church within the nation. Therefore when they take a public stance, as for example in the reaction of each of the three bishops of the San Francisco Bay Area to the 1989 murder of Jesuit priests and their coworkers in El Salvador, they represent the church with particular intensity.

It is such witness and personal faith that provide some substance for the phrase "the paschal presence of the bishop" in my title. For a presence to be "paschal," it must include dying with Christ, as the etymology of the word *pascha* among early Christian writers in Greek shows. The derivation *pascha-passio* (*pascha*-suffering) was superseded by *pascha-transitus* (*pascha*-passage), but as David Power as argued, the earlier etymology has taken on a particular poignancy in a world where we must strive to keep the dangerous memory of Jesus Christ alive.[19]

The Bishop as Preacher

The second aspect of the bishop's image as the leader of sacramental celebrations is his role as preacher. I was impressed to read in Thomas Reese's book *Archbishop* the following words of Archbishop Thomas Kelly of Louisville:

> There is nothing more satisfying to me than to preach to a church full of people and keep their attention. I work hard at my preaching. It is very important to get their attention and hold it and to talk to them about themselves and my experience as their bishop. That is what the pope does. I admire him most for his willingness to be present to the universal church in his preaching. And he does that exceptionally well.[20]

Elsewhere in the book Archbishop Kelly remarks that it is of the utmost importance that he preach well in order to give a good example to priests.[21] Of course this stands to reason. How can priests be expected to get the message that they are to preach well if their bishops do not invest time and energy in preaching? We tend to pick up messages subtly and nonverbally. On that level it is very easy to get the message that preaching is not all that important or that it is not necessary to grapple with the Scriptures in prayer and faith and to work hard at relating them to the experience of the people.

As we begin more and more to respect the power of preaching and to recognize how important it is to speak a word of faith to this particular assembly, I become more sympathetic to bishops who rarely have their "own parish" in which to preach, but must constantly preach in different situations to vastly different assemblies. Nevertheless, since one of the most important values recovered in our recent reform has been the appreciation of the connection between the word of

God and sacramental activities, the bishop's role as preacher in each sacramental situation is crucial.

Style of Presidency

The third aspect of the bishop's role as leader of sacramental celebration I can only call "style of presidency." I think that here the bishop sets an extremely important example and communicates the spirit behind the reformed rites. When I am asked what style I think is most appropriate today, I respond: "High Church." By this I mean High Church-with-a-heart, reverence, solemnity, and formality, but without preciousness or stuffiness that is often associated with these. Liturgical celebration must be characterized by a kind of ease that belies our culture's "heresy" that formality and authenticity are mutually contradictory. For many people formality automatically connotes phoniness and this need not be so. The bishop can set as important an example here as he can do with preaching.

These then are three important aspects that underlie the role of the bishop as "liturgist," namely, as the leader of sacramental worship. I trust I have been clear enough about the importance of the "image" of the person in sacramental activity and of the symbolic role of the bishop in particular.

THE BISHOP AND SACRAMENTAL CELEBRATIONS

Now we can turn to the role of the bishop in the individual sacraments as outlined by Part V of *The Ceremonial of Bishops*. I will follow the order given in the ceremonial itself.

Christian Initiation

Given the increased attention to initiation today, it is no wonder that the role of the bishop is stressed in the celebration of the sacraments of initiation. As the ceremonial states:

> The bishop is the chief steward of the mysteries of God and the overseer of all liturgical life in the Church entrusted to his care. He therefore regulates the conferral of baptism, which brings with it a share in Christ's royal priesthood, and he is the primary minister of confirmation. The bishop also has a responsibility for the entire process of Christian initiation, a responsibil-

ity he carries out either personally or through the presbyters, deacons, and catechists of his diocese.[22]

The text goes on to cite Ignatius of Antioch as an early authority for the centrality of the role of the bishop in initiation. It should be needless to say that with the contemporary emphasis on the Rite of Christian Initiation of Adults (RCIA), it is incumbent upon the bishop to take an active and interested role not only in the liturgical celebrations connected with the RCIA, for example, the enrollment, paschal sacraments, and some involvement in the Easter mystagogy, but also in the process itself. This seems crucial especially when cynical voices like that of Andrew Greeley are raised with regard to the value of the RCIA.[23]

Just as an RCIA which consists only of liturgical ceremonies would ring false in the context of parish celebration, so it seems to me that the bishop's role should be more than that of a ceremonial leader. In the age of video-tape it does not seem unreasonable to suggest that the bishop can participate in the catechesis of candidates for initiation at least by such media.

The same suggestion could be made with regard to confirmation. Confirmation is, of course, the sacrament most associated with the bishop, and one that raises a host of liturgical problems. I have no intention here of entering into the morass of the debate about the theological meaning of confirmation, except to underline the fact that the current rites stress the connection between confirmation and baptism. For that connection to be made clear in a symbolic fashion would ultimately require the restoration of the order of the sacraments of initiation: baptism, confirmation, eucharist. I have great admiration for those dioceses, like that of Sacramento, California, which have taken the bold and tactically difficult step of moving in that direction.[24]

In the meantime it is incumbent upon the bishop and those responsible for the liturgy of confirmation to make that connection as clearly as possible. This would suggest that confirmation best be celebrated in the paschal season, the great fifty days, and certainly not within Lent. Attentiveness to the non-verbal signals given by the liturgical season within which a sacrament is celebrated is at least as important as the words spoken during a celebration—unless I am completely mistaken as to the nature of liturgy. I have no doubt that celebrating confirmation only within the Easter season would raise a host of logistical problems. On the other hand, it might also free the bishop for other kinds of pastoral visitation during the rest of the year.

Holy Orders

Ordinations do not tend to be liturgical experiences in which the vast majority of Catholics tend to participate, at least on a regular basis. Because of their importance and celebratory nature they take on a heightened symbolic value, especially in terms of the bishop as presider. In my experience bishops tend to be either at their best or their worst at ordinations, and this for several reasons.

First, ordinations, because they are occasional, tend to be liturgies with which the bishop may not feel comfortable or at home as a presider. Liturgical presidency in the reformed Catholic liturgy, however, requires that the presider have both a comprehensive grasp of the structure and content of a particular ceremony and the ability to set the pace of the liturgy, namely, to control its flow. It is here that the master of ceremonies has a delicate role to play. Given the complexity and occasional nature of ordinations, a master of ceremonies is necessary. At the same time, the bishop cannot cede the presidency to this person. Presiders who literally look as if they do not know what is coming next invariably draw attention to themselves and not to the prayer of the assembly. They betray the role the church entrusts to them.

Second, by his attitude and demeanor, in addition to spoken words, the bishop communicates what he thinks is going on in an ordination. If he thinks this is raising up of ministers by God above the church, then this is the impression the people will go away with. If, on the other hand, he is convinced that ordained ministry is primarily an empowerment for service to God's people, a sacrament of service all God's people owe to one another, then the church will be enriched. The bishop cannot do everything, but he must take the responsibility of entrusting the arrangement of ordinations to a coordinator who can ensure that the liturgy will "look" more like the church's commissioning to and valuing of service than the reward of a life well-spent.

Third, I would encourage bishops who preside at ordinations to take advantage of the latitude provided by the ritual and the ceremonial to preach in their own words rather than to use the instructions printed in the pontifical. This will enable them not only to speak to the specific situation of the persons being ordained but also to reflect and respond to the message of the Scriptures that have just been read—which is what every liturgical homily should do.

Finally, with regard to one particular element of the rite, the promise of obedience, let me suggest that the National Conference of Catholic Bishops consider choosing a different gesture than the placing of the hands of the ordinand within those of the bishop, as is allowed by the ceremonial.[25] The rite as it is connotes a medieval attitude of fealty which is no longer appropriate with regard to the relation between priest and deacons and their bishop.

Marriage, Penance, Anointing of the Sick

In the final three sacraments treated by the ceremonial, the bishop has no particularly unique sacramental responsibility. Therefore I will make only a few comments.

With regard to marriage, it seems to me that the ceremonial makes an important point when it opens this section:

> Mindful of Christ the Lord's attendance at the wedding feast of Cana, the bishop should make it his concern to bless occasionally the marriages of his people, and particularly those of the poor.[26]

It would be a pity if a bishop acted as the church's witness and officiated only at weddings in his family or for people whose families are in the *Fortune 500*. The symbolic role of the bishop as the leader of the whole local church is so important that he must be sensitive not to give the impression that only the rich and powerful deserve this kind of attention. After all, the Gospel is a counter-sign to what the "world" considers power and prestige.

With regard to penance, there are a number of advantages

to the bishop acting as minister of this sacrament, both in communal and individual settings. In the communal setting he witnesses to the fact that he is responsible "as the one who regulates the penitential discipline."[27] In other words, in this sacramental setting he images the church's continual call to conversion. Moreover, in the individual setting he not only symbolizes the church's solicitude for the repentant sinner, but also stays close to the everyday experience of God's people, especially in their pains and struggles, as anyone who has ever ministered in this sacrament can testify. It is also pertinent to point out that the bishop can give good example to his priests by acting as minister in this sacrament throughout the year and specifically not by hearing confessions during the Triduum, so as to give more attention to the Lenten season which ends before the Mass of the Lord's Supper on Holy Thursday and to enable them to enter more fully into the spirit of the Triduum.

Finally, the anointing of the sick. With the recovery of a more ancient attitude toward this sacrament in our liturgical reform, the bishop's participation can be a significant factor in helping people to appreciate the appropriateness of coming before the Lord for the prayer of faith, the laying on of hands, and anointing with holy oil in serious illness or old age.

* * * * * *

We have dealt, albeit summarily, with the role of the bishop as minister of the sacraments other than the eucharist. I hope that the result has been twofold: first, the conviction that for their effectiveness sacramental celebrations require great care and imagination because God is at work in our assemblies through symbol and ritual; second, a deeper realization of the prominent position of the bishop in sacramental celebration, the bishop who because of his symbolic embodiment of the local church serves as a living image of the paschal presence of the Lord.

Notes

1. Another statement of this thesis is: "The bishop exists as a living sign of Christ's presence in his Church, as one bearing witness to the Word of God and communicating God's life through the sacraments." *Directory on the Pastoral Ministry of Bishops*, no. 11; cited in: Bishops' Committee on the Liturgy, *The Bishop and the Liturgy: Highlights of the New Ceremonial of Bishops* (Washington, D.C.: United States Catholic Conference, 1986) 19. The same ideas are found substantially in the new ceremonial itself, e.g., nos. 6, 7. International Commission on English in the Liturgy, *The Ceremonial of Bishops: Revised by Decree of the Second Vatican Ecumenical Council and Published by the Authority of Pope John Paul II* (Collegeville: The Liturgical Press, 1989). And also in *Sacrosanctum Concilium*, no. 41.

2. For example, John A. Gurrieri and Archbishop Virgilio Noe in *The Bishop and the Liturgy* 3, 8.

3. Neil Postman, *Amusing Ourselves to Death: Public Discourse in the Age of Show Business* (New York: Penguin Books, 1985).

4. Ibid 22.

5. For a particularly fine and lucid treatment of this connection, see Robert F. Taft, *The Liturgy of the Hours in East and West* (Collegeville: The Liturgical Press, 1986) 334-346; on the Paschal Mystery as root metaphor, see George Worgul, *From Magic to Metaphor* (New York: Paulist Press, 1980) 184-195.

6. For a contemporary analysis of doctrinal and theological statements as related to concepts of religion, see George A. Lindbeck, *The Nature of Doctrine: Religion and Theology in a Post-Liberal Age* (Philadelphia: Westminster, 1984).

7. For an excellent summary of the development of sacramental theology, especially in the twentieth century, see Albert Gerhards, "Stationen der Gottesbegegnung: Zur theologischen Bestimmung der Sakramentenfeiern," in M. Klöckener and W. Glade, *Die Feier der Sakramente in der Gemeinde* (Kevelaer: Verlag Butzon & Bercker, 1987) 17-30.

8. On this split, see Alexander Gerken, *Theologie der Eucharistie* (Munich: Kösel-Verlag, 1973) 97-111.

9. Not that there was never any development in Eastern Christian liturgical theology. On the historical development with regard to the eucharistic liturgy, see Hans-Joachim Schulz, *The Byzantine Liturgy: Symbolic Structure and Faith Expression* (New York: Pueblo Publishing Co., 1986) xvii-xxii. For a contemporary Russian Orthodox example of this coherent approach, see Alexander Schmemann, *For the Life of the World: Sacraments and Orthodoxy* (Crestwood, NY: St. Vladimir's Seminary Press, 1973).

10. Odo Casel, *The Mystery of Christian Worship* (Westminster, MD: Newman Press, 1962). For an analysis of Casel's theology and the reaction of the theological world, see Arno Schilsson, *Theologie als Sakramententheologie: Die Mysterientheologie Odo Casels* (Mainz: Mattias-Grünewald Verlag, 1982).

11. David N. Power, *Unsearchable Riches: The Symbolic Nature of Liturgy* (New York: Pueblo Publishing Co., 1984) 98-171.

12. For an attempt to apply the insights of the social sciences to sacramental theology, see Bernard Lee, general editor, *Alternative Futures for Worship*, 7 vols. (Collegeville: The Liturgical Press, 1987), esp. R. Duffy, ed., vol. 1: *General Introduction*.

13. Louis-Marie Chauvet, *Du Symbolique au symbole: Essai sur les sacrements* (Paris: Cerf, 1979) 51.

14. Bishops' Committee on the Liturgy, *Music in Catholic Worship* (Washington, D.C.: United States Catholic Conference, 1972 (1983), no. 6.

15. For the philosophical basis of the relation symbol/reality, see, e.g., Louis Dupré, *The Other Dimension*, 2d ed. (New York: Seabury, 1979) 105-153; Michael G. Lawler, *Symbol and Sacrament: A Contemporary Sacramental Theology* (New York: Paulist Press, 1987) 5-28. For the relation between the sacraments and human life, see Bernard Cooke, *Sacraments and Sacramentality* (Mystic, CT: Twenty-Third Publications, 1983). For the concept of the sacramentality of Christ, Edward Schilebeeckx, *Christ, the Sacrament of the Encounter with God* (New York: Sheed and Ward, 1963). For the relation church/sacrament, Karl Rahner, *The Church and the Sacraments* (New York: Herder & Herder, 1963). For Rahner's basic statement on symbol, Karl Rahner, "The Theology of the Symbol," *Theological Investigations* IV (Baltimore: Helicon Press, 1966) 221-252.

16. *Theological Investigations* XIV (New York: Seabury, 1976) 169-170.

17. For example, *Lumen Gentium*, nos. 26-27; *Christus Dominus*, nos. 4-6.

18. See Schulz, *Byzantine Liturgy* 25-28.

19. See Power, *Unsearchable Riches* 154-158. For the uses of the word *Pascha* in the early church, see Christine Mohrmann, "Pascha, Passio, Transitus," *Ephemerides Liturgicae* 66 (1952) 37-52; repr. in Christine Mohrmann, *Etudes sur le latin des chrétiens*, vol. 3 (Rome: Edizioni di Storia e Letteratura, 1958).

20. Thomas J. Reese, *Archbishop: Inside the Power Structure of the American Catholic Church* (San Francisco: Harper & Row, 1989) 89.

21. Ibid. 138.

22. *Ceremonial*, no. 404.

23. See Andrew Greeley, "Against the RCIA," *America* 161 (10): (14 October 1989) 231-234.

24. For example, Bishop Francis Quinn in a Pastoral Letter, Spring 1989.

25. *Ceremonial*, no. 528.

26. Ibid., no. 598.

27. Ibid., no. 621.

EUCHARIST
AND
MINISTRY

13

Liturgical Renewal after Vatican II: Pastoral Reflections on a Survey

RECENT SCHOLARLY INVESTIGATION HAS SHOWN THAT, IN THE HISTO-ry of the church, councils are only considered ecumenical after they have been received by the church at large. A convenient example is the Council of Chalcedon (451), considered by the Roman and Orthodox Churches as the fourth ecumenical council, but which is of course not considered thus by churches that have been called Monophysite. Today the Second Vatican Council is still in the process of reception by the church. The survey, *Liturgical Renewal 1963-1988*,[1] shows, I think, that this reception process is well along. In fact, in terms of liturgical renewal the council's efforts have achieved a remarkable level of acceptance, except among the smallest minority. It is my intention here to reflect on this renewal in terms of pastoral liturgical theology.

What is the task of the liturgical theologian? Simply put, it is to reflect in a coherent fashion on the church's experience of public prayer and to do this with serious attention to Scripture, history, and the contemporary experience of the church. The pastoral liturgical theologian must do this with a keen eye to the social-psychological conditions that obtain in any particular culture or era. Theology, after all, is always an act of interpretation and, as such, is inevitably governed by the interpreter's background, life-situation, blindspots, and limitations of perspective. This is why theology's task is never complete, never a final synthesis of all that can be said of God and God's relation to the world. The fact that Christian faith keeps on being experienced in different times and different places forces us to reflect anew on the faith in general and on its particular aspects as well.

Nowhere is this more true than in the field of liturgy, affected as it is by cultural conditions, for the church's worship is not a set of texts and rubrics written down in books but the living experience of Christian assemblies. Therefore, as in drama, one can learn a great deal from the script, but true appreciation of liturgy as an event can come only with the experience of the play (liturgy) itself.

The survey, *Liturgical Renewal 1963-1988,* provides us with an opportunity to reflect on the state of post-Vatican II Roman Catholic liturgy as it is experienced in fifteen middle-class American parishes concerned with renewal. The limitations of the data, restricted as they are to parishes that have made a serious effort at renewal, should be obvious. It is also clear that the survey makes no pretense at being scientific in the sociological sense. It seems to me, however, on the basis of my own experience with a variety of parishes around the country that this survey, impressionistic as it is, does provide an opportunity to consider the major pastoral theological issues surrounding the liturgy today. Therefore, in what follows I propose to do the following: first, to ask the formal question "What is the place of 'experience' in liturgical theology?", second, to reflect on the various sacramental images that the survey surfaces, and finally to discuss three fundamental issues in pastoral practice that the survey suggests.

THE PLACE OF "EXPERIENCE" IN LITURGICAL THEOLOGY

It is not too bold to say that today theology in general and with it liturgical theology are in the midst of a paradigm shift, from a classical world view to one that can be characterized as "modern." Some are even willing to argue that theology, having exhausted the modern paradigm, is shifting to one that can be designated "postmodern."[2] In any case, the shift that is taking place can adequately be described as moving from a model of ahistorical truths enshrined in a fundamentally unchanging tradition to the priority of experience in evaluating theological claims. The former model is characteristic of scholastic theology, while the latter "turn to the subject" (to employ a phrase of Bernard Lonergan) is characteristic of theologians after Kant, beginning with Schleiermacher.

One can find this shift well exemplified in two different styles of sacramental theology. The classic form relies first and foremost on the data provided by the doctrinal (even more than the scriptural) tradition, for example in Bernard Leeming's *Principles of Sacramental Theology*.[3] This older style of sacramental theology neatly distinguishes the form and content of liturgical celebration. It is as if sacraments were sacred formulas, actions, and things encased in a changeable liturgy which has little or no bearing on the reality of the sacrament itself. One of the major results of the liturgical reform, especially in the twentieth century, has been the realization that the form of the liturgy (its celebration) and the content of the sacraments are inseparable.

The modern form has taken two directions. The first reflects on sacraments primarily on the basis of a phenomenology of human experience, as in Bernard Cooke's *Sacraments and Sacramentality*.[4] This style of sacramental theology, thoroughly in tune with the renewal of theology in general, represents a significant advance over a "dogmatic" method that tends or remains mired in the disputes of the past, especially those of the sixteenth-century Reformation. But the second direction is even more important for our purposes. This style of sacramental theology is more appropriately called liturgical theology, for it attends not only to the phenomenological data and to the findings of the human sciences, but also analyzes the text and actions of various liturgical celebrations. Raymond Vaillancourt's *Toward a Renewal of Sacramental Theology*[5] is an example of this effort. One should mention here the very different attempts of Aidan Kavanagh, David Power, and Robert Taft in this regard.[6] Finally, the excellent series, *Alternative Futures for Worship*,[7] has provided us with the findings of the human sciences combined with the traditional concerns of sacramental theology and an analysis of liturgical celebration.

Underlying both of these modern views is a wider concept of sacramentality made popular by Karl Rahner who understands the church to be the basic sacrament[8] and Edward Schillebeeckx who sees Christ as the primordial sacrament.[9] In other words, the process of symbolization (in theological terms, sacramentality) is not a mere appendage to the Christian experience of faith but rather an integral dimension of all human knowing and acting.[10]

I want to argue that this modern shift is a necessary correction of a theology that in a one-sided way emphasized extrinsic concerns, that is, based itself on views of positive commands by God that are not grounded sufficiently in an understanding of the human that can make sense to contemporary people. For better or for worse,[11] theology in all its forms must take an anthropological starting point today. This criterion poses an important challenge to the liturgical theologian for in my opinion contemporary liturgical scholarship has placed too high a value on a relatively uncritical recovery of liturgical forms of the past. Two examples will suffice to make my point. The current Order for the Roman Catholic Mass is clearly a copy of the seventh-century *Ordo Romanus Primus* without that document's frills of imperial-ecclesiastical court etiquette, undoubtedly an advance over the "medieval low Mass" model operative prior to Vatican II, but still only one time-conditioned model for what might be possible in the ritualization of the Roman Catholic eucharist. In the area of initiation, the Rite of Christian Initiation of Adults is clearly modeled on the early third-century *Apostolic Tradition* of Hippolytus, a somewhat problematic document that we cannot even be sure was ever really used. Liturgical theologians, myself included, have yet to develop a critical hermeneutic for the study of liturgical history.[12]

The lack of a developed criteriology for liturgical history is paralleled by some assumptions that are implicit in the use of experiential data—a matter on which I wish to focus for the remainder of this section. In his provocative book, *The Nature of Doctrine: Religion and Theology in a Post Liberal Age*,[13] George Lindbeck has questioned the operative definitions of religion which underlie so much of contemporary theology and its theories of doctrine. While I must admit that Lindbeck's theory of doctrine does present some problems, his analysis of the three models employed by students of religion strikes right at the heart of the relation between experience and theology.

The first model is named cognitivist or propositionalist and is characteristic of the view of traditional orthodoxy. It treats the language of the truth claims of a particular religion in realist or objective fashion. The Enlightenment and especially Kant's first philosophical critique have made this a problematic (if not terribly unpopular) view of religion and its function.

The second model Lindbeck terms experiential or expressivist. The fundamental presupposition of this model is a universal religious experience that is merely expressed in different ways by diverse religious faiths. In the field of the study of religion it had its origins in Schleiermacher's "feeling of absolute dependence" and has had its heirs among most of the major theologians popular in the twentieth century—Paul Tillich, Rudolf Bultmann, Langdon Gilkey, to name but a few. It has also been employed by students of religion in general, for example, Rudolf Otto and Mircea Eliade.[14] Lindbeck finds that the experiential or expressivist approach fails to appreciate that there is no one common religious experience universal to humankind in general and for this reason is inadequate. A variation on both of these first two models can be discerned in the theologies elaborated by Karl Rahner and Bernard Lonergan, who for Lindbeck combine the cognitivist and experientialist approaches.

As is usual in the case of typologies, the last given—the cultural linguistic model—is the author's favorite. This postliberal model "places emphasis on those respects in which religions resemble languages together with their correlative forms of life and are thus similar to cultures—that is, as idioms for the construction of reality and the living of life."[15] Proponents of this understanding of religion can be found in the school of thought called the sociology of knowledge (Peter Berger, Thomas Luckmann) as well as in the thought of Karl Marx, Emile Durkheim, Max Weber, Clifford Geertz, Ninian Smart, and (the later) Ludwig Wittgenstein.

The parallel between Lindbeck's cultural-linguistic model

and the nature of liturgy suggests that we are formed by liturgy just as much as (or perhaps even more than) we form it; namely, that liturgy, like religion, is not merely the product of our "extra-liturgical" or "pre-liturgical" experience, but rather shapes all our experience. It is one of the religious ways in which we achieve our most authentic identity.

The implications for the use of the category "experiential" in contemporary liturgical theology are profound indeed. Like any living language liturgy develops and changes. Its "vocabulary" is expanded; new "metaphors" are added to it; new "patterns of speech" emerge. And again as with language, the novel aspects of liturgy are the products of a certain genius, a gift for insight into the nature of the world. But we tend to forget that, like speaking a language, liturgy is something we learn. It is not the "expressive" product of our manipulation—something that we have thought up.

And so, while it would be foolish to discount the element of experience in contemporary liturgy or to fail to be attentive to the needs of worshipers, at the same time it would be equally foolish to neglect the formative powers of the symbols and rituals that go to make up Christian worship. This concern is all the more pressing given the "subjectivist" bias of our age.[16] Never before in the history of the world have so many people been deeply concerned about how they feel. Never before have they been so vocal about it. And, more important, never before have so many been concerned to listen to them. This is not to say that the experiential data provided by the survey is not significant, but rather that it must be sifted in a critical way. Thus when those interviewed report that such and such an aspect of the liturgy was meaningful for them, we must ask: "Just what does 'meaningful' mean here?" It has long been my suspicion that what is truly meaningful about liturgy is experienced on a very subtle level and is not accessible for immediate articulation.

So, when people complain that certain aspects of the liturgy are boring or hold no interest for them, we should be wary about coming to the rapid conclusion that these have no meaning.[17] In other words, attentiveness and meaning are not necessarily synonymous. We are seldom attentive to the patterns which are most formative of our lives. When "they are out of whack," some form of analysis (or even psychoanalysis) is called for to bring them to our conscious attention, but normally these patterns work their subtle effects without much awareness on our part. I am suggesting that liturgy is one of those patterns and that therefore the temptation to constant change which seems to be the constant agenda of so many liturgical planners should be avoided.

If experience is an ambiguous criterion on which to build a liturgical theology, what should characterize the kind of critical theology that is called for? A balance of three factors: the rule of prayer, the rule of faith, and the rule of practice. In recent years much effort has gone into reflecting on the traditional axiom *lex orandi, lex credendi* or the intimate connection between the rule of prayer and the rule of faith. In its original formulation, of course, the principle stated that "the rule of prayer grounds the rule of faith,"[18] but in practice the axiom has been far more dialogical. What Christians believe and how they pray have always affected one another. In fact, as Maurice Wiles has demonstrated, it was actually personal piety more than official liturgical formulations that affected the development of Trinitarian and Christological doctrines in the fourth and fifth centuries.[19] Today, however, we are becoming more and more sensitive to the need for adding a third aspect to the axiomatic *lex orandi, lex credendi*, namely, *lex agendi*, the rule of practice.[20] What kind of (moral) activity is characteristic of people of faith, people who have been formed by liturgical worship? If no notable difference can be discerned on the level of Christian living, then one must ask if there is any significance at all to what goes on in worship or in the faith life of the church.

Let us now turn more directly to the survey itself and some of the issues it raises for liturgical theology in the wake of the council. Perhaps most significant are the sacramental images that surface in the course of the descriptions of the Sunday liturgies and the follow-up interviews. In an impressionistic survey of this sort it would be impossible to define with any scientific exactitude precisely what people are saying is sacramental. But certain words and phrases are repeated with some frequency and point, I think, to a general sacramental vision. The words are: "warmth," "comfortable," "community," "to feel good," "closeness," and "togetherness."

These words and phrases speak volumes about the needs and yearnings of contemporary middle class Americans. It is fairly obvious that many people intensely desire a feeling of belonging and togetherness and that they are happy with liturgy when it provides that feeling. One index of the importance of the need for a feeling of togetherness is the percentage of people in the survey who received communion from the cup. As Gordon Lathrop has perceptively stated in an essay on AIDS and the cup, reluctance to receive from a common cup probably has more to do with the power of symbolic sharing communicated by this action than with germs or viruses.[21] On balance, the parishes surveyed seem to be doing very well in communicating a sense of true community, given the number of people who received from the cup at the liturgies observed.

The question this raises for sacramental imagery is not whether or not people *ought* to feel this way or whether they *ought* to bring an expectation of community and intimacy to liturgy, but how precisely does and should liturgy fit this need. The first thing that must be said is that liturgy cannot make up for the lack of community in other dimensions of life.

One of the most significant dangers of the contemporary renewal of liturgical life is the overblown expectations that many people (including liturgists) tend to bring to it. To expect liturgy to create a community that does not otherwise exist in any way, shape, or form is to confuse symbolic or ritual activity with daily life. These are inseparably interrelated but they are not interchangeable. Of course one of the functions of ritual activity is to enhance community identity—but as we say "grace builds on nature"—community is not created out of whole cloth. The social isolation that we and so many of our contemporaries experience poses one of the most difficult challenges to our appreciation of sacramentality. One of the results is that people are tempted to look to liturgy for immediate gratification and that, when communal identity is accentuated to such a degree, the element of mission is underemphasized. Over-attention to intimacy and warmth also inhibits worshipers from experiencing sacramental action as God's gift, rather than their own creation. Part and parcel of the overblown expectations that are brought to worship is the perverse notion that worship is somehow our good idea in the

first place. It isn't, of course, for it is the result of the prompting of the Spirit—a much neglected aspect of liturgical theology in Western Christianity. There is very little sense in the survey of the church being an *ek-klesia*, an assembly of human
beings that has been convoked by God.

Given the search for intimacy and community as one of the
primary modes of God's presence with us, at least as this is
felt by contemporary worshipers, what does the survey tell us
about how people understand the eucharist? The reactions of
the people interviewed point to a certain limitation on the
meaning of the eucharist. Contemporary reflection on the nature of symbolic activity has taught us that symbols are never
reduced to simple univocal meanings without suffering a loss
of much of their power to evoke feeling, thought, and action.[22]
The richness of multiple meaning involved in the celebration
of the eucharist is evoked by the five meanings named in the
"Eucharist" section of the World Council of Churches' ecumenical convergence document *Baptism, Eucharist and Ministry*
(or the *Lima Document*). These five fundamental aspects of the
eucharist are: thanksgiving to the Father, anamnesis or memorial of Christ, invocation of the Holy Spirit, communion of the
faithful, and meal of the kingdom.[23] Of these five meanings
only the fourth, communion of the faithful, predominates in
the responses of the survey.

The emphasis on communion and community and on the
fellowship meal dimension of the eucharist is indeed a great
and long-overdue gain for Roman Catholics. As I have already
stated, obviously these aspects of liturgical celebration hold an
appeal for today's Catholics. Doubtless, too, each era will concentrate on one or another facet of the rich meaning of eucharistic celebration. The challenge to liturgical theologians (and to
liturgical planners) is to appreciate this contemporary gain in
the worship life of Catholics while at the same time preserving
and reflecting upon the other vital and necessary dimensions
of the eucharist as well.

All of this is not to say that people do not appreciate the
presence of Christ in the eucharistic elements of bread and
wine. Despite their clear inattention to the eucharistic prayer
(a subject we will return to), a deeply ingrained sense of the
presence of Christ in the elements endures. For example, a

number of people, when asked about the eucharistic prayer were embarrassed that they "blanked out" during it since they knew it contained the "consecration." One person, when asked what came next after the preparation of the gifts and table, put it this way: "After this we have the transubstantiation." That such sophisticated language of scholastic theology and the Catholic doctrinal tradition has slipped into a description of what happens in the course of the eucharist is an index of how thoroughly Catholics have been trained to appreciate Christ's presence in the eucharistic elements.

People's reactions to the liturgy thus contain an interesting combination of the old and the new. A rather narrow concentration of the presence of Christ in the transformed bread and wine coexists happily within a more deeply felt framework of the communion meal. The challenge for liturgists (both scholars and practitioners) is to help people through catechesis and above all through liturgical celebration to make the connections between the various dimensions of the eucharist— between the presence of Christ in the assembly, the word, the ministers, and the elements themselves. I am not suggesting that people need to be taught technical terms like *anamnesis*, *eucharistia*, or *berakah*, but rather that the very structure and dramatic presentation of the liturgy ought to help them make these connections on a deeply felt level. For example, appreciating the vertical and horizontal dimensions of participating in communion (that we are bonded with one another as we commune with Christ) ought to lead people to recognize that the eucharist is an anticipatory sign of the coming kingdom of God's justice and peace, and therefore to the daily living out of the justice and peace that witness to that kingdom. Clearly in the parishes that are most serious about liturgical renewal these kinds of connections are being made.

I have spent a good deal of time trying to analyze why I was so perturbed by the fact that the majority of the those interviewed mentioned the exchange of peace and/or the holding hands at the Lord's Prayer as the high point of the Sunday eucharistic liturgy. These are not bad things in themselves. As a matter of fact, they are rather healthy signs that people (for the most part) want to worship together and not in splendid isolation. Clearly, emphasizing the communal dimension of eucharist has made its mark on at least a significant portion of Catholic worshipers. Clearly, people have been profoundly influenced by the Rite of Christian Initiation of Adults, which in my opinion acts as a kind of subtext for the whole survey. At the same time, however, we need to ask whether the most transcendent and the more challenging aspects of the eucharist, as outlined in the *Lima Document* above, need to be heeded. It is clear to me that they do.

Part of the effort to expand the sacramental images that appeal to people in the liturgy must also involve the way liturgical actions, people, and things are described. I noted that the survey questioners consistently employed the term "celebrant" rather than "presider." In this practice they are well within the usage that has been enshrined in Vatican II's Constitution on the Liturgy as well as the General Instruction on the Roman Missal. But experience of the liturgical renewal has made us aware that the assembly is the true celebrant of the liturgy—the assembly, that is, in Christ. The presider plays a necessary but limited and well-defined role in the celebration.[24] This is not a matter of quibbling about technical terms, for words do make a difference as to how people perceive reality. Persistence in using misleading words encourages persistence in a way of thinking that most contemporary students of the liturgy, myself included, consider misguided. Another example is the use of the term "offertory" or the phrase "offertory procession." Once again this corresponds to official usage, at least with regard to the chant that accompanies this portion of the celebration. Once again, it is not quibbling over niceties to suggest that "offertory" connotes an independent action, independent, that is, of the eucharistic prayer. Presentation of the gifts and/or preparation of the gifts and table, though verbally a bit more awkward, connote much better the preparatory nature of this ritual action (and might even someday have the salutary effect of helping presiders to be attentive to the rubrics of the sacramentary which direct an action of placing the gifts rather than offering them up). Gender-inclusive language does not exhaust the areas of linguistic carefulness in contemporary liturgy.

ISSUES FOR PASTORAL REFLECTION

In addition to the more fundamental questions of experience as a category for liturgical theology and sacramental imagery, I want to discuss three areas that call for pastoral reflection. The first two seem to me to be more pressing.

Eucharistic Prayer

It can be stated rather directly and with little doubt that, with the possible exception of its sung acclamations, the eucharistic prayer is experienced by participants in this survey as the dullest part of the eucharistic liturgy. On one level, given what was said earlier about levels of experience being deeper than the superficially conscious, this need not be terribly troubling. People do have a native sense of the importance of the eucharistic prayer, even if they do not attend to it. On another level, however, we must ask: "Must it be so boring?" After all, the General Instruction on the Roman Missal states unequivocally that the eucharistic prayer is the "center and high point" of the celebration.[25] However true this may be theologically, it is certainly not the case experientially.

It could be that the long overdue focus on communion has made the eucharistic prayer seem less important in the minds of any number of Catholic worshipers. And I would even be willing to argue the correctness of that perception—primacy in theory as in practice belongs to the culminating moment of the eucharistic action, the sharing of communion. Yet surely the articulation of the action itself deserves better than to be practically ignored.

That the eucharistic prayer is very little attended to points, in my opinion, to a weakness in the reformed order of the Roman eucharist. From the blessing formulas at the preparation of the gifts to the invitation to communion there are simply too many words, too many prayers. In part this is a result of the compromises that resulted from adopting the *Ordo Romanus Primus* as well as several medieval developments as the model of the eucharistic rite. Here we would do well to learn from the current order of the eucharist of the Episcopal *Book of Common Prayer* (1979) or the *Lutheran Book of Worship* (1978), where the eucharistic prayer can stand out in the eucharistic action because it is not hedged in by other prayers. Were I to be asked to rewrite this part of the liturgy, I would suggest dropping the blessing formulas, the "Pray, brothers and sisters" and its response, the prayer over the gifts, the embolism after the Lord's Prayer, and the prayer preceding the greeting of peace, not to mention the private prayers of the presider which inevitably get spoken aloud contrary once again to the rubrical directives. Perhaps this suggestion reflects my penchant for "minimalist" music, but I am convinced that, were this suggestion taken, nothing important would be lost in the liturgy, and *a fortiori* the eucharistic prayer could stand out as *the* central prayer of the celebration.

Merely highlighting the eucharistic prayer by deleting what ends up seeming like incessant chatter is not sufficient. The lack of attention given to the eucharistic prayer also implies that it is not being prayed well. It is prayed without passion, without a sense of its importance. There is often the sense that a variable preface or particular eucharistic prayer is not chosen so much for its connection to the liturgy of the word as for convenience or simply because the text has not been used for a while. Perhaps public prayer is a lost art; perhaps presiders need to be convinced that if they do not passionately mean what they say when they pray the eucharistic prayer, no one will listen.

My final recommendation with regard to the eucharistic prayer is that people must be invited to active listening. Having worshipers kneel during the prayer not only reinforces a chasm between "celebrant" and assembly, it invites the assembly to be passive. Active participation does not mean that everyone needs to do everything in the liturgy, as Ralph Keifer pointed out,[26] but it does mean that they should be given cues to listen actively. Only the posture of standing will achieve this result in contemporary American culture. In addition, people might also be invited to participate bodily by raising their hands in the *orans* position, a gesture that I have seen work quite effectively in some churches. The renewal of the liturgy in the past twenty-five years has paid far too little attention to what might be called "the choreography of the assembly." Finally, the practice of a number of acclamations in the eucharistic prayers for Masses with children ought to be adapted to all the eucharistic prayers. One thing the survey reveals conclusively is that not only children have short attention spans.

PROCLAMATION OF THE WORD

The second major area calling for reflection is the proclamation of the word. The balancing of more ritual factors with greater attention to the word of God has been one of the crowning achievements of the Second Vatican Council and of the subsequent liturgical reform.[27] The expansion of the Sunday, feastday, and daily lectionaries has without doubt enriched Catholics and inspired a profound desire among them for greater appreciation of the Scriptures. On the other hand, the survey makes it quite clear that the proclamation of the word in the course of liturgical celebration is heard more for the quality and personality of the readers than for its content. In the interviews one finds the consistent comment that the lector read well but the person interviewed cannot really recall the content of the reading, except perhaps for the biblical book from which it was taken. (It would have been interesting to see how much of the liturgy of the word those interviewed recalled without prompting by the interviewers.)

All this calls for some serious analysis. On the one hand, it must be admitted that the proclamation of the word is not a lecture class where students are expected to take notes and recall in detail the content of what was said. (Even the "less active" parishioners selected for the interviews seemed to me to be fairly involved in the church, and therefore one must surmise that the readings are not being heard at all by the vast majority of Catholic worshipers.) On the other hand, if a part of Scripture is proclaimed, it should make some sort of impact. I suspect that, as was the case for the eucharistic prayer, the readings are simply not being heard because they are read ("proclaimed" would be too strong a word) without passion and conviction and without a great deal of interest. In an era when our attention is so clearly dominated by the electronic media, we need to recognize that the word of God will fall on deaf ears if it is not proclaimed with a sense that it is vital, indispensable for authentic human living. The first, but not only, criterion for lectors is that they believe what they are reading. This means not only that they read well but also that they have interiorized the meaning of what is to be proclaimed.

But the fault does not lie with the proclaimers alone. Without some form of introduction to the readings listeners have no content in which to put them. I for one am convinced that our liturgy needs less didacticism and not more, but it seems that some form of catechesis is called for here. This catechesis could be achieved in one of several ways. One approach would be to habituate parishioners to reading an introduction to the next week's Scriptures in the Sunday bulletin. Another would be to provide a brief oral introduction to the three readings either before the liturgy begins or just before the readings themselves.

A more radical solution would involve changing the time-honored sequence of the readings. Currently, and for as long as we have had descriptions of Christian worship, selections from the Bible are read in ascending order, from the least to the most important. There were a number of good reasons for doing this in the early church. The typological and salvation-history view that Christians took made it logical to place the gospel at the culmination of the readings. Perhaps there was also an effort to differentiate the Christian biblical proclamation from that of the Jews, who read the Bible on the Sabbath in descending order—from the Law to the Prophets. The survey shows that if any of the readings "grabs" people it is the gospel. Perhaps we ought to read the gospel first to provide some sort of context for the other readings. I cannot here dwell on the "problem" of the second reading. Except for the major seasons and feasts when all the readings are interrelated, the second reading (from one of the New Testament letters) has no connection with either the selection from the Jewish Scriptures or the Gospel. Despite the advantage of providing greater riches from the Bible, this reading is lost on most people; further reform of Catholic worship should consider dropping this second reading in the Sundays of the Year.

To summarize: our theological statements about the nature and power of the liturgy of the word have not been matched by liturgical efforts or performance. Needless to say, the homily must also be included under this indictment, for it seems both on the basis of the survey and my observation that this is when worshipers are truly eager to hear something significant for their lives. As Bishop John Cummins, then chairman of the Bishops' Committee on the Liturgy, remarked at the 1984

meeting of national liturgical commissions in Rome, homiliz-
ing "has often enough evidenced a mediocre practice."[28] In
this area I would have to say that there has been significant
improvement in the twenty-five years of liturgical renewal. At
least one could come to this conclusion on the basis of the majority of comments made in the survey. A cogent, coherent,
succinct, and passionate homily that relates God's word to
contemporary concerns remains, however, a great challenge to
many preachers. I cannot even begin to analyze here the reasons for this and possible solutions. It suffices to say that
many preachers need to be convinced of the worthwhile nature of their task.

The Importance of Liturgy

The final area I have chosen for analysis is somewhat more
intangible than either the eucharistic prayer or the liturgy of
the word. Do people experience the Sunday liturgy as an important weekly event? On the basis of this survey and the similar study of American parishes undertaken by the University
of Notre Dame,[29] it is difficult to express a simple judgment on
this issue. Yet I believe it is one of the most important questions we need to ask.

The work of Vatican II and the subsequent efforts at renewal undertaken throughout the world point to the vital position
that worship has in Christian life. One does not even need
documents or theological analyses to come to the common
sense conclusion that the weekly assembly of Christians forms
their identity as a people and provides the inspiration for their
common mission. At the same time it has been my frequent
observation that many if not most worshiping assemblies do
not sense the Sunday eucharist as very important. Again this
is a quality that is not easy to pin down. It is analogous to Cardinal Newman's concept of "illative sense" in the arena of
faith. This is to say, when all is said and done, an affirmation
of faith involves not only rationally sound ideas but a sense of
"thatness," an intuition of the inexplicable but nonetheless
real truth of the object of belief, which demands commitment
as well as intellectual agreement.

Why is this liturgical illative sense missing? The answer lies in vague and mysterious terms like "atmosphere" and "aura." It has everything to do with the nature of a liturgical space, the quality of its decorations, the lighting, acoustics, and—above all—the sense of excitement and engagement that animates the liturgical ministers. Such an illative sense is, as they say, caught rather than taught. The lack of it is what I think people refer to when they claim that Catholic liturgy has lost its sense of "mystery"—a common enough complaint. This lament is so wide-spread that there is doubtlessly some truth to it. I fear, however, that what people mean by "mystery" has more to do with a "Wizard of Oz" image of liturgy and with a God whose transcendence is characterized by remoteness and wrath. The awe that the liturgical experience of the living God ought to inspire in us is not that of cringing serfs, but that of a people who pour out their profound gratitude for the mighty acts of God in Jesus Christ, who has set us free; it is the awe and reverence that are called for by the presence of God in the simplest and most human actions when these actions are performed in faith.

Merely to turn to past means for creating this sense is not a solution at all but rather an escape, an admission of defeat. No, the task of engendering an atmosphere in which the public liturgical activity of the church not only is but seems important challenges us to be thoroughly contemporary while standing firm in the tradition. And being contemporary does not mean surrendering to pop culture or the whim of the moment or to a superficial reaction to what people claim they are experiencing. It means being so thoroughly convinced that the ritual symbols of Christian faith are crucial for truly human life in this world that this conviction is contagious and apparent. This is what I mean by "the importance of liturgy."

* * * * * *

Needless to say, there are many other areas of the survey undertaken by the pastoral liturgical centers that could be examined here: the relationship of liturgy and music and the arts, further analysis of the corporate nature of Christian worship, the great change in the image and role of the priest, and the like. But as was stated in one of my favorite comments in the interviews (with regard to the length of the Sunday liturgy): "We can only endure so much." I have surveyed here only a few of the many important issues that surface in the survey—and these from the limited perspective of a liturgical theologian. I readily admit to some "waffling" as I studied the survey itself. At times it seemed to me that the liturgical renewal has proceeded apace and that the gains made by liturgical theology in the past century are well represented at least in these fifteen parishes concerned with providing an excellent liturgy. At times I was struck by how many areas need vast improvement and by how little practice has kept pace with our theory.

If this essay has for the most part concentrated on the latter set of reactions, it is most probably due to the personal predilections of the writer. Much remains to be accomplished, but much has already been accomplished. I believe that we are well on the way toward the definitive reception of the council's work.

Notes

1. The results of this survey and a colloquium held at Georgetown University and sponsored by the Georgetown Center for Liturgy and the Arts, the Center for Pastoral Liturgy at Notre Dame, the Corpus Christi Center of Phoenix, and the Loyola Pastoral Institute of Liturgy in New York, are to be published by Lawrence Madden, ed., *The Gift Understood: The Shape of the Liturgy in the U.S.: Twenty-Five Years after the Second Vatican Council's Reform* (Washington, D.C.: Georgetown University Press and Collegeville: The Liturgical Press, 1991).

2. See Hans Küng, *Theology for the Third Millennium: An Ecumenical View* (New York: Doubleday, 1988) 170-206. On the shift from classical to modern, see Bernard Lonergan, "Theology in Its New Context," in *A Second Collection* (Philadelphia: Westminster Press, 1975).

3. Bernard Leeming, *Principles of Sacramental Theology* (Westminster, MD: Newman Press, 1956).

4. Bernard Cooke, *Sacraments and Sacramentality* (Mystic, CT: Twenty-Third Publications, 1983).

5. R. Vaillancourt, *Toward a Renewal of Sacramental Theology* (Collegeville: The Liturgical Press, 1979).

6. Aidan Kavanagh, *On Liturgical Theology* (New York: Pueblo Publishing Co., 1981); David N. Power, *Unsearchable Riches: The Sym-*

bolic Nature of Liturgy (New York: Pueblo Publishing Co., 1984); Robert F. Taft, chapters on the theology of the liturgy of the hours in his *Liturgy of the Hours in East and West* (Collegeville: The Liturgical Press, 1986).

7. Bernard J. Lee, ed., 7 volumes (Collegeville: The Liturgical Press, 1987).

8. Karl Rahner, *The Church and the Sacraments* (New York: Herder and Herder, 1963).

9. Edward Schillebeeckx, *Christ the Sacrament of the Encounter with God* (New York: Sheed and Ward, 1963).

10. See Karl Rahner, "The Theology of the Symbol," *Theological Investigations* IV (Baltimore: Helicon, 1966) 221-252. On the symbolization process in general, see Peter Berger, *The Sacred Canopy: Elements of a Sociological Theory of Religion* (Garden City, NY: Doubleday, 1967); Ernst Cassirer, *An Essay on Man* (New Haven: Yale University Press, 1944).

11. We have to be rather careful about our judgments of the theology of the past. While in many ways it may not be useful today, it emphasized values that we are apt to ignore. For an even-handed evaluation of models employed in various theologies of the liturgy, see James Empereur, *Models of Liturgical Theology*, Alcuin/Grow Liturgical Study, vol. 4 (Bramcote, Notts: Grove Books, 1987).

12. One exception is David Power, whose *Unsearchable Riches* is a valuable first attempt. Unfortunately Power's presuppositions are not laid out as clearly as one might wish. Another tentative step in the development of such a critical hermeneutic is the work of Margaret Mary Kelleher, for example, her "Liturgical Theology: A Task and a Method," *Worship* 62 (1988) 2-25, based on the theological method of Bernard Lonergan.

13. George A. Lindbeck, *The Nature of Doctrine: Religion and Theology in a Post Liberal Age* (Philadelphia: Westminster Press, 1984).

14. For a critique of Eliade's approach somewhat akin to Lindbeck's point of view, see Jonathan Z. Smith, *To Take Place: Toward Theory in Ritual* (Chicago: University of Chicago Press, 1987), esp. 1-23; also the chapter entitled "The Wobbling Pivot" in his *Map Is Not Territory* (Leiden: Brill, 1978) 88-103.

15. Lindbeck, *Nature of Doctrine* 17-18.

16. What I call here the "subjectivist bias" is treated as the "subjectification of reality in an article by M.F. Mannion, "Liturgy and the Present Crisis of Culture," *Worship* 62 (1988) 102-107. For a similar cultural analysis of the social crisis facing liturgy, see R.T. Scott, "The Likelihood of Liturgy," *Anglican Theological Review* 62 (1980) 103-120.

17. See the perceptive comments on boredom and ritual in Robert F. Taft, "Sunday in the Byzantine Tradition," in his *Beyond East and West: Problems in Liturgical Understanding* (Washington, D.C.: The Pastoral Press, 1984) 33, 43. As Taft says succinctly and quite correctly: "Variety is not the answer to trash."

18. Prosper of Aquitaine, *Indiculus de Gratia Dei* (PL 51:209). See Aidan Kavanagh, *On Liturgical Theology* 3-22. See also Paul DeClerck, "Lex Orandi, Lex Credendi: sens originel et avatar historique d'un adage équivoque," *Questions liturgiques* 59 (1978) 193-212.

19. Maurice F. Wiles, *The Making of Christian Doctrine* (London: Cambridge University Press, 1967).

20. On this subject, see Teresa Berger, "Lex Orandi, Lex Credendi, Lex Agendi: Auf dem Weg zu einer ökumenisch konsensehaftigen Verhaltnisbestimmung von Liturgie, Theologie und Ethik," *Archiv für Liturgiewissenschaft* 27 (1985) 425-432. This is also a concern of David Power, *Unsearchable Riches*.

21. Gordon Lathrop, "Chronicle: AIDS and the Cup," *Worship* 62 (1988) 162-163.

22. See, for example, Susanne K. Langer, *Philosophy in a New Key*, 2d ed. (Cambridge, MA: Harvard University Press, 1978) 54-75; Power, *Unsearchable Riches* 62-70. Several terms have been used for such multiple meaning in symbols. Power employs "polysemy," whereas I prefer "multivalence" or "polyvalence."

23. World Council of Churches, *Baptism, Eucharist and Ministry*, Faith and Order Paper no. 111 (Geneva: World Council of Churches, 1982), Eucharist 3-26.

24. See further comment on this in my "The Eucharist: Who May Preside?", *Commonweal* 115:15 (9 September 1988) 462-466.

25. General Instruction on the Roman Missal, no. 54.

26. Ralph Keifer, *To Give Thanks and Praise* (Washington, D.C.: The Pastoral Press, 1980) 139-151.

27. See, for example, Constitution on the Sacred Liturgy, nos. 24, 35, 51; Introduction to the Lectionary, no. 10.

28. John S. Cummins, "Twenty Years of Liturgical Renewal in the United States: Assessments and Prospects," in *Thirty Years of Liturgical Renewal*, ed., Frederick R. McManus (Washington, D.C.: United States Catholic Conference, 1987) 244.

29. See Mark Searle, "The Notre Dame Study of Catholic Parish Life," *Worship* 60 (1986) 312-333.

14

The Bible
and the Liturgy

SEVERAL YEARS AGO A COUSIN OF MINE TOLD ME THAT ON A RECENT
Sunday the lector at church got up to do the first reading and
announced: "A reading from the Book of the Prophet
Maláchee." The lector's error in giving the prophet Malachi an
Italian surname is actually instructive for our understanding
of the relationship between the liturgy and the Bible. It points
out, even if unconsciously, that the Bible has always been read
and understood within a particular historical context; in other
words, it always needs to be inculturated. We can never pre-
sume that the Bible will be understood automatically. In fact,
the varieties of understandings that have been attributed to
the Bible down through the centuries are partly what makes
the study of the Bible itself and its relation to the liturgy so
fascinating.

Basically I want to ask the question: What shall we read in
church, *and why*?

Let me deal with the "why" first. Our topic is important because it touches one of the most pressing issues in theology
today: What is the status of the Bible as an authority for theology? I hope that raising this and all the right questions surrounding it will help anyone concerned with liturgy to get a
better grasp on the vital issues of the relation between the
Bible and the liturgy.

My basic question then is: What should we read in church? But it seems to me that I have to deal with two other questions before I get to that one. First, just how authoritative is or should be the Bible for the church today? Second, given what we say about the status of the Bible, how are we to understand the relationship of the Scriptures to the liturgy, which I will define here simply as the ongoing worship life of the church.

THE STATUS OF THE BIBLE TODAY

In 1982 Edward Farley, a systematic theologian at Vanderbilt University, published an important but much neglected book entitled *Ecclesial Reflection*. In it he discussed the question of just what authoritative status the Bible, doctrine, and church officials have. It is his conviction that "the house of authority" has fallen. In other words, theology after the Enlightenment of the seventeenth and eighteenth centuries can no longer take the authority of church doctrine, a living officialdom, or even the Bible for granted. None of these is automatically a criterion for understanding and living out the Christian faith. This is, of course, a question that has been asked by Protestant theology for at least two hundred years—and it is still a burning issues for Protestant theologians. Catholics have come to this point a bit more slowly. One has only to recall the struggles over Modernisn in the Roman Catholic Church at the beginning of this century to realize how recently Catholic biblical scholars have been given the freedom to investigate the Scriptures in a critical fashion. Only recently have Catholic interpreters "received permission" to get behind the biblical texts themselves and ask questions about the social and intellectual background of the books that make up the Jewish and Christian Bible. Only in the last half of the twentieth century have Catholic researchers been given the freedom to recognize what is surely a common view today— that the Bible, even the New Testament, does not contain a unified theology or Christology so much as theolo*gies* or Christolo*gies* or ecclesiolo*gies*. And when one analyzes the use of biblical material in such Roman Catholic documents from the Congregation for the Doctrine of the Faith as the 1976 statement on women's ordination, the 1982 document on the minister of the eucharist, or the 1986 statement on homosexu-

ality, one wonders if anything at all has been learned at all in
official circles about biblical research.

The absoluteness of the biblical witness—by which I mean
reading the Bible purely at face value—has been relativized today by critical scholarship. It fact, it seems to me that the profoundly radical discoveries of critical scholarship with regard
to important issues like the virginal conception of Jesus, the
resurrection narratives, or the ecclesiologies of the New Testament have made many Catholic biblical scholars nervous
about translating their findings for church practice and teaching today. A piece of advice: If you want to be a radical theologian in the church today, study the biblical witness with the
appropriate tools—original languages, archeology, history
with an open mind—and see what happens.

So, our appreciation of the Bible today is heavily dependent
on a critical reading of the scriptural texts that tells us often—
if not what the text does say—at least what the text *does not
say*. Such critical reading also alerts us to the necessity of understanding the biblical text in its context—social, economic,
political—and helps us to realize that often the questions that
we bring to the scriptural text are not the questions the biblical
writers were addressing.

What about the Bible as Revelation?

The Bible is supposed to be revelation, isn't it? I am not
about to deny that, for the role of the Bible in the church has
been improved immeasurably in the course of the last century
and especially in the years just before and since the Second
Vatican Council, whose Constitution on Divine Revelation has
given it such a new breath of life. But what do we mean when
we say that the Bible is revelation?

When we talk as Christians about revelation, we discuss
revelation not primarily as the history of God's dealing with a
people (like Israel or Judaism), nor are we treating primarily a
book (as is the case with the Qu'ran of Islam), but primarily
revelation is about a person, Jesus of Nazareth. Primary—first
level—revelation for Christianity is a person, not history or a
book or a set of propositions. Only in second place can we talk
about the faithful witness to this person through whom God
has been definitively revealed in the Scripture and in the tradition of the church. Vatican II's Constitution on Divine Revela-

tion supports this view when it claims that the Bible as the word of God *contains*—not *is* revelation.[1]

This is what makes fundamentalism so fundamentally, (if I can pun), so basically wrong. It substitutes second level revelation for the primary revelation; it substitutes a book for the person of Jesus of Nazareth. Of course, you don't have to be a biblical fundamentalist to be a fundamentalist. Fundamentalism comes in a variety of shapes and sizes that includes the kind of traditionalism that divides churches today. I do not intend to attack tradition, but I will repeat the wise words of Jaroslav Pelikan, who in the first volume of his history of Christian doctrine states: "Tradition is the living faith of the dead, while traditionalism is the dead faith of the living."[2] Fundamentalism cannot be regarded as anything other than idolatry, and a pernicious idolatry at that, for it replaces the revelation of the living God with a religious form: a book, a doctrine, or a church office.

After all, the very formation of the Christian Bible defeats the fundamentalists' claim. Christian exegesis of the Jewish Scriptures, which were what the earliest generation of Christians considered to be the Bible, was an exegesis that was not at all self-evident, but had to be transformed in light of a new principle of interpretation, Jesus himself as the center and focus of the history of God's dealings with humankind. And the documents that go to make up what we call the Christian Scriptures themselves offer a most varied witness to this person of Jesus[3] and the churches the apostles left behind.[4] Moreover, in addition to the need for a new exegesis of the Jewish Scriptures and the variety inherent in the Christian Scriptures themselves, we have to add another factor: for the first century and a half of Christianity, it was not at all clear just what the official Christian Scriptures were. The canon, the definitive collection of books that we call the New Testament, was not settled until the end of the second century, and that after bitter struggles with Gnostics, Marcionites, and Montanists about just exactly how one could interpret Jesus as the Christ. In the words of a number of recent writers as diverse as Willi Marxsen and Gerard Sloyan, the Bible is the church's book. It does not precede Christianity historically nor does it come down from heaven whole and entire like some excellent divine gift.

Rather, it is the product of struggle, division, controversy, and witness of faith. We call it inspired, not because God or an angel or some such divine intervener guided the various writers' hands but because in this collection of diverse writings the church has recognized its faith in Jesus.

The Bible therefore is revelation only in a secondary sense; it contains a great deal of diversity that we can no longer ignore. This means that the Bible itself is always interpretation, not the mere recounting of facts. It is always in some sense theology. Finally, the Bible is the product of the primitive church's experience of what it means to live with the risen Jesus of Nazareth as the focus of human existence.

What I have just done is to cast great doubt on the so-called scripture principle of the Protestant Reformation. That reform, although I cannot deny that it enriched the Christian faith by a necessary return or retrieval of biblical sources, argued that the Bible is the *norma normans non normata* or, to put it in English, the norm that cannot be governed by any other norms. I hope to show that this has never been true and it cannot be true, especially with regard to the liturgy. The Christian faith, though necessarily dependent on the biblical witness as the element that offers best access to Jesus Christ, was governed by other considerations as well, including the historical, social, and political situations in which Christians lived.

How Do the Faithful Approach the Bible?

Scripture is always approached with some form of interpretation. In a lucid way, Elizabeth Schüssler-Fiorenza has outlined three major approaches that are taken in biblical interpretation (hermeneutics) today.

Doctrinal Approach. The first way (or *paradigm*, to use her word) is the doctrinal one. In this interpretive approach the Bible contains doctrines or truths that are necessary to salvation, or it contains truths about how to live one's life. It can be mined for data. An extreme example of this can be found in the practice of opening up the Bible, placing one's finger on a passage, and deriving guidance or consolation from it—a practice that has more to do with magic and superstition than with Christian faith. Schüssler-Fiorenza calls this "instant inspiration" and compares it to instant coffee. The danger inherent in this approach is, of course, that the Bible can become a series of proof texts for one's already-formed theological or religious opinions.

There are two variants within this approach. The first is the illustrative approach that uses the Bible to prove something else. A favorite method of this way of reading the Bible is called allegory, where the text stands for another kind of truth altogether. An example of allegorical exegesis is the treatise of the fourth-century Cappadocian theologian, Gregory of Nyssa, entitled *On the Life of Moses*. In this treatise Gregory considers the life of Moses as an allegory for the progress of the human soul in its ascent to God. Needless to say, this is almost certainly not what the biblical writers of the various traditions of the Pentateuch had in mind.

A second variant is the psychoanalytic approach in which the text is made to symbolize a psychological state. How am I like the man born blind or the paralytic, or the prodigal son, for example? According to Schüssler-Fiorenza, the liturgy itself is a good example of this illustrative approach because it forces the biblical texts into themes that the text itself does not warrant.

So, the doctrinal paradigm of biblical interpretation looks to the Scriptures for certain kinds of data that will make the Scriptures relevant to contemporary concerns. I part company with Schüssler-Fiorenza in that I don't think these approaches are necessarily bad (except for putting one's finger on a biblical text for instant inspiration). The Bible does contain facts and doctrines. It can be an excellent starting point for themes that may not have been the original author's concern. It has, in the great spiritual classics of writers like Origen and Gregory of Nyssa, provided the basis for profoundly moving reflections on the Christian faith and human life. On the other hand, Schüssler-Fiorenza is correct in pointing out that this approach does not render *the* meaning of a biblical text and so must always be regarded with some caution.

Historical Approach. A second major approach is the historical paradigm. It offers what Schüssler-Fiorenza calls "value-neutral" exegesis; that is, it limits itself purely and simply to the best and most accurate understanding possible of the texts in question as well as their historical and social background. The trouble with such an "objective" or objectivist approach to the biblical text is that is encourages people to believe that only what can be stated as literally true in Scripture is really true. In other words, if the magi from the east did not really bring gifts of gold, incense, and myrrh to the child Jesus, then there is no historical truth to the passage at all. For the purposes of religious faith, if this approach were taken to its extreme, the vast majority of the biblical writings would have to be considered as nothing more than mere pious twaddle. Schüssler-Fiorenza has correctly pointed out that most American graduate departments of biblical studies favor this historical approach to the Scriptures and leave their students, who often become seminary professors, in a quandry as to what to teach their students. The seminary professors of course tend to take the approach that was taught to them, leaving their students who will become preachers in a similar quandry as to what to preach.

Pastoral-Theological Approach. There is a third approach, the one that Schüssler-Fiorenza herself espouses, an approach that can avoid the pitfalls of the doctrinal and the historical paradigms. This third approach she calls the pastoral-theological paradigm. In it the biblical texts are given their due as documents that respond to pastoral problems in a theological way. In other words, the biblical critic tries to understand the original context for this or that portion of Scripture and then to apply it to appropriate parallels in contemporary life. For example, St. Paul in 1 Corinthians 10 treats the question of meat sacrificed to idols and whether Christians should eat it. This particular problem has little relevance today, but Paul's solution to the question does provide contemporary Christians some principles on how to act in the face of a culture that is at least sometimes opposed to Christian faith. For Schüssler-Fiorenza this approach also brings critical questions to bear upon the documents themselves, understanding their context in order to assess their value for various Christian communities today. She puts it:

> We have to learn that not all texts speak to all situations and to everyone. It is therefore necessary for the minister to learn how to determine the situation and needs of his or her congregation with the same sophistication he or she applies to the study of biblical texts. Moreover, he or she must be aware of the sociological, psychological, cultural and political influences that shape

the world and the understanding of the self and of the community of faith. A repetition of biblical texts will not suffice. [5]

The net result of the pastoral-theological paradigm is an insistence that the Bible must be approached with a certain amount of reserve and suspicion. Indeed, the phrase "hermeneutics of suspicion" has become quite popular today and points correctly, in my opinion, to the need to suspect that a document may well have some self-serving purpose in mind, a purpose that must be unearthed and examined if the text itself is to speak to us in an authentic manner. The dilemma for believers, of course, is that at the same time that we bring a critical eye to these texts, we also approach them with faith. Despite my attempt to relativize the position of the Bible as an absolute authority in Christian faith and doctrine, it retains a privileged status among all the sources of theology as the source that is closest to the original or primary revelation in Jesus. Though it is a grave error to approach the Bible as a fundamentalist, we still owe to it our obedience of faith, and it governs every aspect of theology and practice, including liturgy. In that sense, the Bible is a norm that cannot be superceded.

BIBLE AND LITURGY: THEIR INTERRELATION

The relation between the Bible and the liturgy requires, as I have shown, that the Bible be read critically. It is necessary to avoid a naive approach to biblical inspiration, as if the Bible were the directly dictated word of God to us. This raises some important questions about how the Bible is used in the liturgy. I want to deal with four issues: (1) how the liturgy is thoroughly biblical; (2) how the liturgy, calendar, and lectionary have governed and continue to govern the understanding of the Bible; (3) what biblical passages we read in the liturgy; and (4) how we read them in the liturgy.

The Liturgy Is Thoroughly Biblical

Let me quickly name those parts of the eucharist of the Roman Rite that are taken directly from Scripture or relate to it closely: entrance psalm, greeting (at least in the form "May the grace . . ."), readings and intervening chants, the acclamation

"Holy, Holy, Holy" (from Isaiah 6 and Psalm 118), institution narrative of the eucharistic prayer (though not word-for-word), Lord's Prayer, Lamb of God, and communion psalm. This comprises a considerable portion of what is said or sung during the liturgy, which should not surprise us. Because religious forms are inherently traditional (they link the present believers to the experience of past generations), it stands to reason that the charter documents of the community of faith will be used extensively in its worship. Hence, readings from the Scripture as well as use of biblical material in liturgical texts is one of the ways that the community experiences continuity with the past and identity in the here and now.

That the liturgy is biblical also means that its *tone* is biblical. By this I mean not merely that it employs biblical material but also that the liturgy itself performs much the same function as Scripture, not by looking back to a founding event as a piece of history, as if they were dead and past, but by rendering that event present again through its enactment. In liturgy it is the repetition of the pattern, a ritualized form, that molds people's lives as a community of faith. This is precisely what happens with the reading or proclamation of Scripture.[6] We do not read Scripture so much to discover what we don't know or have forgotten, as to let the pattern of the biblical story continue to form us.

So then the liturgy is thoroughly biblical both in its context and in its form. At the same time we need to recognize that the Bible is liturgical. We are accustomed to think of the Bible as a book (indeed, that is what the word *Bible* means). But in its origins as oral material and in its influence over the ages, Scripture has had an effect on the Christian community more by being heard than read. (I am not going to go into the theories about various biblical books like 1 Peter or Revelation as examples of early Christian liturgies. Nor do most scholars find those theories that hold that the various Gospels were originally lectionaries to be persuasive.) My only point is to underline the part that Scripture has played by being proclaimed. Think, for example, of St. Anthony, the founder of monasticism, who according to his biographer became a monk after hearing *in church,* "if you wish to be perfect, go, sell all you have, and follow me." I cannot deny that the Bible has had great impact on its readers. Think, for example, of three figures, all in their thirties, who changed the course of Christian history because of their experience of reading the Letter to the Romans: Augustine of Hippo, Martin Luther, and John Wesley. Of course, these men were not merely scholars in their libraries but had been exposed to the word of God proclaimed liturgically. In fact, hearing Romans read in church was a part of Wesley's own conversion experience. For the majority of Christians, the Bible has had its greatest influence by being heard, and being heard in a liturgical setting.

Often the liturgy takes both its forms and content directly from the Scripture. This can be demonstrated by appealing to Gregory Dix's famous description of the fourfold shape of the liturgy,[7] or by citing Cyril of Jerusalem's reasoning for the anointing after baptism (as contrasted with the usual Syrian practice of only prebaptismal anointing). Cyril argues that the anointing is done at this point because this was the sequence of the Jordan event where the Spirit descended upon Jesus after he came up from the water.[8] In other words, Scripture acts as a warrant for the liturgical pattern even when that pattern is not exactly duplicated by liturgical ceremony. A host of other examples, particularly of how the liturgy was interpreted by the early Christian writers, is provided by Jean Daniélou in his book on the liturgy and biblical typology, which has the same title as this chapter, *The Bible and the Liturgy*.[9]

The liturgy is biblical, and the Bible is (among other things, to be sure) liturgical. Moreover, the Bible and the liturgy belong together because the reading of the Scripture provides the setting and motivation for liturgical actions. I am speaking of the pattern of proclamation and response that characterizes every sacramental activity, from baptism and eucharist to weddings, ordinations, anointing, and reconciliation. Liturgical preaching, therefore, always connects the proclamation of the community's story with the action that is about to take place. Sadly, this seems to be a principle that is more often than not ignored.

How Liturgy Governs Biblical Interpretation

Let us examine how the liturgy, particularly by means of the lectionary and the assignment of feasts, has affected the understanding of the Bible. It is well known that the earliest use of scripture readings in the liturgy followed the principle of *lectio continua,* continuous reading. In fact, some of the early commentaries on various biblical books, like those of Origen, reflect this practice. The books would be commented on in sequence because they were read chapter by chapter in church.

Thomas Talley has recently proposed a theory that reading the Gospel in sequence, beginning with Epiphany, accounts for a number of features in the development of the liturgical year.[10] Be that as it may, by the end of the fourth century we begin to find developments in the lectionary that depart from the principle of continuous reading. Many of these developments had less to do with feasts or the content of the books of the Bible than with the goal of situating the community in the *place* where the readings were being read.

A few examples will suffice. When Christians celebrated the octave of Easter at Jerusalem in the early fifth century, they made the rounds of the various churches and shrines of the holy city. On Easter Wednesday they celebrated the eucharist at the church called Sion, which had originally been the headquarters of the Christian community. On that day they began reading from the Letter of James, surely a strange piece of Scripture to read during this week. The reason that James was chosen is quite simple and has little to do with Easter festivities. Sion, the type of the heavenly Jerusalem, a traditional Easter-time theme, was represented by its first bishop, James (the brother of the Lord), and thus reading from the letter of James seemed appropriate. The next day the liturgy took place at the church called Eleona atop the Mount of Olives. Here the gospel reading is what attracts the attention of anyone studying the Jerusalem lectionary. The gospel passage for that day was Matthew 5:1-12, the beatitudes. Why the beatitudes during Easter week? Simply because of the association of the Mount of Olives with the Sermon on the Mount of which the beatitudes are the introduction.

Lest we think that Jerusalem represents an isolated instance, let us turn briefly to the church at Rome and a lectionary that still affects us today. The medieval lenten lectionary of the city of Rome is fascinating, and one of its most interesting asspects is that there is no rhyme or reason to the choice of weekday readings. No rhyme or reason, that is, until one pays attention to the churches in which the readings were proclaimed. Like Jerusalem, Rome had a liturgy that was called stational, meaning that different churches or shrines were used for the main liturgy, depending on the specific Sunday or the particular feast being celebrated.[11]

The choice of biblical readings has traditionally been governed less by the narrative of the Bible itself, less by a choice of seasonal themes, but more by specific, local, contextualized situations. The liturgy itself takes the scripture passage out of context to bring its own interpretations. The lectionary *is* a biblical interpretation. This is why preachers need to do far more than technical exegesis of passages selected in the lectionary. They have to attempt to understand why the liturgy is employing such passages on a particular day. The clearest example of this is the use of the three great Johannine passages (the woman at the well, the man born blind, and the raising of Lazarus) on the third, fourth, and fifth Sundays of Lent in Cycle A. Not to understand that these three chapters of the Gospel of John are used because of their significance for initiation at the approaching Easter Vigil is to miss the point of their inclusion in the lenten liturgy. The joining of the Bible and the liturgy cannot be understood if we fail to appreciate the fact that the lectionary is already an interpretation of Scripture.

What Should We Read in Church?

The Public Broadcasting System once aired a provocative two-part film dealing with the evangelical right in America, entitled *Thy Kingdom Come, Thy Will Be Done*. The second part of the film focused on the First Baptist Church of Dallas, a kind of evangelical empire unto itself. In this part the interviewers talked to a professor at the church's bible college who had recently been fired for promoting social justice concerns. Now, mind you, this man was a card-carrying evangelical; he believed in the inerrancy of the Bible. What had been his "sin"? Simply that he insisted on teaching courses on the Gospels. He told the interviewer that the Gospels were rarely treated in the First Baptist Church of Dallas, because if you read them seriously, they raised too many questions about social justice. What *is* read and what *isn't read* in church makes a great deal of difference to the formation of Christian life.

What Are We Reading?

First, there can be little doubt that the current three-year Roman Catholic lectionary (which for the most part has been adopted by other mainline Christian Churches) represents a significant advance over the one-year lectionary of the past. The motive in the reform of Vatican II was perfectly clear: "The treasures of the Bible are to be opened up more lavishly, so that a richer share in God's word may be provided for the faithful. In this way a more representative portion of holy scripture will be read to the people in the course of a prescribed number of years."[12] Of particular value in the restructuring of the lectionary has been the decision to read the synoptic Gospels in three consecutive years, enabling Christians to hear a Gospel more or less as a continuous narrative. More questionable, however, was the decision to retain an exclusively Christological focus when it came to selecting readings from the Jewish Scriptures. The first reading for Sundays in Ordinary Time was taken from the Jewish Scriptures. But this reading was selected by means of what the Introduction to the Lectionary for Mass (no. 66) calls the principle of harmony: the relation of the reading to the gospel reading of the day. The basis for this principle of harmony is the practice of typology, which I addressed in the first part of this article. The second reading (taken from a non-Gospel passage of the Christian Scriptures) has a sequence of its own.

The problem is clear enough. With everything we have learned from the critical study of the Bible, including our recovered respect for the heritage of Israel, should not the Jewish Scriptures get their due? Are they to be interpreted solely by means of typological exegesis, while their own historical context is ignored?

Recently an attempt has been made to rectify this situation. The ecumenical North American Consultation on Common Texts (CCT) has published a three-year lectionary in which the readings from the Jewish Scriptures are selected with a view toward narrative integrity so that, for example, in Cycle A, twenty Sundays have semi-continuous selections from the Pentateuch that are read in conjunction with semi-continuous selections from the Gospel of Matthew, not an unhappy marriage in my opinion. I do not mean to abandon the Christological focus of the liturgy. In fact, as Christians we can legitimatey read the Jewish Scriptures through the lens of Christ. But it seems to me that the CCT proposal moves in the right direction as far as respecting the heritage of the faith of Israel, a direction that our own time and culture call for. Therefore, it seems to me that at least occasionally the Jewish Scriptures should be read as stories that have a legitimate meaning of their own in the story of salvation.

Second, how are the selections made? Let us look at a most important reading from the Christian Scriptures: 1 Corinthians 11, the institution narrative according to the Pauline tradition. This passage is always read in the Roman liturgy for Holy Thursday and in Cycle C for the Solemnity of the Body and Blood of Christ. These are the only times that this passage is read outside the regular weekday cycle. It begins with verse 23: "For I received from the Lord what I also handed on to you, that the Lord Jesus . . ." But the passage cannot be understood adequately if we fail to pay attention to its context. Paul is not merely repeating the institution narrative for its own sake. He is speaking about the setting in which the Corinthians celebrate the Lord's Supper, a setting in which inequality flourishes and the very meaning of the supper is betrayed, as biblical interpreters Elizabeth Schüssler-Fiorenza, Jerome Murphy-O'Connor, and others have noted. Here we have an excellent example of the liturgy so narrowing a biblical text as to change its meaning profoundly. In my opinion, this kind of narrow selection takes Holy Thursday out of the context of the paschal mystery as a whole and reinforces a kind of historical interest in the institution of the eucharist that the reform has generally been concerned to avoid.

How Are We Reading?

Let me turn to the issue of inclusive language. I will pass over the question of inclusive language that deals with human beings. I consider it axiomatic that all such language is to be inclusive. The real issue before us today is what to do with inclusive language that deals with God—not only in the texts of prayers and songs but also in the biblical text itself. How can we remain faithful to the biblical texts that are being proclaimed and at the same time be sensitive to the problems that are raised by the overwhelming male imagery of the Jewish and Christian Bible? I think it would be a serious error for the most part to reinterpret male images like King and Lord, at least in the oral proclamation of the Scripture itself. But perhaps something can be done with regard to the overwhelmingly male tone conveyed by the constant use of the male pronoun with regard to God. I agree with Gail Ramshaw's and Gordon Lathrop's attempt to translate the lectionary in such a way that "he" or "his" is never used for God. Their *Lectionary for the Christian People,*[13] now published for all three of the Sunday and festal cycles, is a model of both inclusive translation of the Scripture and solid principles of translation and interpretation. As human beings we are what we say, and what we say in church must be consistent with standards of justice, respect, and equality.

There is another difficult problem, for example, in Ephesians 5:21-33. In this passage the author illustrates spousal love by a comparison with Christ's love for the church. The passage is read on the 21st Sunday in Ordinary Time in Cycle B, on Tuesday of the 30th Week in Ordinary Time in even numbered years, and it may be used in the liturgy of the word for the sacrament of matrimony. I owe a good deal of my reflection on whether Ephesians 5:21-33 ought to be read in church to a conversation (actually it was more like an argument) that I had with a colleague, who one morning said: "Did you hear that awful thing that was read in church yesterday?" The burden of my colleague's remarks to me was that liturgists had no reasonable basis upon which to defend the validity of the formation of the lectionary. I tried to defend it as best I could, arguing that to excise texts from reading in church would be to create a canon within the canon of Scripture. My last line of defense was that I myself had alluded to the text in a homily the day before and that I thought it was necessary to differentiate the valid and powerful point the author was making about Christ's love for the church from the sexist implications of wives being subservient to their husbands. I argued that this passage could be read in church, but that the preacher had a responsibility to comment on it in its proper context and to deplore any sexist connotations the reading may have.

Today I would go further. It seems to me, since the liturgy has always been selective about what is read from the Bible, that we might well consider that a passage like Ephesians 5, which has so much potential for being misunderstood, should not be read in church. At least I am willing to counsel that it should never be selected for use at weddings. In examples such as these, *what* we read and *how* we read it in the liturgy are related.

* * * * * *

There are more questions here than answers, and the answers themselves are fairly tentative. Perhaps my musings on the relationship of the Bible and liturgy have been able at least to raise some of the right questions—difficult questions that need to be asked in the contemporary church. One thing is certain: Christians have had to struggle with this relationship since the dawn of Christianity, and will continue to do so until the sun rises and sets no more.

Notes

1. Constitution on Divine Revelation, no. 11; see also nos. 8-9.

2. Jaroslav Pelikan, *The Emergence of the Catholic Tradition* (Chicago: The University of Chicago Press, 1971) 9.

3. See James D.G. Dunn, *Unity and Diversity in the New Testament* (Philadelphia: Westminster Press, 1977).

4. See Raymond E. Brown, *The Church the Apostles Left Behind* (New York: Paulist Press, 1984).

5. Elizabeth Schüssler-Fiorenza, *Bread Not Stone: The Challenge of Feminist Biblical Interpretation* (Boston: Beacon Press, 1984) 35-36.

6. See Robert F. Taft, *Beyond East and West: Problems in Liturgical Understanding* (Washington, D.C.: The Pastoral Press, 1984) 1-13.

7. Gregory Dix, *The Shape of the Liturgy* (London: Dacre, 1945) 103-140.

8. Cyril of Jerusalem, *Mystagogical Catechesis* 3:1.

9. Jean Daniélou, *The Bible and the Liturgy* (Notre Dame: University of Notre Dame Press, 1956).

10. Thomas J. Talley, *The Origins of the Liturgical Year* (New York: Pueblo Publishing Co., 1986) 129-134.

11. See my *The Urban Character of Christian Worship: The Origins, Development and Meaning of Stational Liturgy*, Orientalia Christiana Analecta, vol. 228 (Rome: Pontificium Institutum Studiorum Orientalium, 1987).

12. Constitution on the Sacred Liturgy, no. 15.

13. *Lectionary for the Christian People: The Roman, Episcopal, Lutheran Lectionaries*, eds., Gordon Lathrop and Gail Ramshaw (New York: Pueblo Publishing Co., 1986, 1987, 1988).

15

The Liturgical Homily: Nature and Function

IN HIS ELOQUENT MEMOIR OF THE TWENTIETH-CENTURY LITURGICAL movement, Dom Bernard Botte describes the state of preaching in Belgium at the turn of the twentieth century:

> The clergy were poorly prepared for the ministry of the word of God by such substandard teaching. Neither the classes of theology, nor those of Scripture, nor those of the liturgy offered material for preaching. The clergy had nothing to say except for moralizing sermons, the kind they themselves had heard over and over again. They preached out of duty, because it was prescribed, just as they observed the rubrics. I remember the remark of an old Jesuit priest for whom I always had great esteem: "preaching is a bore: you repeat the same thing all the time and that bores everybody." Priests no longer believed in preaching.[1]

No doubt Botte must be exaggerating. Surely there were good preachers somewhere. The general state of preaching, however, seems to be accurately described in his dismal account. It does not take much experience to know that preaching has vastly improved in our own day. In good part this improvement is due to the new vision of the connection between liturgy and preaching fostered by the Second Vatican Council's Constitution on the Sacred Liturgy.[2]

And yet many people remain dissatisfied with what they hear in church. It seems that, for the most part, Roman Catholic preachers are on their way from moralizing sermons which bore everyone to truly liturgical preaching. This essay will deal with what that preaching might look like. Note, it is not about preaching in general but rather about the homily in the context of liturgical celebration.

What is specific to liturgical preaching? The answer is obvious but seems lost on so many preachers that it must be expressed clearly. The homily is liturgical when it takes place in the context of the church's liturgy, namely, as the Introduction to the Lectionary for Mass puts it with regard to the eucharist: "it must always lead the community of the faithful to celebrate the eucharist wholeheartedly."[3] This is to say that the homily is an integral part of the liturgical act; it does not float out there somewhere independent of the service as a whole. When one is preaching liturgically, people should have some sense of why we then proceed to make eucharist, to witness marriage vows, to baptize, and the like. In what follows I hope to fill out this basic principle on the basis of my experience as a listener, a preacher, and as a student of the church's worship. My reflection will focus on seven main points: (1) purpose; (2) subject; (3) length; (4) getting interest; (5) the preacher's own experience; (6) strategic preaching; and (7) credibility. Thus these reflections are not so much about the actual preparation of the homily, since abundant literature exists on this subject,[4] as about getting clarity on the purpose and nature of the liturgical homily as a whole.

Purpose

What purpose does the liturgical homily serve? All too often one gets the impression that the homilist thinks that the preacher has to instruct the people about the meaning of the biblical text, that is, to do exegesis in the pulpit. The result is stultifying. Such a dry examination of the text presumes a basic biblical illiteracy and corresponds to a basic error in our contemporary approach to liturgy, namely, that the liturgy must accomplish everything that the church must do. Thus the liturgy becomes a tool for adult education, social action, and community building. In significant ways the liturgy does enhance these activities of the church, but it cannot bear this weight alone. Worse still, liturgy committees, planners, presiders, and homilists begin to get the impression that their task is to instruct the assembly about some worthy theme with the result that the assembly itself is alienated, sensing that it is being imposed upon by "experts." Simply put, much of contemporary liturgical celebration suffers from forgetting that the liturgy is God's service to us before it is our service to God.[5]

If this mistake is to be avoided, the homily can be conceived of neither as a direct exegesis of the biblical texts nor primarily as instruction, but rather as prayer-filled reflection on the scriptural text in the context of this particular assembly by a person whom the church as a whole has certified as a competent witness. This is in part what ordination does (or better, should) mean. The homilist's task, therefore, is not to instruct the assembly about something with which it is unfamiliar but to inspire and deepen the faith that is already there. The purpose of the homily is invitation to deeper faith, or as the excellent document prepared by the U.S. Catholic Bishops' Committee on Priestly Life and Ministry, *Fulfilled in Your Hearing*, puts it:

> What the preacher can do best of all in this time and this place is to enable this community to celebrate by offering them a word in which they can recognize their own concerns and God's concern for them.[6]

Therefore, the question the preacher must ask is: How is my understanding of the scriptural readings of the day going to enable *this* community both to celebrate and to deepen their faith in daily life? There is no such thing as an all-purpose homily, suitable for every community at every time. This requires the homilist to know the community well. A visiting homilist is an "extraordinary" preacher, regardless of ordination.

Subject

Once one has realized that the purpose of the liturgical homily is the expression of faith by the preacher in order that the members of the assembly might celebrate the liturgy and lead deeper Christian lives, an important question arises as to the subject of the homily. Here my experience as listener, preacher, and student of liturgy has convinced me that each Sunday homily can only be about one aspect of the Christian life. The key word here is *modesty*. For some reason many preacher tend not to realize that the liturgical life of Christians is cumulative in its impact. Everything does not happen all at once every Sunday. Rather, the liturgical experience is the gradual process of people being formed more deeply into what they already are—the Body of Christ. And the effective preacher is one who does not expect "on the spot" results, but rather communicates the patient confidence that the word of God will do its work when it is attended to week after week. As George Guiver has rightly written with regard to daily liturgical prayer: "It is missing the point of the exercise always to expect a pay-off on the nail."[7] We read only discrete portions of the Scripture a Sunday at a time because we can only absorb so much on any one occasion.

My rule of thumb is that people walking down the street after the Sunday eucharist ought to be able to respond to questions from their acquaintances regarding the subject of the Sunday homily with "the preacher talked about such and such today." Of course this requires that the preacher be very clear in preparation about what it is exactly that he wants to get across. This procedure has the further advantage of convincing the preacher beforehand that one has something to say. In my experience people have a much easier time listening to someone who looks and sounds as if that person has something to say. At times, when I am doubtful that I am getting my main point across, I will even ask the congregation if I am making myself clear. No verbal response is needed; the very faces and bodies of members of the assembly give me the answer. I think that even verbal response should be welcome in our churches. It is clear, for example, from the transcripts of the homilies of St. Augustine that the people felt very free to respond with laughter, applause, tears, and shouts. This tradition is maintained particularly in African-American churches and could well be incorporated into other racial/ethnic groups as well.

Length

How long should a homily be? The correct but facetious and somewhat unhelpful answer is: as long as it needs to be. This is dependent upon the listening habits of the assembly.

Among some groups a homily that lasts only ten minutes would be an insult to the assembly. Among others a homily that goes on for twenty minutes would be unconscionably long. In my opinion, the average length of time of an effective homily in a middle-class suburban American parish ought to be from seven to nine minutes, which happens to be the average length of time between commercial advertisements on American television. But other factors are important as well: for example, the length of the liturgy as a whole; having something particular to say that will take either a shorter or longer period of time; a significant occasion or an event in the public sphere. Here too the body language of the assembly should be an indication to the preacher as to how long to continue. Preachers who cannot "read" the body language of a congregation are poor communicators. And poor communicators make dreadful preachers.

Getting Interest

In my experience, if I hear the homilist begin with the words: "In today's three readings . . .," I have already received automatic permission to let my mind wander to what I am cooking for supper, or how the car is running, or what I will be doing in my next class or lecture. This introduction is (almost always) a signal that the preacher is going to do a rather dry textual exegesis with no significant point to it all. Especially in parishes where people have been positively anaesthetized by poor preaching, it is necessary to begin with something—a phrase, a story—that will capture the assembly's interest. I think many homilists regard this simply as a gimmick, but I fear that they overestimate the ability of ordinary people to listen to reasoned argument. In order for people to be "rendered benevolent," as they used to say, they must be grasped by an image, namely, more than their reasoning abilities must be engaged. This is not to say that there is absolutely no room in the homily for reasoned argument, but rather that such argument will only be heard if the imagination of the people has been alerted.

To accomplish this, the assembly's interest must be "piqued" from the outset. Otherwise people will drift off immediately into cloud-cuckoo-land, as I do more often than I want to admit. If this happens to me (who after all has a deep existential and professional stake in these matters), I assume that such is the case with the vast majority of other listeners. An interest-getting beginning to a homily also alerts me to the fact that the homilist has thought out rather thoroughly what will be said, and that, even if I do not get the point at the outset, there will be something of interest for me here somewhere down the line.

The ability to capture and maintain the interest of the assembly also has a great deal to do with the stance of the homilist. By this I mean the homilist's use of a text as well as literally where and how the homilist stands. First the text. I find that most often a text works only to distance myself from people with whom I wish to communicate. People seem much more engaged when preachers know what they want to say well enough to dispense with a text. When a text must be used, and this depends upon the occasion as well as the ability of a homilist to remember, then it should be used as the way an effective politician uses a written speech, namely, as a jumping-off point for communication. After all, even scholarly papers at academic conferences do not come off very well when they are simply read.

On a more basic level, the stance of the preacher also involves where and how the preacher stands. A pulpit as well as a text can act as a shield to block the homilist from the people. It would be more effective for the preacher to have nothing physical intervene between the preacher's body and the assembly—depending, of course, on sight-lines, the overall architecture of the church, portable microphones, and acoustics. In any case, stance also has to do with the body-language of the homilist. The most effective preachers I have heard use their very bodies, not just their mouths, faces, and arms to communicate what they are saying. Perhaps homilists need to see themselves preaching on videotape—once with the sound on and then again with the sound off—to know how they are communicating bodily. These comments about stance also apply to the voice modulation of the preacher. There are certain (monotone) speech patterns which render the listeners practically comatose.

The Preacher's Own Experience

Storytelling has become one of the most popular and effective ways of getting the interest of the assembly and avoiding the pitfalls of arid exegesis in the pulpit. It has the added advantage of capitalizing on the narrative nature of the Gospel itself, that is, to tell a story is to respect the way that Jesus himself preached, thus rendering the homilist at least potentially a more faithful witness in proclaiming the good news.

The more I hear young preachers, many of whom have forgotten the point that telling stories is an effective means of preaching, the more I become convinced that we need to reflect further on the relation between stories and the preacher's own experience. All too often homilists seemed to have gained the impression that the only authentic way of proclaiming the Gospel is to relate it to their own experience. The end result is that they end up seeming to preach about themselves rather than about the Lord; instead of preaching *out* of their experience, they preach more *about* it.

To be genuine, to preach as one person of faith to the whole community of faith assembled, is surely to preach out of one's experience. As Karl Rahner once wrote somewhere, each priest has only profoundly appropriated a few insights into the Gospel and must preach out of these. We must preach out of the core of our human experience of faith or not preach at all. As one priest friend once remarked: "My preaching got an awful lot better when I decided that I would only preach what I believe." But there is a fine line between preaching out of that experience of faith and preaching about one's experience. This is not to say that homilists should not occasionally refer to themselves and their own experience or that of their families and close friends. It is rather to argue that a homilist must be aware of whether or not one is becoming solipsistic in communicating the gospel message. The temptation to become solipsistic is exacerbated by the fact that people tend to like hearing stories about the preacher because such stories render the preacher more accessible, more human. Thus preachers tend to be rewarded emotionally when they preach about themselves. I fear that many people might find this cute. And being cute is not the same as sharing one's faith and interpreting the faith of the community.

Strategic Preaching

In recent years I have become more and more convinced that the key to understanding liturgy is to realize that the liturgical experience of the assembly is cumulative. Everything cannot be accomplished all at once on a particular Sunday. Ritual is about patterns that emerge in the faith life of the community, patterns that are based on the root metaphor of Jesus Christ, who died and rose for us and continues to live in us through the power of the Holy Spirit. Thus planning for major liturgical feasts and seasons that does not respect the ongoing experiences of the celebrating assembly is off the mark. The trick, I tell parish liturgy committees, is not preparing for the Easter Vigil so much as it is understanding and preparing for the "Seventy-seventh Sunday in Ordinary Time."

By the same token, liturgical preaching requires strategic planning. This problem does not (or should not) usually arise when the assembly is accustomed to hear the same person preach week after week. But it does arise when there are a number of regular preachers and (with a vengeance) when a number of "guest" homilists are brought in from the outside. When I am asked to be a guest homilist, I am well-served by attending the community's celebration for several weeks in advance, so that I can build on what other preachers have been saying. Otherwise, no matter how rhetorically brilliant the homily, the assembly is not being respected as an ongoing community of faith.

Strategic preaching also requires a sense of the wholeness of a Gospel (during Ordinary Time) and of the integrity of the liturgical seasons. The current Roman Catholic lectionary is far from perfect, but there is a rhyme or reason in the selection of scripture passages for the various seasons. The lectionary itself, as well as the context of a passage in its original biblical setting, is a hermeneutical key or principle for homiletic interpretation. All too often one gets the impression that the preacher is unaware that anyone might have preached the good news last week, or last month, or last year. Often enough one finds that the preacher has no idea, to use an obvious example, that the proclamation of John 4, Jesus and the Samaritan woman, in the lectionary's Cycle A is connected liturgically with the illumination of candidates for baptism, the scrutinies, and the subsequent gospels from John 9 and 11 as well as the passion narrative.

I do not mean to say that the preacher can ignore what has happened this week to the community or in the community, but that the on-going worship life of the community and the way it is formed by the church's annual celebration of the liturgical cycle are a vital means of respecting the assembly's experience as a whole.

Credibility

I have saved the most important and most intangible feature of the liturgical homily for last. In a way, all the other aspects of the homily surveyed here depend on it. In a way, if it is present and a number of the other features are disregarded, it still covers a multitude of sins. I mean the credibility of the homilist as a person of faith. Rhetorical skills, tactics, strategies, exegetical knowledge, and knowledge of doctrine and theology, none of these suffice if the assembly cannot perceive the preacher as a person of deep faith committed to communicating the Gospel. Every time I hear a homilist, I ask myself if this person is believable. If yes, I listen. If no, I feel free to wander. No technique can take the place of the credibility of the preacher. This means that the homilist must be above all a person with a passionate commitment to prayer and to the people of God. If this be the case, then whatever comes out of the homilist's mouth in the pulpit will have a beneficial effect that the community's faith will have deepened. If this not be the case, then the exercise of liturgical preaching, or any preaching at all, is futile.

* * * * * *

These brief pages have been an attempt on my part to reflect on the status of liturgical preaching in our churches today, and on those elements which preachers need most attend to. If I have seemed to concentrate most on the problems, it is because there are a number of simple considerations which will surely be of value to preachers in our current situation. On the whole, however, we can be grateful that the situation described by Dom Botte at the beginning of our century is no longer true. We do believe in the value of preaching—and that is a giant step forward.

Notes

1. Bernard Botte, *From Silence to Participation: An Insider's View of Liturgical Renewal*, trans., John Sullivan (Washington, D.C.: The Pastoral Press, 1988) 7.

2. Constitution on the Sacred Liturgy, nos. 51-52, also no. 24; see also General Instruction on the Roman Missal, nos. 41-42; and Introduction to the Lectionary for Mass, nos. 24-25.

3. General Instruction on the Lectionary, no. 24.

4. See John A. Melloh, "Publish or Perish: A Review of Preaching Literature, 1981-1986," *Worship* 62 (1988) 497-514.

5. This notion is well conveyed by the German word for worship, *Gottesdienst*, which can mean both God's service to human beings and the service of human beings to God.

6. National Conference of Catholic Bishops, *Fulfilled in Your Hearing: The Homily in the Sunday Assembly* (Washington, D.C.: United States Catholic Conference, 1982) 8.

7. George Guiver, *Company of Voices: Daily Prayer and the People of God* (New York: Pueblo Publishing Co., 1988) 24.